# Active Asset Allocation

## Gaining Advantage in a Highly Efficient Stock Market

Walter R. Good

Roy W. Hermansen

Jack R. Meyer

**McGraw-Hill, Inc.**

New York   San Francisco   Washington, D.C.   Auckland   Bogotá
Caracas   Lisbon   London   Madrid   Mexico City   Milan
Montreal   New Delhi   San Juan   Singapore
Sydney   Tokyo   Toronto

332.6
G64a

**Library of Congress Cataloging-in-Publication Data**

Good, Walter R.
  Active asset allocation : gaining advantage in a highly efficient
stock market / Walter R. Good, Roy W. Hermansen, Jack R. Meyer.
       p.    cm.
  Includes index.
  ISBN 0-07-023730-1 (acid-free paper) :
  1. Portfolio management.   2. Investment analysis.   3. Stock price
forecasting.   4. Hermansen, Roy W.   I. Meyer, Jack R.   II. Title.
HG4529.5.G66   1993
332.6—dc20                                                     93-19450
                                                                   CIP

1 2 3 4 5 6 7 8 9 0   DOC/DOC   9 9 8 7 6 5 4 3

ISBN 0-07-023730-1

*The sponsoring editor for this book was Caroline Carney, the editing
supervisor was Jane Palmieri, and the production supervisor was Donald
Schmidt. It was set in Palatino by McGraw-Hill's Professional Book Group
composition unit.*

*Printed and bound by R. R. Donnelley & Sons Company.*

This book is printed on recycled, acid-free paper con-
taining a minimum of 50% recycled de-inked fiber.

# Contents

## 2. The Radical Assumption Underlying Passive Management                                          **29**

# Part 3. Understanding the Pitfalls and Opportunities

# Part 4. Confronting the Future

## 11. The Three Prime Variables in Operation                      269

## 12. Examining the Alternative: Back-Door Market Timing                      283

# Preface

## Targeting the Critical Decision

For most investors, the critical asset-allocation decision is the commitment to common stocks. How should this commitment be determined? And how should it change as the investment outlook changes? To respond to these questions, this book establishes an innovative approach to active asset allocation in the framework of a long-term policy plan. *Policy asset allocation*, conforming to the principles of passive investing, diversifies widely among asset groups. The broad objectives of the investor—rather than the changing prospects for the financial markets—drive policy. *Active asset allocation*, in contrast, looks to superior skill to secure competitive advantage. The time horizon is usually 6 to 18 months. Almost always, the key decision concerns exposure to the stock market. Transactions in highly liquid fixed income markets ordinarily provide offsetting changes.

## Why a New Approach?

Continuing pressures to develop new approaches to asset allocation reflect the limitations and contradictions that characterize two familiar alternatives. At one extreme is the traditional view, which has long provided the foundation of mainstream active management. It holds that the stock market, often responding irrationally to available information, is frequently mispriced. Despite opportunities implied by this assumption, the accumulating evidence shows that active asset allocation too often proves counterproductive. Discouragement with active asset allocation, meanwhile, contributes to the growth of passive investing. The continuing shift to index funds and other forms of passive investing builds on the efficient market hypothesis. Since the efficient market hypothesis identifies the current market price as the best estimate of market value, it precludes—at least in theory—all efforts to manage actively. Yet, passive investing, particularly as it applies to asset allocation, can never be completely passive. Efforts to operate passively without a formal role for active asset allocation almost inevitably burden the fund with significant unplanned episodes of "back-door market timing." As we argue in this book, back-door market timing is a poor substitute for a carefully planned program of active asset allocation. In this light, the practical question concerning active asset allocation shifts from "whether" to "how."

The innovative active decision process presented in this book makes use of the radical principle underlying passive investing. Most investors regard active and passive management as mutually exclusive disciplines. Our active decision process, differing from both traditional active management and passive investing, recognizes that the stock market is highly efficient but not completely efficient. In this philosophical framework, it accepts the current market price as a "storehouse of information." The result is a reordering of the active decision process. The current market price serves as the point of departure, permitting concentration on the probability of change over the year ahead.

## What Does the Investor Really Need to Know?

Although written from the perspective of institutional fund management, this book also aims to serve enterprising individual investors. In support of this goal, we stress the readily understandable logic of the decision process and its ease of implementation. We limit the inputs to the decision process to a short list of objective measures, routinely available in the financial press. A one-page worksheet, included in Chapter 11, organizes these inputs to assess their significance for market valuation. An accompanying decision matrix translates worksheet relationships into active asset-allocation decisions.

Peter Drucker, in a recent comment, succinctly describes the goal that we also apply to this book. Writing in late 1992, Drucker observed, "Executives have become computer literate. The younger ones, especially, know more about the way the computer works than they know about the mechanics of the automobile or the telephone. But not many executives are information literate....Few executives know how to ask: What information do I need to know to do my job?"* While Drucker's remarks address the broad area of business management, they apply equally to the valuation of the stock market. For those of us concerned with practical investment decisions, the explosion in information and information handling that continues into the 1990s underscores the importance of Drucker's question (our rephrasing): "What do we really need to know?" To this end, our book focuses on three objective measures which logic, historical simulation, and real-time experience identify as critical to stock market valuation.

## Acknowledgments

Readers with widely disparate points of view have generously provided us with the benefit of their advice and suggestions. Frank E. Block, CFA, is a coauthor of *Graham & Dodd's Security Analysis* (McGraw-Hill, 1988) and a former member of the Financial Accounting Standards Board. Jack L. Treynor, president, Treynor Capital Management, Inc., earlier served as editor in chief of the *Financial Analysts Journal*. Both Mr. Block and Mr. Treynor wrote at length with very thoughtful comments. J. Parker Hall III, CFA, president of Lincoln Capital Management Company, pro-

*Peter F. Drucker, "Be Data Literate—Know What to Know," *The Wall Street Journal*, December 1, 1992, p. A-16.

vided another extremely valuable point of view but from yet a different vantage point. We greatly appreciate the reactions provided by highly qualified managers of major tax-exempt funds. We very much thank David A. White, treasurer and chief investment officer, and Webb Trammell, assistant treasurer, of the Rockefeller Foundation; C. J. Wolfe, managing director of the IBM Retirement Fund; and Sudeep Anand, treasurer of the Smithsonian Institution. We are very pleased to have a British perspective from John W. Hawkins, group treasurer, Vestey Group and John F. Pike, NMC-Management Consultants. Along with many helpful observations, they pointed out that certain terms, such as "back-door market timing," have an entirely different meaning in the United Kingdom. We also are very pleased to recognize the important roles of our sponsoring editor, Caroline Carney, and our editing supervisor, Jane Palmieri. We greatly appreciate their help.

*Walter R. Good, CFA*
*Roy W. Hermansen, CFA*
*Jack R. Meyer*

# Introduction: Changing View of Market Efficiency Creates Opportunity

## Powerful Forces Challenge Traditional Active Management

### Reshaping the Investment Framework

Powerful forces have converged over the past quarter century to reshape the framework in which investment management operates. The revolution in computer technology has facilitated research into the workings of the publicly traded financial markets and has also contributed to the quickening pace of change in day-to-day operations. The increasingly dominant investment role of the large financial institutions, particularly retirement funds, has generated demand for more rational, systematic approaches to investment. New investment vehicles, including futures, options, and various types of index funds, have broadened opportunities to implement investment policies and strategies. In this rapidly changing environment, investment management has had to strain to keep pace with the new opportunities and to avoid the penalties of falling behind.

**1**

The innovative approach to stock market valuation described in this book draws on the changing understanding of how prices are established in the financial markets. Thus far, active asset allocation has gained little advantage from clues provided by passive investing. Most knowledgeable investors look at passive investing and active management as mutually exclusive disciplines. *Active management* seeks to gain advantage through superior forecasts of future investment returns. *Passive investing*, in contrast, accepts the consensus forecast already incorporated in market prices. It has no use for additional information concerning prospects for the economy or other factors bearing on the financial markets. Its purpose is simply to achieve the balance of assets which most appropriately meets the fund's investment objectives (in terms of risk and expected return). Our approach, contrary to established practice, makes use of the concept which underlies passive investing to secure critical inputs for the active decision process. The goal is not only substantial simplification of the decision process but improved probability of success.

This book specifically addresses the active allocation of assets between common stocks and cash equivalents. Active management, in its many different forms, seeks opportunity in a wide range of investment decisions. It aims at skillful selection of individual investments within each asset group as well as the timely shifting of funds from one asset group to another. Active decisions in each of these highly competitive areas require a high degree of specialization. Our specialized focus on stock market valuation—as distinguished from the many other issues confronting active management—is consistent with the dominant influence of aggregate stock holdings on investment performance.

Common stocks are by far the most important asset group in most institutional portfolios, often accounting for about half the market value of total investments. *Pensions & Investments*, commenting on a survey of the largest 200 defined-benefit pension funds, reported that common stocks (primarily domestic issues) averaged 48 percent of the aggregate asset mix on September 30, 1992.[1] Since returns on common stocks are generally more volatile than those for fixed-income alternatives, they provide, for the same dollar of investment, substantially larger opportunities for gain—and for loss. Other investments, such as foreign stocks or real estate, may demonstrate returns as volatile as those of the domestic stock market, but they ordinarily account for a much smaller segment of the total fund.

## Understanding the Underlying Logic

Our discussion of active asset allocation stresses the underlying logic concerning stock market valuation as well as the details of the decision process. The decision process itself is straightforward, requiring access only to statistics reported routinely in the financial press (such as in *Barron's* or *The Wall Street Journal*). Equally important, however, is understanding why this highly selective use of information is likely to produce results. The underlying logic is critical, because the decision process departs from the conventional framework of traditional active management. By way of explanation, our starting point is a brief overview of the relationship between the efficient market hypothesis (EMH) and the burgeoning growth of passive investing.

The EMH, which first received widespread attention in the late 1960s, has provided the philosophical basis for the subsequent growth of passive investing. In its strongest form, it states that all available information that could matter to the financial markets has already been discounted. Under these circumstances, active management would be futile and should give way to passive management. This extreme conclusion requires modification, however, since the theoretical model of a completely efficient stock market is a less-than-perfect representation of how the financial markets actually work. In describing the stock market, we therefore apply the term *highly efficient* rather than *completely efficient*.

A stock market that is highly efficient—but not completely efficient—leaves the door open for both active and passive management. In recent years, fund managers have increasingly accepted index funds and other forms of passive management as a rational alternative to active management. A logical case for the coexistence of active and passive management—because it redefines the assumptions underlying the operation of the financial markets—must necessarily alter the approach to active management itself.

## Changing View of How the Stock Market Works

The inroads of passive management—at the expense of traditional active management—provide highly visible evidence of the impact of the EMH on day-to-day investment operations. For the most part, fund managers do not articulate a formal assessment of the EMH in order to justify acceptance of passive management. They are practical decision makers, primarily concerned with investment performance rather than theoretical explanations. What they do in their own self-interest, nevertheless, provides a measure of their convictions. Passive investing implies acceptance of the current market price as the best estimate of value in the light of currently available information. Fund managers that accept passive management for a particular portfolio role acknowledge by their actions that they cannot confidently identify a better estimate of value.

By way of contrast, consider the state of mind of fund managers prior to the widening influence of the EMH. Not so long ago, the generally accepted assumption among investors was that all investment management is, or at least should be, active. The prevailing understanding of how the financial markets work allowed for huge discrepancies between "true" value and actual market prices. Professional investment opinion frequently attributed this price gap to poorly informed investors or extreme swings of mass psychology. The "madness of crowds"[2] resulted in "crazy" market prices. Under these conditions, passive management could not be a legitimate alternative. For the professional investment manager, acceptance of passive management, which routinely takes the current price as the best current estimate of value, would have been an abdication of responsibility.

From very small beginnings in the early 1970s, passive investing has grown rapidly over the subsequent years. The shift to passive investment has been under way at two levels. Figure I-1 addresses the explosive growth of equity index funds held by tax-exempt institutional investors. These funds, which passively aim to match the performance of the S&P 500 or other designated index, have increased more than 60-fold since 1980. They now account for about 30 percent of the equity holdings of these institutions. Foreign-stock index funds, although still a relatively small proportion of the total, have expanded at a particularly rapid rate in recent years. Note that the estimates shown in Fig. I-1 do not include fixed-income index funds, which are also

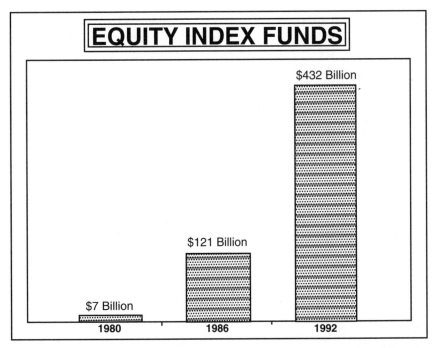

**Figure I-1.** The growth of equity index funds from 1980. (*Source: Pensions & Investments, Crain Communications, Inc., copyright 1993*)

growing rapidly but from a smaller base. At another level, passive assumptions play a major role in planning asset allocation. Fund managers increasingly base long-term asset allocation—the policy plan—on the assumption that the stock market is efficient. A fund that adheres strictly to passive asset allocation as stated in the policy plan implicitly accepts current market price as the best estimate of stock market valuation.

Increasing reliance on passive investing by the large financial institutions, although reflecting the widespread influence of the EMH, constitutes something less than its full acceptance. Table I-1 compares three contrasting views of how the stock market works. Very few fund managers would agree that the stock market is completely efficient, as indicated by the middle column of the table. To our knowledge, no major retirement or endowment fund has attempted complete elimination of active management. Yet, there has been growing recognition that the stock market is much more efficient than implied by the traditional views of active management, as represented by the left-hand column. As a practical matter, increasing sophistication in performance measurement has demonstrated how difficult it is for active management to achieve superior results that cannot be readily explained by chance. Increasingly, institutional fund management is moving toward the concept of a highly efficient stock market, as described in the right-hand column of Table I-1.

**Table I-1.** Three Contrasting Philosophies

|  | Traditional active management | Completely efficient market | Highly efficient market |
|---|---|---|---|
| Investor consensus | Often irrational | Completely rational | Highly rational |
| Current price | Not necessarily related to value | Best estimate of value | Starting point for valuation |
| Required estimate | "True" market value | None | One-year price change |

## Redefining the Decision Process

### Identifying Information Embedded in Stock Prices

Recognition that the stock market is highly efficient requires fundamental readjustment in traditional approaches to valuation. As discussed in Chap. 1, traditional approaches aim to assess the proper *level* of stock prices. They have no choice, since they view the stock market as subject to irrational forces which may result in wide disparities between "true" value and current market price. There is no way to make use of information already embedded in stock prices. In a highly efficient stock market, in contrast, the current price level, which incorporates the combined judgments of investors, becomes the point of departure for the analysis of the stock market outlook. In general, the current market price provides the best estimate, based on information generally available to investors, of the relative value of the stock market. (We shall address in Chap. 2 the distortions resulting from actions of misguided or error-prone investors.)

With the current market price as the starting point, the valuation of the stock market focuses on *change*. As discussed in Chap. 5, modern capital theory provides a framework for analyzing the probability of change. Three key factors, listed in Table I-2, drive stock prices. The left-hand column displays the technical terms, and the right-hand column lists the more famil-

**Table I-2.** Key Factors That Drive Stock Prices

| Technical term | Common term |
| --- | --- |
| Dividend-growth rate | Business outlook |
| Risk-free rate | Interest rates |
| Risk premium | Investor confidence |

iar language which is approximately equivalent. The analysis consists of two steps. The first step is to identify measures which will shed light on the likelihood of change for each of these factors. The second step assesses the net effect of these changes on the overall valuation of the stock market.

## How the Decision Maker Benefits

The shift in the orientation of stock market valuation from level to change offers two important advantages to active management:

**What's Important Now.**   The approach presented in this book recognizes that stock prices discount much of the information traditionally involved in investment decisions. Our decision process therefore aims to dispense with time-consuming, unnecessary, and even counterproductive efforts to evaluate such already discounted information. The goal is to concentrate on the critical information that has not yet been discounted. This narrowing of focus strengthens the likelihood of identifying prospective change in the key factors that drive stock prices.

**Automatic Updating.**   Risks of overlooking an important new influence are better controlled. There is no longer a reason to be captive to yesterday's mistakes, since the starting point for each day's analysis is the closing price of the previous day. At the same time, reliance on objective data for information relating to the probability of change establishes a firm discipline. The flow of objective data, rather than the bullish or bearish biases of the decision maker, drives changes in stock market valuation.

## Taking the Measure of the Stock Market

Our objective in the following pages is to spell out lessons derived from our experience in tracking the forces that drive stock prices. Our efforts include development of a quantitative stock market model, which we have operated on a real-time basis since the beginning of 1982. Back testing of our conclusions, moreover, has covered more than 6 decades of stock market history. Over both the real-time operations of the past decade and the simulations extending for a much longer period, three economic and financial variables (three "prime" variables) have provided continuing practical guidance. We direct attention to these measures not just because they have proved useful in the past. Equally important, the underlying logic gives reason to expect that they will continue to be useful.

## Straightforward Implementation Encourages Broad Use

### Who Should Read This Book

Prospects for the stock market, as addressed in this book, rank near or at the top among the issues confronting most investment programs. Writing from the vantage point of the institutional investor, we stress the rigor required by those involved in, or responsible for, day-to-day investment management. At the same time, we present our decision process in a manner that aims to encourage use by individual investors working to improve their investment skills. To this end, we have avoided technical terms so far as possible and, where they are used, have provided explanation.

**Pension, Endowment, and Foundation Funds.**  A primary aim is to meet the needs of pension, endowment, and foundation funds. The book specifically targets the managers of these funds and their professional staffs. At the same time, it offers a fresh perspective for those in broad policy-making positions with oversight responsibility for such funds. This group includes the chief financial officer of the sponsoring organization as well as members of the various committees with ultimate responsibility for fund investments.

**Investment Specialists Who Serve the Institutional Funds.**  This closely associated group includes (1) the investment managers, along with their professional staffs, who are responsible for the portfolios which make up the institutional funds; (2) the institutional brokerage firms, especially the analysts and strategists, who advise these funds and their portfolio managers; and (3) the consultants, who develop investment policies, select managers, and analyze performance.

**Faculty and Students.**   Both faculty and students of the graduate schools of business have reason to read this book. It addresses one of their primary objectives: the improvement of investment practice.

**Individual Investors.**   Although we write from the vantage point of the institutional investor, we expect our book to be useful to those knowledgeable individual investors who stress improvement of their investment skills. The individual investor, seeking to avoid costly mistakes and to gain advantage, can benefit from the same conceptual framework useful to the institutional investor.

### How This Book Is Organized

The book is organized in four main sections.

**Reconciling Two Conflicting Views.**   In order to make clear the need for a fresh approach, the first section highlights the contradictory assumptions underlying current approaches to active and passive management. *Chapter 1* identifies the long-established concept of stock market pricing that underlies virtually all fundamental methods of stock market valuation. This generalization applies to the dividend-discount model as well as other familiar quantitative approaches to active asset allocation introduced in recent years. *Chapter 2*, in sharp contrast, explores the very different concept which makes the case for passive management. It underscores the conflict between active and passive management. *Chapter 3* outlines the separate but complementary roles of policy, which is managed passively, and active management, which represents a series of departures from the policy plan.

**Adapting Active Management to a Highly Efficient Stock Market.** The second section presents an approach to stock market valuation that exploits the efficient market principle underlying passive investing. *Chapter 4* differentiates between "fast" and "slow" information. The former, readily discounted by stock prices, conforms to the efficient market model. Most of the information that concerns investors, since it is discounted by market prices almost as soon as it becomes available, qualifies as fast. Only a slim margin of slow information offers opportunity to active management. *Chapter 5* addresses the mechanism of price change in a highly efficient stock market. It identifies the three key factors that, although hidden from view, drive stock prices. *Chapter 6* considers the economic variables that provide clues to change in these three key factors. We explain the selection of three of these variables (designated *prime* variables) as critical to the decision process.

**Understanding the Pitfalls and Opportunities.** The third section discusses in detail the three prime variables and their interaction with each other. *Chapter 7* warns of the earnings trap—how earnings forecasts, even when accurate, mislead investors. It presents an alternative method to track the effect on the stock market of changes in the business outlook. *Chapter 8* differentiates between useful and not so useful measures of the changing influence of interest rates. *Chapter 9* compares alternative approaches to gauging change in investor confidence. *Chapter 10* brings together the individual measures considered in the previous three chapters to provide a logically coherent approach to stock market valuation.

**Confronting the Future.** A final section examines specific application in practical investment operations. *Chapter 11* shows how market valuation translates into a specific asset allocation decision within the framework of the fund's long-term policy plan. Using the three prime variables to assess bias, it also explains the vulnerability of a decision process that concentrates on only one or two of the three key factors that drive stock prices. *Chapter 12* warns of the dangers of "back-door market timing," particularly for investors who are most committed to passive management. It explains the burden that back-door market timing will likely impose on fund performance. It stresses the difficulty of avoiding back-door market timing in the absence of a complementary role for active asset allocation.

## References

1. Christine Philip, "Top 1000 Funds Increase by 9%," *Pensions & Investments,* January 25, 1993, p. 34.
2. Charles Mackay, *Extraordinary Popular Delusions and the Madness of Crowds,* L. C. Page, Boston, 1932. (Initially published in 1841.)

# PART 1

# Fund Manager's Dilemma: How to Reconcile Two Conflicting Views

# 1

# How Traditional Active Management Strives to Add Value

## Understanding the Traditional View of Stock Prices

### Operating in an Irrational Stock Market

Active management has long operated on the "commonsense" principle that the stock market is irrational—and, at times, highly irrational. According to this view, the mistakes of the many investors who participate in the stock market result in frequent mispricing. Investor errors may result from lack of diligence in seeking information, limitations on skill in interpreting information, or mass psychology that overwhelms otherwise sound individual judgment. As a result, stock prices are often irrationally high or irrationally low. Irrational market prices imply continuing opportunity. It follows that skillful investment decision makers, insulated from the follies of the marketplace, gain advantage through a rational process of stock market valuation. The greater the difference between the rational estimate of value and the irrational market price, the greater is the opportunity.

### Listening to Benjamin Graham

For an authoritative pronouncement of the philosophical assumption which underlies traditional active management, we
turn to Benjamin Graham. We focus on Graham because of his
extraordinary place in the history of investment analysis. Having
made his mark on Wall Street as well as in the academic world, he
became widely accepted, beginning in the mid-1930s and through
several decades after World War II, as the leading authority on
the theory of investments. As summed up by an editor of the
*Financial Analysts Journal*, "He became the acknowledged teacher
of at least two generations of security analysts and investors."[1]

Graham's reputation in the financial world remains formida-
ble almost 2 decades after his death. Early in his career, he
achieved notable financial success in arbitrage and hedging. He
was able to start his own firm in 1926, just 12 years after gradua-
tion from Columbia University. The firm, which eventually
evolved into the Graham-Neuman Corporation, established a
highly favorable reputation for its value approach to investing.
By 1927, Graham had returned to Columbia as a part-time lec-
turer in finance and, subsequently, served as professor until his
retirement in 1956. He was the principal author of *Security
Analysis*,[2] which was issued in four editions between 1934 and
1962. It remained the leading textbook on investments for some
years thereafter. Although Graham's influence has diminished
in recent years, he continues to receive enthusiastic support
from a substantial number of dedicated adherents. A revised
edition of *Security Analysis*,[3] prepared after his death by three
well-experienced students of his approach, has achieved sales
since 1988 of more than 50,000 copies (bringing the total for all
editions to more than 800,000 copies).

Because of Graham's special place in the history of investment
analysis, his unambiguous assessment of the irrationality of
stock prices is noteworthy. It represents the mainstream view of
traditional active managers, even though other aspects of investment philosophy may vary widely from one manager to another.
Many traditional active managers do not subscribe to Graham's
value-oriented approach. Value managers who regard Graham as
their model, moreover, may depart in important ways from the

textbook version of the discipline. Yet, most traditional active managers begin with the assumption concerning stock prices which Graham spelled out in the following quotation:

> The behavior of stock prices departs radically from the concept of intrinsic worth....Thus we reach our conclusion, with its overtones of a scriptural paradox, that the investor can profit from market fluctuations only by paying them little heed. He must fix his eye not on what the market has been doing—or what it apparently is going to do—but only on the *result* of its action as expressed in the relationship between the price level and the level of underlying or central values.[4]

## Long History Provides Many Anecdotes

Anecdotes supporting the irrationality of stock market prices abound in the long history of the financial markets. John Kenneth Galbraith recounts in a recent book several classic episodes of folly in the financial markets.[5] Speculation in tulip bulbs in seventeenth-century Netherlands serves as an early example.

**Tulipmania.**   Introduced in western Europe in the sixteenth century, tulip bulbs were soon prized for the beauty of their blossoms, with particular value attributed to certain rare types. As Galbraith noted, "...appreciation of the more exceptional of the flowers rapidly gave way to a yet deeper appreciation of the increase in the price that their beauty and rarity were commanding." As the speculative fever infected the range of social classes—from nobles to chimney sweeps—a single bulb, according to one example, was valued at the equivalent of $25,000 to $50,000 in current dollars. The inevitable crash, after many had mortgaged their assets or secured other borrowings to support purchases at extremely inflated prices, occurred in 1637. It brought ruin to a large segment of the population as well as depressed economic conditions throughout the country.

**Other Examples.**   Galbraith focuses on a number of other examples, including accounts of John Law and The Banque Royale, the South Sea Bubble, and numerous episodes of financial folly from the North American continent. These latter anecdotes range from colonial times through the early years of the Republic to the events of more recent years. Galbraith accords special emphasis to the role of speculation in bringing about the 1929 stock market crash.

> In the larger history of economics and finance, no year stands out as does 1929. It is...like 1066, 1776, 1914, 1945, and, now, perhaps with the collapse of Communism, 1989—richly evocative in the public memory. That is partly because the speculative debacle that then occurred was of special magnitude, even grandeur, and more because it ushered in for the United States and the industrial world as a whole the most extreme and enduring crisis that capitalism has ever experienced.[5]

With a characteristic irony, Galbraith takes strong exception to those who claim that market prices react rationally to changing circumstances:

> The market in October 1929 was said only to be reflecting external influences. During the previous summer there had been, it was belatedly discovered, a weakening in industrial production and other of the few currently available economic indices. To these, the market, in its rational way, had responded. Not at fault were the speculation and its inevitable aftermath; rather, it was those deeper, wholly external influences. Professional economists were especially cooperative in advancing and defending this illusion. A few, when dealing with history, still do....They were not, however, completely persuasive.[5]

The record 1-day market drop of October 19, 1987, serves Galbraith with a more recent illustration of market irrationality. He concludes,

> There was, as before, little that was new in this speculative episode. All of the elements were again predictably in place....That the crash of 1987 and its results were predictable, well in the established pattern, I can avow, for, as I have earlier noted, I ventured the relevant prediction. In early 1987, I dealt with it and the parallels with 1929 in *The Atlantic* and spoke of a day of reckoning....I also suggested in the article, however, that the crash, when it came, would be less devastating in its economic effect than that of 1929.[5]

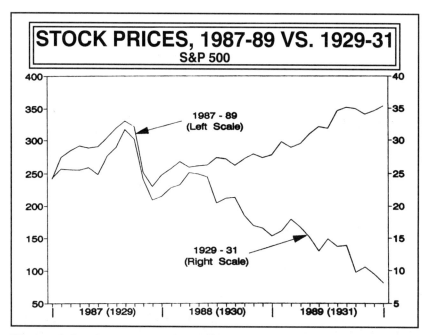

**Figure 1-1.** Comparison of the course of the stock market over 1929 to 1931 with 1987 to 1989.

By way of perspective, Fig. 1-1 compares the course of the stock market over 1929 to 1931 with 1987 to 1989. The measure of stock prices is the S&P 500 (which, in earlier years, included fewer issues).

## Explaining Why History Repeats

In assessing the record of the financial markets over five centuries, Galbraith offers a conclusion very much like that presented by Graham:

> The circumstances that induce the recurrent lapses into financial dementia have not changed in any truly operative fashion since the Tulipmania of 1636–1637. Individuals and institutions are captured by the wondrous satisfaction from accruing wealth.

The associated illusion of insight is protected, in turn, by the oft-noted public impression that intelligence, one's own and that of others, marches in close step with the possession of money....The upward movement confirms the commitment to personal and group wisdom. And so on to the moment of mass disillusion and the crash...[5]

## Confronting the "Index-Fund" Mentality

In recent years, many voices, echoing the traditional view of market irrationality, have warned against the "index-fund" mentality. James R. Hamilton, CFA, president of Hamilton & Company (a New York consulting firm), addressed a union meeting in late 1989. His remarks[6] focused on index funds in the amount of $16 billion held by the New York State Common Retirement Fund:

All indexers share one overwhelming characteristic. They have never heard of prudence or of risk. Obviously, they have never heard of anything; they have no ears or brains; they are simply compilers of past prices of one conglomeration of stocks or another. By investing to imitate them, is the system becoming deaf to prudence, at least with respect to the $16 billion invested this way?

What protection does the system's S&P 500 index fund have against a debacle? The answer is none. Under a passive approach, no investment manager will be trying to shift to stocks that will better weather the storm, or to switch to cash equivalents when no stocks look attractive. Active equity managers, on the other hand, will be buying cash equivalents and even government bonds in place of stocks.[6]

## Traditional Active Management in 1992

As this chapter is written in the summer of 1992, the prevailing assumption underlying active management continues the traditional view that stock markets are often highly irrational. The financial press[7] reports that The Columbia Graduate School of Business sponsored a second annual breakfast honoring two former faculty members, Benjamin Graham and Clarence Dodd. According to this report, "200 Columbia Business School alumni and other Wall Street types" attended the meeting. The speaker, Seth A. Klarman, president of Baupost Group, forcefully supported the concept of a stock market that is irrational and inefficient.

> "At this moment, the financial markets are characterized by an extraordinary smugness," states Klarman. Every price dip, regardless of cause, is seen as a buying opportunity. Bad news such as write-offs and layoffs is cheered. And investors pitch their money into an already frothy market with the expectation that, if things get too bad, the government will step in to solve every problem, even those it helped to create.
>
> In such a market, Klarman concedes, value investing can be difficult at best: "It is very frustrating right now to be a value investor, but not because markets are efficient." Rather, bargains have become scarce even as the markets have become more inefficient, and undervaluation has ceased to exist "not because investors today are so sophisticated but, instead, because they are the opposite."
>
> The culprit, Klarman believes, is the "mindless investing known as portfolio indexation," which eschews fundamental analysis in favor of matching the market. "To value investors, the concept of indexing is at best silly and at worst quite hazardous."[7]

# Looking for the Message in Market-Price Change

## Underlying Assumption Shapes the Decision Process

A central issue which we raise in this book is whether a substantial change in market price, other things equal, is itself of any significance to stock market valuation. Traditional active management, viewing the stock market as highly irrational, shapes the investment decision process accordingly. In this traditional framework, there is no well-defined relationship between market price and information available to investors. Consequently, there is no logical way to use market price to assess information already embedded in stock prices. In sharp contrast, a highly efficient stock market implies a strong relationship between the information available to investors and current market prices. Revision of this basic assumption concerning how the stock market works creates opportunity for reordering of the decision process.

The following example restates the question in practical terms. Suppose traditional active management, based on a decision process that completely ignores the developing information discounted by current market price, values the S&P 500 at 360. Assuming the current market price is 325, the stock market is undervalued by about 10 percent. Over a relatively short period, the market price rises to 360, confirming the initial valuation. Then, with still no change in the inputs to the valuation model, market price increases to 400, resulting in an overvaluation of about 10 percent. In this example, stock prices change by close to 25 percent with no change in the inputs to the decision process. If the market is often irrational, as assumed by traditional active management, the change in market price does not qualify as a useful input to stock market valuation. The decision maker, under this assumption, is well advised by Graham and other representatives of the traditional point of view to insulate the determination of stock market valuation from the changing level of market price. If the stock market is highly efficient, in contrast, another answer is likely to prove advantageous. In our view, as addressed in Chap. 2, the accumulating evidence indicates that the stock market is much more efficient—and therefore much more rational—than assumed by traditional active management. We have developed our approach to active asset allocation in the light of this evidence.

## How Market Prices Influence Traditional Decision Makers

While the concept of a highly efficient stock market disagrees sharply with the traditional view of market irrationality, traditional active managers do not totally escape the influence of changing market prices. Frequently, they use market price as an input—or at least a supplement—to the decision process. Such actions tacitly acknowledge that stock prices discount information which may be missed—or at least be wrongly interpreted—by a traditional market valuation. The three examples which follow highlight the discrepancy between the irrational market assumption stressed by traditional active managers and their actions in day-to-day operations. In each example, the investment decision maker infers a message from the market-price change itself.

## Capitulating to a Contrary Trend

A familiar example of the influence of market-price change on the decision process is capitulation to a trend that carries far beyond expectations. Such capitulation often takes place after mounting losses in a bear market, but it may also reflect pressures resulting from missing out on large gains in a bull market. Suppose, by way of example, the decision maker is bearish. Subsequent to arriving at this conclusion, the stock market rises—first by 20 percent, and then, as time passes, by an additional 20 percent, and eventually by a further amount. At some point, the decision maker may conclude that the market knows something that has been overlooked by a decision process that attempts to remain independent of stock prices. The resulting capitulation to a market trend is, in effect, a poorly planned effort to make use of information embedded in stock prices. By way of example, note the following account from *The Wall Street Journal.*[8] It concerns a large firm which, for some months previously, had been on the wrong side of the market (our emphasis): "Six weeks ago, not a cent of the $3 billion...[that this] firm manages was invested in stocks. Now, 50% of the funds in aggressive accounts are committed to stocks, *even though the quantitative analysis on which...[the firm] usually bases its investment decisions shows the market seriously overvalued.*" A key decision maker for the firm pointed out that it now "is paying more attention to sentiment: The market's continued success, he figures, should make more and more investors feel like buying again."

## How Technical Analysis Looks
## to Market Prices for Guidance

Technical analysis seeks guidance from market prices in a more systematic way. The goal is to forecast future market prices through patterns of stock prices and other indicators. Dedicated practitioners sometimes pride themselves on complete indifference to fundamental considerations, such as earnings, dividends, interest rates, and inflation. Others combine analysis of stock-price movements with a wide range of other indicators, including measures which are also followed by fundamental analysts.

For large institutional funds, technical analysis plays only a marginal or supplementary role. Many funds accept the negative verdict on technical analysis presented by the preponderance of academic research. They therefore disavow, at least officially, any interest in technical analysis. To our knowledge, none of the large institutions manage—or have others manage—a significant portion of investable funds *solely* on the basis of technical analysis.

Despite the dominant role of economic fundamentals in active management, technical analysis enters into the decisions of the major financial institutions in various ways. Managers of some funds, although relying primarily on fundamental analysis, routinely keep an eye on technical analysis for a second opinion. Alternatively, they may use it as a timing device for decisions supported in a general way by fundamental analysis. In either case, they are looking to market prices themselves as a source of inputs to the decision process.

Market technicians may take into account scores of indicators as well as market-price changes, and they are likely to stress the individual skill required in interpreting such information. For a simple example that relies entirely on market prices, note a recent report in the "Abreast of the Market" column in *The Wall Street Journal.*[9] The chief investment officer of an often-quoted investment firm

> ...cautions that long-term investors shouldn't try to time the inevitable temporary declines that occur in bull markets...."What you want to be able to do is catch most of the

rise in a bull market and avoid most of the losses in a bear market." The tool that works best for that, he says, is a simple chart comparing where the market ends each week with the average performance of the market during the previous 53 weeks... "technical analysts have determined that as long as the market finishes every Friday at a level above the 53 week moving average, owning stocks is fine. When it falls below the moving average, its time to sell."[9]

## Using Market Prices as an Economic Forecaster

Changing market prices may also indirectly influence stock market valuation through the effect on the economic forecast. The stock market is widely recognized, despite substantial limitations, as a leading indicator of economic activity. Prospects for economic activity, meanwhile, bear on the outlook for the stock market.

The extreme example in recent years of the impact of a sharp change in market prices on the perception of the economic outlook is the market break in October 1987. In the third quarter of 1987, prior to the break, the S&P 500 established a succession of new highs, reaching a closing peak of almost 337 on August 25. Although the market then began working lower, the correction attracted limited attention until October 19. On that day, the S&P 500 registered a record 1-day loss of more than 20 percent, dropping from the previous day's close of 283 to a new closing price of 225. Compared with the record high attained less than 2 months earlier, this broad measure of stock prices had plunged by 33 percent. Investment managers, together with economists who advised them, rapidly took this steep drop in stock prices into account in assessing the economic prospects underlying the valuation of the stock market. *Blue Chip Economic Indicators,* which collects data from a large sample of leading business forecasters, summarized data assembled shortly thereafter: "The CONSENSUS forecast for Real GNP growth *next year* took the biggest 'month-from-prior-month' dive in our 11 year history— sliding nearly a full percentage point from 2.8% to 1.9%...."[10] *Barron's,* meanwhile, reported on the impact the market crash had on investment decision makers. The title of an article in early December, representative of many that appeared about this time, summarized the conclusion: "Bloody but Bowed: Money Managers Remain Badly Shaken by the Meltdown."[11]

## Exploiting a Highly Efficient Stock Market

These brief examples raise two crucial questions. The first question concerns the likelihood that useful information is embedded in stock prices. Chapter 2 responds affirmatively. It makes the case that the stock market, while not completely efficient, is highly efficient. Current stock prices therefore discount most of the information generally available to the investor consensus. The second question follows from the first. If a highly efficient stock market incorporates useful information, how can active asset allocation exploit it? The remainder of the book spells out our answer.

## References

1. Nicolas Molodovsky, "Portrait of an Analyst: Benjamin Graham," *Financial Analysts Journal*, January–February 1968.
2. Benjamin Graham and David L. Dodd, *Security Analysis*, McGraw-Hill, New York, 1934, 1940, 1952, and 1962. (Sidney Cottle was included in the authors of the 1962 edition.)
3. Sidney Cottle, Roger F. Murray, and Frank E. Block, *Graham and Dodd's Security Analysis*, McGraw-Hill, New York, 1988.
4. Benjamin Graham, *The Intelligent Investor*, Harper Brothers, New York, 1949, pp. 184–186.
5. John Kenneth Galbraith, *A Short History of Financial Euphoria*, Whittle Direct Books, Knoxville, 1990.
6. James R. Hamilton, "Indexers turning deaf ear to risk, prudence," *Pensions & Investments*, September 3, 1990, p. 17.
7. Edward A. Wyatt, "Bacon, Eggs, Graham & Dodd," *Barron's*, July 27, 1992, p. 18.

8. Douglas R. Sease, William Power, and James A. White, "Persistent Rally After Months of Doubt, Long Rise in Stocks Finally Gains Converts," *The Wall Street Journal,* May 28, 1989, p. 1.

9. Douglas R. Sease and Robert Steiner, "Taking Stock: Here Are Simple Tools for Gauging the Health of the Market," *The Wall Street Journal,* February 8, 1992, p. C-11.

10. Robert J. Eggert, editor, "Forecast for 1988 GNP Drops Sharply," *Blue Chip Economic Indicators,* Vol. 12, No. 11, November 10, 1987, p. 1. (Copyright 1987, Capitol Publications, Inc.)

11. Jay Palmer, "Bloody but Bowed: Money Managers Remain Badly Shaken by the Meltdown," *Barron's,* December 7, 1987, p. 18.

# 2

# The Radical Assumption Underlying Passive Management

## Understanding the Highly Efficient Market

### Assessing the Implications for Active Management

The efficient market hypothesis (EMH) radically departs from the traditional view of how the stock market works. When the EMH first attracted public attention more than 20 years ago, practical decision makers heatedly opposed both the theory itself and its implied support for passive investing. Even today, few institutional investment managers commit to the hard-line version of the theory, which defines a completely efficient market. Yet, burgeoning growth of index funds and other forms of passive investing, especially over the past decade, has provided hard evidence of changing attitudes. There is growing recognition that the stock market, although it does not conform precisely to the rigid assumptions of the EMH, is much more efficient than implied by the traditional view of a highly irrational market.

We direct attention to the concept of a highly efficient stock market because of its implications for active investment management. Already, passive investing has made major inroads in the market share of active management. Competition from passive investments has also affected active practices relating to transaction costs and risk control. A logical next step, as we argue in this book, is the formal application of the concept underlying passive management to the active decision process. Passive investing is incompatible with the traditional view of the stock market (highly irrational) outlined in Chap. 1. *To the extent active asset allocation operates in the same stock market as passive management, it cannot logically proceed under a different assumption concerning how the stock market works.* How we apply the concept underlying passive management to the active decision process determines in large measure our approach to active asset allocation.

### A Short Definition Gets at the Heart of the Matter

For a concise definition of the EMH, we turn to Professors Lorie and Hamilton: "An efficient market is one in which prices always fully reflect all available, relevant information. Adjustment to new information is virtually instantaneous."[1] Although much more can be said by way of elaboration, this short definition gets at the heart of the matter. It identifies the current market price, in a completely efficient stock market, as the best measure of value.

Note that the Lorie and Hamilton definition applies specifically to the theoretical concept of a *completely* efficient market. Under this extreme assumption, no investor, however skilled, could expect to gain advantage other than by chance. An alternative assumption describes the stock market as *highly* efficient. This point of view, gradually gaining support among institutional investors, represents the point of departure for the approach to active asset allocation presented in this book. It views the stock market as less than completely efficient but only by a narrow margin.

## Explaining Variations in Market Efficiency

To distinguish a *highly* efficient market from a *completely* efficient version, we refer to Jack Treynor's bean-jar experiment.[2] It involves efforts of university students to guess the number of beans in a transparent jar. The first set of experiments reported by Treynor models the operation of a completely efficient market. A second set illustrates the workings of a highly efficient market.

By way of introduction, Treynor points out that

> ...the accuracy of market prices (in a completely efficient market)...comes from the faulty opinions of a large number of investors who err independently....But what assurance do we have that investors' errors are really independent?... Fortunately, the mechanism whereby a large number of error-prone judgments are pooled to achieve a more accurate "consensus" is not confined to finance, or even economics. The mechanism is present even in traditional "bean-jar" contests...
>
> Results of a bean-jar experiment conducted in the author's investment classes indicate that the mean estimate has been close to the true value. In the first experiment, the jar held 810 beans; the mean estimate was 841, and only two of the 46 guesses were closer to the true value. In the second experiment, the jar held 850 beans, and the mean estimate was 871: only one of the 56 guesses was closer to the true value.
>
> These results suggest that, in situations where the subjects have not been schooled in a "correct" approach, the bulk of the individual errors will be independent, rather than shared. Apparently, it doesn't take knowledge of beans, jars or packing factors for a group of students to make an accurate estimate of the number of beans in the jar. All it takes is independence.

Treynor illustrates the workings of a less-than-efficient market through a second set of experiments. As reported by Treynor,

> ...the observers were cautioned to allow (after recording their original guesses) for, first, air space at the top of the bean jar and, second, the fact that the jar, being plastic rather than glass, had thinner walls than a conventional jar. The means of the guesses after the first and second "warnings" were 952.6 and 979.2, corresponding respectively to errors of 102.6 and 129.2.

Although the cautions were not intended to be misleading, they seem to have caused some shared error to creep into the estimates.

Although the Treynor article does not specifically address active asset allocation, the bean-jar experiment serves as a framework for describing a stock market that is highly, but not completely, efficient. Table 2-1 compares three alternatives. The very inefficient market, as discussed in Chap. 1, may slip into periods of extreme irrationality from time to time. In contrast, a completely efficient market, reflecting the textbook version of the EMH, is always perfectly rational. The highly efficient market conforms closely to the completely efficient market but not perfectly. It includes shared errors, reflecting information flow which the investor consensus does not discount "almost instantaneously." Although shared errors are rare—or at least hard to identify—they open the door to opportunity for active asset allocation.*

**Adding Up Changes to Date**

Over the past 20 years, the concept of a highly efficient market has gradually impacted the operations of investment manage-

**Table 2-1.** Degrees of Stock Market Efficiency

|  | Very inefficient | Completely efficient | Highly efficient |
| --- | --- | --- | --- |
| How perceived | Traditional view | Theoretical model | Evolving view |
| Shared errors | Normal | None | Rare or hard to identify |
| Management role | Active only | Passive only | Passive and active |

*Appendix 2-1 addresses the evolving pattern of academic research relating to market efficiency.

ment in a number of ways. The changes are particularly evident among the several hundred largest institutions, since they tend to be best situated to monitor new ideas and introduce innovative investment programs. Most visible has been the substantial shift of business to passive management. One result has been a significant subtraction from the revenues which active managers otherwise would have received. At the same time, increasing competition from passive management has contributed importantly to innovations in active management.

# Tracking the Growth of Passive Investing

### Early Efforts Meet Intense Resistance

For the most part, the professional investment community vigorously resisted the early evidence offered in support of the EMH. At the beginning of the 1970s, few investors paid attention to the academic work on market efficiency published in the 1960s. There was no passive investment management, little talk of the benefits of diversification, and a lack of rigor in the interpretation of investment performance. Fund sponsors held high expectations that active management could readily outperform the broad market indexes. Clearly, the EMH threatened the financial interests of established investment managers. At the extreme, complete acceptance of EMH would rule out any possibility of active management. Even the concept of a *highly* efficient market conflicts with many of the traditional approaches to active management.

### Pioneering Index Funds

Initial attempts at passive management date back to the early 1970s. The Wells Fargo Bank (currently operating in this area as Wells Fargo Nikko Investment Advisors) created the first index fund in July 1971, a portfolio designed to track the equally weighted New York Stock Exchange Index. In 1973, Wells started an S&P 500 index fund, which was easier to manage. It required fewer maintenance transactions since it was capitalization-weighted.

The first index funds were not unqualified successes. Primitive sampling techniques were used to track the approximately 500 issues which make up the S&P 500. Both significant tracking error and high transaction costs burdened performance. The reaction of most investment management firms was, at best, patronizing and, more often, hostile. Why would investors accept index-fund returns when they expected active management to add at least several percentage points to performance?

While the literature on efficient markets grew and quantitative management techniques improved dramatically in the 1970s, passive management did not achieve broad acceptance until the mid-1980s. Table 2-2 traces the explosive growth of equity index funds held by tax-exempt institutions. They increased 10-fold from $7 billion at year-end 1980 to $75 billion by the end of 1985. Over the subsequent 7 years ended 1992, they reached an estimated $432 billion.

**Table 2-2.** Equity Index Funds*

| Year end | $ Billions |
|----------|-----------|
| 1980 | $  7 |
| 1985 | 75 |
| 1986 | 121 |
| 1987 | 191 |
| 1988 | 198 |
| 1989 | 286 |
| 1990 | 282 |
| 1991 | 380 |
| 1992 | 432 |

*Held by tax-exempt institutions, includes foreign-stock index funds.

SOURCE: *Pensions & Investments,* Crain Communications, Inc. (Copyright 1993.)

## How Performance Comparisons
## Drive Market Share

While the academicians who provided the theoretical background for passive management might point to this trend with pride, they recognize that investors have been largely convinced by practical considerations rather than theoretical arguments. The rush to passive management did not really begin until performance comparisons made clear that most active managers were underperforming relative to the S&P 500. In the second half of the 1970s and the early 1980s, many active managers, measured against the S&P 500, benefited from the superior performance of small-capitalization stocks included in their portfolios. Table 2-3, in contrast, shows the results of the median equity manager relative to the S&P 500 over 1983 to 1992. The median equity manager underperformed the S&P 500 in 7 of these past 10 years. This adverse turn in the performance of active

**Table 2-3.** Active Manager Performance

|  | S&P 500 | Median manager | |
| --- | --- | --- | --- |
|  | Total return | Total return | Rel. S&P 500 |
| 1983 | 22.4% | 20.1% | −2.3% |
| 1984 | 6.1 | 3.0 | −3.1 |
| 1985 | 31.7 | 29.6 | −2.1 |
| 1986 | 18.3 | 16.8 | −1.5 |
| 1987 | 5.1 | 3.8 | −1.3 |
| 1988 | 16.7 | 17.0 | +0.3 |
| 1989 | 31.7 | 26.5 | −5.2 |
| 1990 | −3.2 | −4.1 | −0.9 |
| 1991 | 30.6 | 31.8 | +1.2 |
| 1992 | 7.7 | 9.1 | +1.4 |

SOURCE: Wilshire Associates, Inc., Santa Monica, CA, Trust Universe Comparison Service (5000 institutional accounts representing $600 billion of pension plan assets in custody at 39 institutions). (Copyright 1993.)

managers over much of the 1980s reflected in large part an extended period of superior returns for large-capitalization stocks. Beginning in 1983, large-capitalization issues, which dominate the S&P 500, performed well relative to small-capitalization issues. Some investors attribute the superior performance of the S&P 500 to strong demand for large-capitalization stocks created by the rush to index funds. Whatever the reason, investors were made increasingly aware of the underperformance of active management as a result of improvements in performance measurement.

Plan sponsors seem certain to move additional assets into various forms of index funds in the years ahead. Analysis of active-manager performance has included periods, such as late 1970s and early 1980s, when active management achieved superior returns relative to the S&P 500. Such favorable performance comparisons are virtually certain to recur. When they do, they will likely limit, or interrupt, for a time the further shift to index funds. Slowing of gains for S&P 500 index funds, however, may be partially offset by continued rapid gains for other index funds representing such broad stock categories as small capitalization, growth, and value. Currently, tax-exempt institutional investors hold about 30 percent of equities in index funds. We look for further gains in market share in the 1990s, although at a much slower average rate of increase than over the past decade.

## Reshaping the Way Active Managers Operate

### Competition Forces Change

The shift to passive management has profoundly affected active-management techniques as well as the profitability of investment management firms. Active management has adapted in various ways to the vigorous growth of passive management and the accompanying implications for stock market efficiency. The following pages focus on changes affecting active management attributable at least in part to these influences.

## Subtracting from Revenues

The inroads of index funds over the past 2 decades represent a major limitation on the revenues of active managers. As shown in Table 2-2, about $432 billion of equity funds are now managed passively, mainly in S&P 500 index funds. The net subtraction of active-management fees, assuming an average of about 35 basis points, represents a reduction of more than $1 billion in annual revenues to active managers from what, other things equal, they otherwise would be.

The loss of active-management fees cannot be offset by acquisition of an equal amount of index fund business, even where the manager handles both types of business. Management fees for equity index funds (domestic stocks) range from about 2 to 10 basis points, depending on portfolio size. Because intense competitive pressure has turned index funds into a commodity-type business, profit margins for even a very large passive operation are likely to be much smaller than for the more successful active managers.

A shift to index funds exerts similar pressure on brokerage revenues. Transaction costs are greatly reduced for index funds for two reasons. Turnover of shares (greater of sales or purchases) may average as low as 30 percent for some active managers to over 100 percent for others. This ratio drops to 3 to 5 percent for an index fund once established and no longer subject to additions or withdrawals. Index funds do not completely eliminate turnover. Dividend payments require reinvestment, changes will occur from time to time in the index, and the fund itself may be subject to additions and/or withdrawals. Equally important, passive investment incurs much lower costs per transaction than active management. Transaction costs, including brokerage commissions and the impact on prices of buying and selling the shares, average about 30 basis points for index funds transactions compared to an estimated 100 to 150 basis points for a typical active-management trade.

## Lowering Expectations

A highly efficient market implies that it is more difficult to achieve superior performance than suggested by the traditional claims of investment managers. Until recently, many active managers claimed that they could outperform the broad market averages by large margins, perhaps by as much as 4 or 5 percentage points per year. Traditional active managers did not pay close attention to transaction costs or benchmark portfolios, since the margin of expected superior performance would swamp such subtleties. Many studies in the universities and professional investment community have stressed the role of chance in explaining superior performance. In the face of the accumulating evidence bearing on the efficiency of the stock market, active managers have had to revise their expectations accordingly. Many now target performance in excess of their respective benchmarks of 1 to 2 percentage points.

## Recalibrating Performance Measurement

Prior to the 1980s, most active managers paid little attention to the composition of the benchmark they were trying to outperform. They bought stocks they liked and ignored those they did not know much about. Many managers demonstrated distinctive styles—such as growth, value, or small-capitalization. They pursued these styles regardless of the fact that their portfolios bore little resemblance to the performance benchmark, usually the S&P 500. The underlying logic stressed a "market cycle" lasting 3 to 5 years. While active managers recognized that their individual styles might underperform for a year or two, they expected that their portfolios would outperform by a substantial margin over a complete market cycle.

Unfortunately for the traditional active managers, the evolving performance measurement techniques of the 1980s increasingly demonstrated that active managers were not outperforming the broad market indexes—not over the short term and not over the long term. Often superior performance was shown to be due entirely to the manager's style. The manager's performance would deteriorate as soon as the associated style was out of favor.

Academics and consultants began to measure the performance of active managers relative to their respective styles. For instance, if a manager routinely bought growth stocks, performance would be measured relative to a universe of growth stocks. If a manager bought small-capitalization stocks, then a universe of small-capitalization stocks would represent the benchmark portfolio. These benchmark portfolios came to be called "normal portfolios" since they represented securities that the manager would normally hold.

Institutional clients have forced active managers to pay much more attention to the performance benchmark. If the normal portfolio is the S&P 500, they have to recognize as their positive bets the stocks overweighted relative to the S&P 500. Similarly, they have to look at their negative bets as stocks underweighted relative to the S&P 500. If a growth bias characterizes the normal portfolio, the objective becomes superior performance relative to the appropriate growth-stock universe. Where performance measurement utilizes normal portfolios, the manager's style, and whether it is in or out of favor, no longer is very significant. Performance is measured relative to the appropriate style, and the objective is to outperform the designated style.

## Tying Fees to Performance

As performance measurement became more precise and the ability of active managers to outperform became more suspect, a few institutional clients began to press their portfolio managers to accept "incentive" or "performance" fees. While performance fees have been around for a long time, they were generally structured as an option. The manager received a base fee and a positive incentive fee if performance exceeded a specified hurdle. The new performance fees had an important structural difference. In addition to a positive incentive fee for superior performance, there was a negative fee for underperformance. The interests of the manager and the client were now in parallel. If the manager performed well, fees would be high—usually higher than fees earned under the traditional fee schedule. If, however, the manager performed poorly, fees would drop, perhaps even as low as zero. Appendix 2-2 illustrates application of an incentive fee to an actively managed portfolio.

It is difficult for managers to argue against this type of performance fee. Since passive management is now a clear alternative, the only reason to hire an active manager is superior performance. Does an active manager deserve a traditional fixed fee for underperforming his or her normal portfolio? More and more clients are saying no. The result is escalating pressure on active managers to outperform their normal portfolios.

## Containing Transaction Costs

Normal portfolios and performance fees draw attention to transaction costs. Active managers have a continuing incentive to control transaction costs, since they are a direct subtraction from portfolio performance. The incentive is increased materially when more realistic performance measurement, with the aid of carefully selected normal portfolios, underscores the burden of transaction costs on total return. Performance fees contribute to further scrutiny of transaction costs. If, by way of example, the manager stands to earn (or forfeit) $100,000 per 100 basis points of performance, transaction costs can look extremely important.

Active managers have begun to look much more closely at transaction costs over the past 5 years. Many have turned to discount brokers (who do not offer research services) and off-exchange trading techniques. Pressure on transaction costs likely will continue as money managers and their clients experiment with electronic trading and other new trading techniques.

For active asset allocation, the opportunities to reduce transaction costs have been enhanced by informationless trades and the use of futures contracts. Purchase or sale of individual stocks as components of an index fund represents an informationless trade. Under such circumstances, the trade depends only on the broad decision to adjust the level of stock holdings rather than on specific information relating to a particular security. Brokers, relieved of the concern that they are taking the opposite side of a transaction from an investment manager who may have advantageous information supporting the purchase or sale of a specific stock, are willing to trade at a much lower rate of commission than would otherwise apply.

Futures contracts on the S&P 500 provide an even larger potential for savings. One futures contract covers a basket of securities equivalent in dollar value to 500 times the level of the S&P 500. With the level of the S&P 500 at 400, for example, one contract covers equities with a total dollar value of 500 times 400, or $200,000. To cover a buy or sell transaction in underlying stocks with a total value of $10 million, the commission on S&P 500 futures contracts would amount to about $625. The total commission for transactions in the individual components of the S&P 500 with an aggregate market value of $10 million would likely be in the area of $7500 to $10,000.

## Seeking Increased Risk

Paradoxically, the growth of passive investing, which attempts to eliminate unnecessary risk, has encouraged active management to increase risk taking. Now that passive management has become a respectable investment alternative, investment managers can focus active management on investments subject to a high degree of conviction. Where the conviction is no more than moderate, passive management logically substitutes for active management. Where increased risk is warranted in the actively managed portfolio, it is balanced by the lower risk in the passive segment.

The passive-active strategy established by several major pension funds provides an example. A core of equity holdings is managed passively, supplemented by a number of aggressively managed, highly concentrated, active portfolios. The managers of these active portfolios are asked to limit their holdings to a relatively few issues. The active manager may choose, for example, up to 15 issues considered to be the most attractive among the 40 or 50 issues which might otherwise constitute an institutional portfolio. The concentration of holdings aims to increase the potential gain, but, since the portfolios are not well diversified, also increases the downside risk. The lack of diversification by the active managers is balanced by the highly diversified passive portfolio.

In a similar way, asset allocation policy may partition holdings between a larger passive segment and a smaller, actively managed segment. The passive segment eliminates risk associated with opportunistic changes in asset allocation. Consequently, the active segment may be encouraged to take correspondingly larger risks. Suppose, for example, the asset allocation for 80 percent of the portfolio regularly conforms to long-term policy. For the remaining 20 percent, designated as the swing portfolio, active management may depart from policy as the outlook for the financial markets changes. Guidelines may be established to require aggressive risk taking within the confines of the swing portfolio. The most extreme guidelines (among many possible alternatives) would stipulate that 100 percent of the swing portfolio must be held in stocks or 100 percent in Treasury bills. If the transactions were accomplished with futures contracts (to minimize transaction costs), limits on turnover could be set correspondingly high.

## Targeting Incremental Performance with Limited Risk

Investors have shifted assets to passive management as they realized that the markets are highly efficient and that superior performance is often an elusive goal. In this environment, the possibility of a small but consistently positive increment of performance relative to straight passive management is particularly seductive. Opportunities to enhance returns relative to those achieved by the underlying index fund have evolved over the past 7 or 8 years. In most cases, these enhancements offer only small increments of positive performance, but the strategies typically involve very little risk. The enhancement strategies are unlikely to result in performance inferior to the index return.

The most common technique for enhancing equity returns has been the arbitrage between the S&P 500 stocks and the S&P 500 index futures. When futures are undervalued, investors hold futures rather than the underlying stocks. When futures are overvalued, investors hold the underlying stocks and sell futures. During the mid-1980s, futures were often mispriced and investors capable of handling the immense transaction flow of futures arbitrage profited handsomely, earning as much as 200 to 400 basis points annually over the S&P 500. As the success of this arbitrage became apparent, more and more investors set up procedures to take advantage of the mispricing. By the end of the 1980s, there were few mispricings and, hence, few arbitrage possibilities left in the market.

As one opportunity for enhancement evaporates, investors look hard for the next opportunity. The possibility of an incremental 20 or 30 basis points is a strong incentive. In recent years, investors have occasionally found significant mispricing for put and call options. Accordingly, they could virtually assure incremental returns over the underlying security through a series of transactions defined as a forward conversion. Appendix 2-3 presents an example executed in 1988. At the end of 1989 and in early 1990, the Japanese market offered similar opportunities. Investors who noted that Japanese warrants were sharply undervalued were able to enhance returns through replacement of stocks with warrants.

### Next Step Addresses the Decision Process

A logical next step in the evolution of investment management addresses the active decision process itself. We refer to the examples cited above to underscore the shifting emphasis as decision makers increasingly recognize that the stock market is highly efficient. So far, however, the active decision process has made little use, at least in a systematic way, of information already discounted by a highly efficient market. The approach to active asset allocation presented in this book exploits this opportunity. Before focusing specifically on the active decision process, the next chapter places active asset allocation in the perspective of the passive policy plan.

# Appendix 2-1
# Evolving Second
# Thoughts Concerning the
# EMH

After the rapid accumulation of evidence supporting the EMH during the 1960s, academic research increasingly focused on studies which aimed to modify the initial conclusion. Consider the reflections* of Gary G. Schlarbaum, CFA, an investment decision maker who had earlier taught investments at Purdue University and currently serves a major investment management firm.

> The two pillars of modern portfolio theory were newly—and firmly—established in 1970 when I first taught investments at Purdue University. The capital asset pricing model (CAPM) had been set forth by Bill Sharpe (1964) and others, and Gene Fama (1970) had just provided a cohesive framework and some firm conclusions about market efficiency.
>
> The two pillars are less solid in 1987. There is now a viable alternative to the capital asset pricing model—the arbitrage pricing model (APT)—which is perhaps the better of the two models. Many types of anomalies (perceived inefficiencies) have been discovered and many different strategies have been developed to capitalize on them.

In support of these initial observations, Schlarbaum subsequently summarized several academic studies which conflict with the hard-line version of the EMH. They are generally consistent with the increasingly accepted view that the stock market is something less than completely efficient.

### Efficient Market
### Research: The 1970s

During the 1970s, there was a major change in the direction of market efficiency research. Suddenly everything that was so well established—the twin hypotheses of the CAPM and market efficiency—looked a lot less firm.

*Reprinted with permission, from *Equity Markets and Valuation Methods.* Copyright 1988, The Institute of Chartered Financial Analysts, Charlottesville, Va. References are listed on page 49.

The first question posed in this period was: Does the market always respond quickly to public announcements? Several studies were published that shed doubt on that conclusion. Jaffe (1974) studied whether insiders make abnormal profits using their information set, and concluded that they do. He went on to test whether information in the Official Summary, based on what insiders are doing, may be used to make above-average profits. He concluded that it was possible. This made a small dent in the armor of the efficient market theory—at the semi-strong-form level at least.

Latané and all of his associates and students, many of whom are very well known in their own right today, studied whether the market responded efficiently to the announcement of quarterly earnings. His tests used Standardized Unexpected Earnings (SUEs). These studies attempted to determine how the market responded to differences between expected and actual earnings. Figure 2-1 illustrates the results. In this study, the

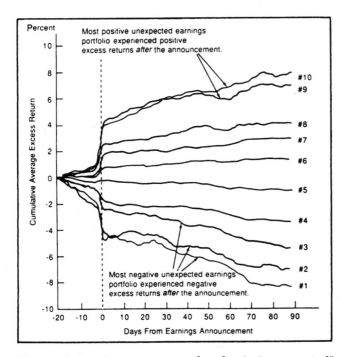

**Figure 2-1.**  Excess return after firm's "unexpected" earnings announcement. (*Source: Rendleman, Jones, and Latané, "Empirical Anomalies Based on Unexpected Earnings and the Importance of the Risk Adjustments,"* Journal of Financial Economics, *November 1982.*)

earnings surprises (differences between actual and expected earnings) were divided into 10 categories—or deciles. The top decile indicates the most positive earnings surprises; the bottom is the worst earnings surprises. The important thing for purposes of thinking about semistrong-form efficiency is what happens after the day of announcement. There are some rather systematic drifts. Those stocks with positive surprises drift upward; those with negative surprises drift downward. There was an adjustment before announcement, but there was also a kind of systematic adjustment afterwards.

These findings are not consistent with the notion of efficiency at the semistrong level. They indicate that there was an opportunity to create a trading system based on earnings estimates. There were also studies of reaction to listing on exchanges, which provided very puzzling results.

There is one argument in favor of market efficiency that must be addressed. Some people will say that markets are efficient no matter what evidence is uncovered, because we still do not understand asset pricing. Therefore, all tests of market efficiency are tests of a joint hypothesis. Rejection of the joint hypothesis means that either markets are inefficient *or* the asset pricing model that is being used to test market efficiency is not correct. So, if someone holds a very strong prior belief in market efficiency, it is easy to conclude the latter.

By this time, there was a growing body of evidence that was not consistent with that joint hypothesis. One watershed event of the 1970s, from an efficient markets point of view, was the publication of the anomalies issue of the *Journal of Financial Economics* (June 1978). Ten or twelve different anomalies were reported in that issue. By the late 1970s, the profession was moving away from the conclusion that the market was not efficient only at the strong-form level, toward the conclusion that it was not efficient at the semistrong form level.

The second question asked in the 1970s was: Are there profitable selection rules that rely on public information? This kind of selection rule really has a much longer history than the 1970s. An example of the selection rule which relies on public information would be a selection rule using price/earnings (P/E) ratios. There has been a long history of research into P/E ratios, some of which was done by Paul Miller and Jay Sherrerd in the 1960s. Nicholson published a piece on the subject in the *Financial Analysts Journal* in the early 1960s. The finding was that low P/E stocks perform better over a market cycle.

The low P/E studies continue. The profit opportunity did not go away after the results of early P/E studies were published in the early 1960s. This body of literature was capped by the very careful work of Basu in the mid-1970s. In a piece that was published in the *Journal of Finance,* he tested the low price/earnings strategy. Basu examined a number of different asset pricing models and used a carefully selected data set. His results showed that buying low price/earnings ratio stocks was a good idea.

Fischer Black's piece on the Value-Line Survey was another important addition to the efficient market literature. It was published as a letter to the editor in the *Financial Analysts Journal* called "Yes, Virginia, There Is Hope: The Value-Line Investment Survey." Quite simply, he looked at the rankings published in the Value-Line Survey and said, "Here's something that appeared to have worked in the past." A colleague and I did a similar test on Ben Graham's selection criteria (Oppenheimer and Schlarbaum, 1981). Ben Graham, a very well known investor, periodically published his advice to people he called defensive investors in his book *The Intelligent Investor.* So we did an experiment; we followed Graham's advice as if we had purchased *The Intelligent Investor* every time it was published. Sure enough, that advice had value. It had more value than Graham claimed, because he was quite modest in talking about his advice to the defensive investor.

Finally, the question was posed: Do insiders earn excess positive returns? The answer was yes. There were several studies on this topic, including Jaffe's work on insiders. All of them found that insiders earned positive excess returns.

## Efficient Market
## Research: The 1980s

In the 1980s, efficient market research has come full circle. The first question of the decade was: Are there patterns in returns that are exploitable? We ruled out these patterns in the 1960s; now we come to the 1980s, and we have said that there is evidence not consistent with semistrong-form efficiency. Suppose we went back to look at the weak form? One of the first papers of this phase actually appeared in 1976; it is a paper on seasonality by Rozeff and Kinney (1976). They noted that returns in January were higher than returns in other months. In the 1980s, we also discovered the size effect: Small firms tend to do better than large firms in ways that are not readily explainable by risk measures. (Yale Hirsch in the *Stock Traders Almanac* seems to have discovered this pattern long ago, as he had many of the patterns that academics discovered later.) Seasonality and size

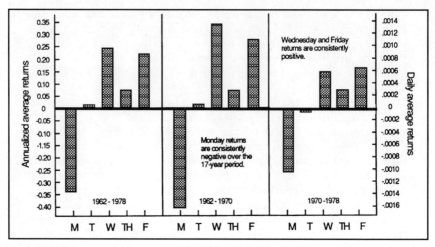

**Figure 2-2.** S&P returns by day of the week. (*Source: Jacob and Pettit,* Investments, *1984, Homewood, Ill.: Richard D. Irwin. Calculated from Gibbons and Hess, 1981.*)

combined form the turn-of-the-year effect, a pattern which repeated itself throughout the 1960s and 1970s. Then we came to something as simple as the day-of-the-week effect, which said that Monday is not a very good day (see Fig. 2-2). How can we explain that? Certainly it will go away because everyone is exploiting it—or so it seems.

There is a second question posed here: Do security prices fluctuate too much? Bob Schiller concludes that they do. That is clearly a source of controversy. There are others who think it is not so obvious.

So the conclusions have come full circle, from a point around 1970 when the market was believed to be totally efficient, to the point in the mid-1980s when the market appears much less efficient.

Schlarbaum concludes his remarks on a positive note:

In the end, our views on market efficiency will continue to evolve over time. The efficient markets hypothesis will continue to have its advocates and its detractors. New anomalies will be discovered. New strategies will be employed. Many questions remain to be answered, and as these are answered, more will arise. This continuing interest in market efficiency is healthy for the profession, because it is here that ideas from the academe and experiences from the real world come together to create synergies that represent progress in the business of investment management.

## References

Sharpe, W. F. 1964. Capital Asset Prices: A Theory of Market Equilibrium Under Conditions of Risk. *Journal of Finance* 19 (September): 425–442.

Fama, E. F. 1970. Efficient Capital Markets: A Review of Theory and Empirical Work. *Journal of Finance* 25 (May): 383–417.

Jaffe, J. A. 1974. Special Information and Insider Trading. *Journal of Business* 47 (July): 410–428.

Nicholson, S. F. 1960. Price-Earnings Ratios. *Financial Analysts Journal* 16 (July/August): 43–45.

Basu, S. 1977. The Investment Performance of Common Stock in Relation to their Price/Earnings Ratios: A Test of the Efficient Market Hypothesis. *Journal of Finance* 32 (June): 663–682.

Black, F. 1973. Yes, Virginia, There is Hope: Tests of the Value Line Ranking System. *Financial Analysts Journal* 29 (September/October): 10–14.

Oppenheimer, H. and G. G. Schlarbaum. 1981. Investing with Ben Graham: An *Ex Ante* Test of the Efficient Market Hypothesis. *Journal of Finance and Quantitative Analysis* (September): 341–360.

Rozeff, M. S. and W. R. Kinney, Jr. 1976. Capital market seasonality: The case of stock returns. *Journal of Financial Economics* 3 (October): 379–402.

Hirsch, T. *The Stock Trader's Almanac.* The Hirsch Organization.

# Appendix 2-2
# Performance Fees

The schedule of performance fees shown here has been used by a large tax-exempt fund in determining the compensation for outside portfolio managers.

## Fee

The manager will be paid a base fee plus an incentive according to the following schedule:

| Value-added* | Fee,† % |
|---|---|
| −800 or lower | 0 |
| −600 | 20 |
| −400 | 40 |
| −200 | 60 |
| 0 | 80 |
| +200 | 100 |
| +400 | 120 |
| +600 | 140 |
| +800 | 160 |
| +1000 | 180 |
| +1200 or higher | 200 |

*Performance relative to normal portfolio (basis points).

†As a percent of standard fee schedule: 0.70% on first $10 million, 0.60% on next $25 million, 0.50% thereafter.

## Payment Schedule

The fee will be paid according to the following rate and schedule:

| | | |
|---|---|---|
| 1st Quarter 1992 | 100% of standard fee | April 20, 1992 |
| 2nd Quarter 1992 | 100% of standard fee | June 20, 1992 |
| 3rd Quarter 1992 | 100% of standard fee* | October 20, 1992 |
| 4th Quarter 1992 | Remainder of fee due under incentive schedule† | January 25, 1993 |

*Will not be due until January 25, 1993, if performance for the first 9 months lags the normal by more than 300 basis points.

†Negative fees will be applied first against first-quarter 1993 fees, next against second-quarter 1993 fees.

## Example 1

| | |
|---|---|
| Performance of client account | +21.65% |
| Less performance of normal | +15.41% |
| Value-added | +6.24% |

| | |
|---|---|
| Standard fee on average assets of $32,514,219 | 0.631% |
| Times incentive fee factor for +624 basis points | ×1.424 |
| Incentive fee rate | 0.899% |

| | |
|---|---|
| Incentive fee rate times average assets | $292,303 |
| Less payment in first three quarters | 153,814 |
| Due on January 25, 1993 | $138,489 |

## Example 2

| | |
|---|---|
| Performance of client account | +7.21% |
| Less performance of normal | +8.71% |
| Value-added | − 1.50% |

| | |
|---|---|
| Standard fee on average assets of $30,829,324 | 0.632% |
| Times incentive fee factor for −150 basis points | ×0.650 |
| Incentive fee rate | 0.411% |

| | |
|---|---|
| Incentive fee rate times average assets | $126,709 |
| Less payment in first three quarters | 146,131 |
| To be applied against first-quarter 1993 fee | − $19,422 |

# Appendix 2-3
# Arbitrage Opportunities

## Forward Conversion

The following example of a forward conversion uses closing prices for Kraft on October 27, 1988. The net outlay is the net negative cash flow as shown below:

| Transaction | Cash flow |
|---|---|
| Buy stock | $ –94.50 |
| Sell December 100 call | +3.625 |
| Buy December 100 put | –8.00 |
| Pay commissions | –0.175 |
| Net cash flow on 10/27/88 | $–99.05 |
| Dividend on 11/14/88 | $ +0.51 |

### Outcome 1: Hold Until Expiration on 12/15/88

A. If stock price exceeds strike price, the call is exercised, the stock is delivered, and the put expires. The investor receives the strike price plus one dividend.

$$\frac{\text{Strike price + dividends}}{\text{Net outlay}} = \frac{100 + 0.51}{99.05} = 1.015$$

$$= 11.50\% \text{ annualized rate of return}$$

B. If strike price exceeds stock price, the put is exercised, the stock is delivered, and the call expires. The investor receives the strike price plus dividends (same as above).

$$\frac{\text{Strike price + dividends}}{\text{Net outlay}} = \frac{100 + 0.51}{99.05} = 1.015$$

$$= 11.50\% \text{ annualized}$$

### Outcome 2: Call Is Exercised Before Ex-Dividend Date.
The stock is called 11/13/88, and the put is sold. The investor receives the strike prices of 100 and the proceeds from the sale of the put, but no dividends.

$$\frac{\text{Strike + put*}}{\text{Net outlay}} = \frac{100 + 0}{99.05} = 1.010 = 22.70\% \text{ annualized}$$

*Assume put is worthless (the worst case).

# References

1. James H. Lorie and Mary T. Hamilton, *The Stock Market: Theories and Evidence*, Richard D. Irwin, Inc., Homewood, IL, 1973.
2. Jack L. Treynor, "Market Efficiency and the Bean-Jar Experiment," *Financial Analysts Journal*, May–June 1987, p. 50.

# 3

# Divide and Conquer: Unambiguous Roles for Active Management and Passive Policy

## Developing the Policy Framework

### Understanding the Need for a Dual Approach

Recognition that the stock market is highly efficient opens the door to both active management and passive investing. The traditional view of the irrational, inefficient stock market, as discussed in Chap. 1, excludes consideration of passive investment. Why would anyone commit funds to the stock market without a careful analysis of the outlook if market prices may at any time "go crazy"? Conversely, the textbook version of the completely efficient market, described in Chap. 2, excludes all opportunity for active management. Under this extreme assumption, no investor, no matter his or her qualifications, benefits from a forecasting advantage. Allocation of assets to common stocks, as well as other diversifying assets, therefore depends on the risk tolerance of the fund rather than on a specific appraisal of the current investment outlook. The third alternative, increasingly accepted among institutional investors, views the stock market as highly efficient but not completely efficient. This point of view, which we share, accords complementary roles to two very different approaches. A passive policy plan, reflecting the views of the investor consensus already incorporated in market prices, determines the long-term framework for asset allocation. Active management, meanwhile, seeks incremental returns through opportunistic departures from policy. This chapter first considers the development of the policy plan and then focuses on operation of active asset allocation in the policy context.

## Gaining Advantage through Diversification

The fund manager who recognizes that the financial markets are highly efficient will broadly diversify the policy plan among many asset classes. Returns from different asset classes, such as stocks and bonds, vary substantially from each other from one measuring period to the next. When stock returns decline sharply, by way of illustration, returns from bonds do not move in lock step. Part of the time they improve, and part of the time they do not. Similarly, there are times when bond returns falter but stocks will still achieve or exceed their expected returns. Risks for stocks and bonds, when combined in the same portfolio, partially offset each other. Portfolios consisting of both assets therefore achieve ratios of expected return to risk superior to that for either asset held separately. In general, expanding the asset groups included in the policy plan enhances the advantages to be achieved by diversification.

Our stress on diversification does not mean that all policy plans should have the same asset mix. Policy plans may vary widely since the objectives of fund sponsors vary widely. At one extreme, policy may be characterized by very low risk. To meet this definition, the asset mix would ordinarily reflect heavy emphasis on high-grade, shorter-maturity, fixed-income securities and limited use of equities. Alternatively, a policy plan may qualify as high risk, based on the skewing of investments toward common stocks and other more aggressive investments. *Neither policy plan—low-risk nor high-risk—is inherently better.* The choice depends on the return goals and risk tolerance of the fund. For example, a public retirement fund typically is more risk averse than a philanthropic foundation. Public funds must rely on tax dollars to make up for unexpected shortfalls in investment returns. Foundations, in contrast, can cut back on grants if returns falter. Policy plans may also vary widely within any category of funds. Differences depend in part on the specific values of the decision makers responsible for fund performance. Other critical factors include differences in sources of fund assets and in the obligations related to their disposition.

**Establishing the Policy Plan**

The policy plan defines the trade-off between the consensus views of risk and return which most appropriately serve the fund's objectives. Recognition that policy is the primary determinant of fund returns underscores its central role in fund management. In support of this central role, policy fulfills four important functions. First, the development of a policy plan requires that management define its financial goals in specific quantitative terms. Second, the policy plan links the financial goals of the fund sponsor to the management of the portfolio. Without a clearly defined portfolio plan, this link is fuzzy and may lead to misunderstandings. Third, the policy plan highlights the importance of diversification. Finally, the policy plan provides the benchmark against which the performance of the actual portfolio is measured. In the absence of a previously determined policy plan, it is difficult to determine whether active management is adding or subtracting value.

The first step in establishing the policy plan is to identify the various financial objectives of the plan sponsor, some of which will be in conflict with each other. Since no policy plan will be able to satisfy fully each of these conflicting objectives, the final selection will represent the choice of the most appropriate compromise. For a private pension plan, individual objectives relate to funding status, the timely payment of plan benefits promised to participants, and the interaction of the plan with corporate profit goals. For a foundation or endowment fund, the objectives include maintenance of the real value of the endowment into the indefinite future, support of a given level of annual spending, and avoidance of situations where spending has to be cut. Clarification of objectives at the beginning of the process provides criteria necessary to assess the relative attractiveness of the various policy alternatives.

## Defining Capital Market Assumptions

Policy alternatives depend on the capital market assumptions for the relevant asset classes. These assumptions include expected returns for each asset class, the measure of risk associated with each estimate of future returns, and the correlation of returns between asset classes. The assumptions are not meant to forecast the near-term. Rather, they are long-term forecasts based, to the extent possible, on unbiased sources of information. On the basis of these assumptions, portfolio optimization (accomplished with the aid of a standardized computer program) identifies the portfolio with the highest level of expected return for each level of risk. These portfolios (which together comprise the "efficient frontier") provide the alternatives from which the appropriate policy portfolio will be chosen.

The method used to select assumptions is critical. Poorly selected assumptions may result in large distortions in asset allocation. Nobel laureate William F. Sharpe effectively states the danger:

> Statistics professors teach the saving graces of the "law of large numbers." For example, the average of a series of numbers, each subject to a large error, may nonetheless be quite accurate. Optimizers, unhappily are subject to what might be termed the law of *small* numbers: if there is an error, an optimizer will find it (and probably suggest that you invest most of your money in it!). It is thus crucial that sensible inputs be used.[1]

How can the investment manager identify, to use the words of Professor Sharpe, "sensible inputs"? Individual estimates of the long-range future are subject to errors which may greatly distort the optimization process. These errors become particularly destructive when they are reinforcing. For example, suppose the return estimate for stocks is too high while the return estimate for bonds is too low. Even if each error is relatively small, the combined effect is likely to shift policy asset allocation sharply away from bonds and in the direction of stocks.

The widely used method of developing capital market assumptions makes use of individually developed estimates for each asset group. It seeks to determine each assumption in the light of historical experience and the various considerations which point to modification of the historical experience. The process, nevertheless, remains something less than an exact science. Appendix 3-1 presents adjustments to historical returns as compiled by a prominent consultant on institutional investment. Such adjustments aim to reduce sampling errors in historical data, although there can be no assurance that they will achieve this goal. Consequently, most large funds make use of constraints, particularly for asset groups where confidence concerning the accuracy of the input data is low. Development of constraints may take into account peer-group practice as well as the testing of proposed policy portfolios under market extremes recorded in the past. Suppose, by way of example, most similar institutions hold 5 to 10 percent in foreign stocks, but the designated set of capital market assumptions indicate a policy allocation of 30 percent. Under the circumstances, a limitation of 15 or 20 percent allows considerable leeway for emphasizing foreign stocks while moderating the more extreme risks associated with the target figure of 30 percent.

Appendix 3-2 summarizes an alternative approach to the identification of capital market assumptions. It aims to reduce error by deriving capital market assumptions, to the extent possible, from the consensus views of investors as reflected in market prices. A change in stock prices relative to bond prices, for example, translates into an objective measure of relative change in capital market assumptions. This method cannot eliminate error, but, as outlined in App. 3-2, benefits from internal consistency. Specifically, a significant error for one asset group tends to be offset by related errors for other asset groups. At the same time, estimates derived in this way provide a discipline which facilitates periodic policy revision. This approach, despite these advantages, is not widely used. Practical obstacles include the additional calculations required and the necessary focus on the fundamentals of modern capital theory.

Table 3-1 lists a set of capital market forecasts recently used by Harvard University in a study to determine an appropriate policy plan for its $6 billion endowment fund. The assumptions are consistent with the premise that investors are risk-averse and will price assets accordingly. The relevant risk-however, is that which cannot be offset through diversification. Since the contribution to diversification depends on the lack of correlation of returns for the individual assets relative to other portfolio assets, assumptions concerning correlations between the various asset groups are as important as assumptions concerning return and risk.

**Simulation Differentiates
between Policy Alternatives**

The next step utilizes a simulation program to review the future implications of various policy alternatives. For a retirement fund, the simulation aims to estimate the likely range of company contributions required to achieve targeted funding levels in the light of anticipated benefit payments. In a similar way, the simulation for an endowment fund relates policy alternatives to projected levels of spending and funded assets. In either case, an important consideration is the sensitivity of projections to the various levels of risk associated with the alternative policy plans.

The Harvard University Endowment Fund illustrates the application of simulation to a large investment portfolio. Tables 3-2 through 3-4 present data from simulations run by Harvard based on the capital market assumptions shown in Table 3-1. Table 3-2 shows the five alternative portfolios included in the study. Note that the portfolios are arranged in order of ascending expected return (and risk). Table 3-3 displays projections based on portfolio C. These projections assume spending at 5.25 percent of the average market value of assets over the previous 12 months, annual deposits equal to 1.5 percent of market value,

**Table 3-1.** Capital Market Assumptions, Harvard University Endowment Fund

| Asset classes | Real return* | Risk† | Correlation coefficients | | | | | | | | | | |
|---|---|---|---|---|---|---|---|---|---|---|---|---|---|
| | | | 1 | 2 | 3 | 4 | 5 | 6 | 7 | 8 | 9 | 10 | 11 |
| 1. Domestic stocks | 6.8% | 20.0% | 1.00 | .65 | .75 | .45 | .20 | .25 | .60 | .35 | .50 | -.10 | -.05 |
| 2. Foreign stocks | 6.5 | 22.0 | .65 | 1.00 | .75 | .30 | .60 | .35 | .35 | .30 | .45 | -.10 | -.05 |
| 3. Foreign stocks—hedged | 6.2 | 18.0 | .75 | .75 | 1.00 | .35 | .25 | .30 | .45 | .35 | .50 | -.10 | -.05 |
| 4. Domestic bonds | 3.4 | 10.0 | .45 | .30 | .35 | 1.00 | .50 | .80 | .45 | .40 | .20 | -.25 | -.20 |
| 5. Foreign bonds | 3.3 | 14.0 | .20 | .60 | .25 | .50 | 1.00 | .65 | .40 | .30 | .15 | -.15 | -.10 |
| 6. Foreign bonds—hedged | 2.9 | 8.0 | .25 | .35 | .30 | .80 | .65 | 1.00 | .50 | .40 | .20 | -.15 | .10 |
| 7. High-yield fixed income | 5.0 | 17.0 | .60 | .35 | .45 | .45 | .40 | .50 | 1.00 | .30 | .30 | -.10 | .10 |
| 8. Real estate | 5.0 | 16.0 | .35 | .30 | .35 | .40 | .30 | .40 | .30 | 1.00 | .30 | -.05 | .10 |
| 9. Venture capital | 9.5 | 35.0 | .50 | .45 | .50 | .20 | .15 | .20 | .30 | .30 | 1.00 | -.05 | .00 |
| 10. Commodities | 4.0 | 20.0 | -.10 | -.10 | -.10 | -.25 | -.15 | -.15 | -.10 | -.05 | -.05 | 1.00 | -.10 |
| 11. Cash equivalents | 1.5 | 4.0 | -.05 | -.05 | -.05 | .20 | -.10 | .10 | .10 | .10 | .00 | -.10 | 1.00 |

*Inflation assumption is 5.0 percent.

†Risk as measured by annual standard deviation of return.

SOURCE: Harvard Management Company, Inc. Used with permission.

**Table 3-2.** Policy Alternatives, Harvard University
Endowment Fund

|  | A | B | C | D | E |
|---|---|---|---|---|---|
| Domestic equities | 30% | 33% | 35% | 37% | 40% |
| Foreign equities | 10 | 12 | 15 | 18 | 20 |
| Foreign equities—hedged | 0 | 0 | 0 | 0 | 0 |
| Total equities | 40% | 45% | 50% | 55% | 60% |
| Real estate | 10% | 10% | 8% | 8% | 6% |
| Venture capital | 6 | 8 | 10 | 12 | 14 |
| Commodities | 4 | 5 | 7 | 5 | 5 |
| Total private | 20% | 23% | 25% | 25% | 25% |
| Domestic bonds | 25% | 20% | 17% | 14% | 10% |
| Foreign bonds | 10 | 8 | 6 | 4 | 3 |
| Foreign bonds—hedged | 0 | 0 | 0 | 0 | 0 |
| High-yield fixed income | 0 | 1 | 2 | 2 | 2 |
| Cash equivalents | 5 | 3 | 0 | 0 | 0 |
| Total fixed income | 40% | 32% | 25% | 20% | 15% |
| Total | 100% | 100% | 100% | 100% | 100% |

SOURCE: Harvard Management Company, Inc. Used with permission.

and inflation at an annual rate of 5 percent. If all these assumptions hold, the expected growth in the real value of the endowment would amount to 2.54 percent annually.

Table 3-4 takes into account the uncertainty of fund returns. It displays fund spending in real dollars based on alternative assumptions concerning investment returns. The columns labeled A through E refer to the five portfolios shown in Table 3-2. Projections are shown for 5-, 10-, and 20-year intervals. The table lists median projection for real spending opposite the 50th percentile. The odds are only 5 percent that real spending will be less than the 5th percentile or more than the 95th percentile.

Table 3-5 shows the policy portfolio that Harvard selected. It is similar to policies C and D shown in Table 3-2 but makes allowance for *negative* cash of 5 percent. Harvard's studies indicated that the best portfolio to meet its return and risk targets could be created by "borrowing" cash and spreading it across other asset classes. Harvard does not actually borrow the cash but creates a

**Table 3-3.** Forecast of Cash Flow, Harvard University Endowment Fund

| Year begin | Year number | Nominal dollars (millions) | | | | Real dollars (millions) | | | |
|---|---|---|---|---|---|---|---|---|---|
| | | Income | Market value | Spending* | Deposits | Income | Market value | Spending | Deposits |
| 7/90 | 0 | $ 250.00 | $ 5,000.00 | $ 244.05 | $ 75.00 | $250.00 | $5,000.00 | $244.05 | $ 75.00 |
| 7/91 | 1 | 268.72 | 5,374.36 | 256.25 | 80.61 | 255.92 | 5,118.43 | 244.05 | 76.78 |
| 7/92 | 2 | 289.16 | 5,783.13 | 272.33 | 86.75 | 262.27 | 5,245.47 | 247.01 | 78.68 |
| 7/93 | 3 | 311.33 | 6,226.61 | 292.88 | 93.40 | 268.94 | 5,378.77 | 253.00 | 80.68 |
| 7/94 | 4 | 335.22 | 6,704.42 | 315.26 | 100.57 | 275.79 | 5,515.75 | 259.36 | 82.74 |
| 7/95 | 5 | 360.95 | 7,219.02 | 339.44 | 108.28 | 282.81 | 5,656.29 | 265.96 | 84.84 |
| 7/96 | 6 | 388.66 | 7,773.13 | 365.49 | 116.60 | 290.02 | 5,800.43 | 272.73 | 87.01 |
| 7/97 | 7 | 418.49 | 8,369.77 | 393.54 | 125.55 | 297.41 | 5,948.24 | 279.68 | 89.22 |
| 7/98 | 8 | 450.61 | 9,012.21 | 423.75 | 135.18 | 304.99 | 6,099.82 | 286.81 | 91.50 |
| 7/99 | 9 | 485.20 | 9,703.97 | 456.28 | 145.56 | 312.76 | 6,255.26 | 294.12 | 93.83 |
| 7/00 | 10 | 522.44 | 10,448.82 | 491.30 | 156.73 | 320.73 | 6,414.66 | 301.62 | 96.22 |
| 7/05 | 15 | 756.18 | 15,123.63 | 711.11 | 226.85 | 363.74 | 7,274.72 | 342.05 | 109.12 |
| 7/10 | 20 | 1,094.50 | 21,889.96 | 1,029.26 | 328.35 | 412.50 | 8,250.09 | 387.92 | 123.75 |
| Increase | | 844.50 | 16,889.96 | 785.21 | 253.35 | 162.50 | 3,250.09 | 143.87 | 48.75 |
| Annual % change | | 7.66% | 7.66% | 7.46% | 7.66% | 2.54% | 2.54% | 2.34% | 2.54% |

*Spending rate is 5.25 percent of average market value over previous 12 months with a 1-year budget lead.

SOURCE: Harvard Management Company, Inc. Used with permission.

**Table 3-4.** Spending in Real Dollars (millions), Harvard University Endowment Fund. Stochastic simulation based on 5.25 percent spending rate.

| | Investment policy | | | | |
|---|---|---|---|---|---|
| | A | B | C | D | E |
| **5 Years:** | | | | | |
| 5th | 186.3 | 186.4 | 183.9 | 180.5 | 177.7 |
| 10th | 195.7 | 200.4 | 198.7 | 196.2 | 194.0 |
| 25th | 228.0 | 229.1 | 229.5 | 229.1 | 228.5 |
| 50th | 256.5 | 262.8 | 266.0 | 268.7 | 270.3 |
| 75th | 300.1 | 297.3 | 303.5 | 309.7 | 314.0 |
| 90th | 340.6 | 335.8 | 345.8 | 356.3 | 363.9 |
| 95th | 374.3 | 376.5 | 391.0 | 406.7 | 418.4 |
| **10 Years:** | | | | | |
| 5th | 168.0 | 168.9 | 166.9 | 163.3 | 160.0 |
| 10th | 186.0 | 191.6 | 191.2 | 189.0 | 186.7 |
| 25th | 209.6 | 230.7 | 233.3 | 234.3 | 234.1 |
| 50th | 285.6 | 287.4 | 295.4 | 302.0 | 306.1 |
| 75th | 355.1 | 369.9 | 387.2 | 404.2 | 416.3 |
| 90th | 433.7 | 441.1 | 467.8 | 495.5 | 515.9 |
| 95th | 519.7 | 493.5 | 527.7 | 564.0 | 591.4 |
| **20 Years:** | | | | | |
| 5th | 141.4 | 153.3 | 153.2 | 150.2 | 146.8 |
| 10th | 167.6 | 184.6 | 187.1 | 186.3 | 184.3 |
| 25th | 244.8 | 234.7 | 242.0 | 245.8 | 246.8 |
| 50th | 344.3 | 355.1 | 377.4 | 396.6 | 408.7 |
| 75th | 491.7 | 504.9 | 550.6 | 595.4 | 627.4 |
| 90th | 611.8 | 674.9 | 751.9 | 833.0 | 894.1 |
| 95th | 707.4 | 845.8 | 958.4 | 1082.3 | 1178.6 |

SOURCE: Harvard Management Company, Inc. Used with permission.

**Table 3-5.** Policy Plan, Harvard
University Endowment Fund

| | |
|---|---|
| Domestic stocks | 40% |
| Foreign stocks | 18 |
| High-yield fixed income | 2 |
| Real estate | 7 |
| Venture capital | 12 |
| Commodities | 6 |
| Domestic bonds | 15 |
| Foreign bonds | 5 |
| Cash equivalents | −5 |
| Total | 100% |

SOURCE: Harvard Management Company,
Inc. Used with permission.

negative cash position through security lending, repurchase agreements, or derivative contracts such as S&P 500 futures.

The fund sponsor must decide which policy alternative best matches fund objectives. The final selection is a trade-off. It limits expected return in order to limit risk to acceptable levels. Large endowments and foundations generally favor more aggressive investment programs than pension plans. Table 3-6 compares the policy portfolio of the Harvard University Endowment Fund with sample portfolios for four other institutions. Taxpayer criticism in the event of adverse market-price fluctuations has historically limited the risk assumed by public pension funds. While the gap between public and private pension funds has narrowed in recent years, public funds remain somewhat more conservative.

### Calculating the Return of the Policy Plan

Calculation of the return for a policy plan requires a performance benchmark for each asset class. An appropriate benchmark should be broadly representative of the asset class and easy and inexpensive to replicate. To illustrate, Table 3-7 lists the benchmarks chosen by Harvard for its policy portfolio. Harvard calculates the return on its policy portfolio at the end of each

**Table 3-6.** Sample Policy Portfolios

|  | Harvard endowment | University | Foundation | Corporate pension | Public pension |
|---|---|---|---|---|---|
| Domestic stocks | 40% | 45% | 50% | 45% | 40% |
| Foreign stocks | 18 | 15 | 15 | 8 | 3 |
| High-yield fixed income | 2 | 0 | 0 | 0 | 0 |
| Real estate | 7 | 10 | 10 | 7 | 5 |
| Venture capital | 12 | 10 | 5 | 3 | 2 |
| Commodities | 6 | 0 | 0 | 0 | 0 |
| Domestic bonds | 15 | 20 | 15 | 30 | 45 |
| Foreign bonds | 5 | 0 | 0 | 2 | 0 |
| Cash equivalents | –5 | 0 | 5 | 5 | 5 |
| Total | 100% | 100% | 100% | 100% | 100% |

SOURCE: Harvard Management Company, Inc. Used with permission.

**Table 3-7.** Policy-Plan Benchmarks, Harvard University Endowment Fund

| Asset class | Weight | Benchmark |
|---|---|---|
| 1. Domestic stocks | 40% | S&P 500 |
| 2. Foreign stocks | 18 | EAFE* |
| 3. High-yield fixed income | 2 | Salomon High-Yield Flash |
| 4. Real estate | 7 | Russell-NCREIF; 50% leverage† |
| 5. Venture capital | 12 | Venture Economics |
| 6. Commodities | 6 | Adjusted PPI + 4% |
| 7. Domestic bonds | 15 | SBIG‡ |
| 8. Foreign bonds | 5 | J.P. Morgan Non-U.S. |
| 9. Cash equivalents | –5 | T-bills + 0.5% |
|  | 100% |  |

*Index of European, Australian, and Far East stocks maintained by Morgan Stanley.

†Index of over 1500 properties maintained by Frank Russell Company and the National Council of Real Estate Investment Fiduciaries. Benchmark assumes index is leveraged 50 percent at prime rate.

‡Salomon Broad Investment Grade Bond Index.

SOURCE: Harvard Management Company, Inc. Used with permission.

month. The total policy return is the weighted average of the individual returns for each asset group. The linking of monthly returns determines returns for longer periods, such as a quarter or a year.

# Operating Active Asset Allocation in a Policy Context

## Adding Value through Superior Insight

Active asset allocation depends on superior insight concerning the valuation of the financial markets. The point of departure is the policy portfolio. The appropriate weighting for an asset class, in the absence of a superior insight, is that specified by policy. Once the policy plan is in place, however, fund management is in a position to consider active asset allocation. A weighting which differs from policy becomes appropriate when the fund manager concludes that the asset group is either undervalued or overvalued. Active management seeks to gain advantage by translating valuation into overweighting or underweighting. The degree of underweighting or overweighting depends on both projected return, net of prospective transaction costs, and risk.

To control risk at acceptable levels, active asset allocation operates within moderate ranges. Given complete certainty, the decision maker would commit the entire fund to the asset with the highest expected return net of transaction costs, no matter how small the advantage. In a highly efficient market, however, risk warrants as much attention as expected return. No decision is a "sure thing." No matter how skillful the decision maker, the prospective return advantage implied by valuation must be balanced against the risk that it may not materialize.

Consider a simple example. Suppose the policy plan provides for 50 percent stocks and 50 percent bonds. This policy represents the asset allocation that best meets fund objectives absent superior insight. How much should active management raise

the stock percentage in the light of a judgment that the stock
market is undervalued? As asset allocation deviates from policy,
the advantages of diversification deteriorate rapidly.
Consequently, an extreme increase in stocks from 50 to 100 percent would likely increase risk of loss to an intolerable level
should the active decision prove wrong. An upper limit of 60 or
70 percent, in contrast, would accordingly limit the damage to a
more acceptable level. Operating in this framework, skillful
active asset allocation would still have opportunity to overcome
the results of a wrong decision through a balance of correct decisions over an extended period.

Separate ranges apply to each asset group in the policy plan. To
illustrate, Table 3-8 lists ranges for the Harvard Endowment
Fund. Implementation within these ranges depends on market
liquidity and transaction costs as well as valuation. Domestic
stocks provide an example of a generally liquid market with
moderate transaction costs. The active manager, confronted by a
negative valuation for domestic stocks, will reduce the percentage to less than the policy standard of 40 percent. An extremely

**Table 3-8.** Ranges for Harvard University
Endowment Fund

| Asset class | Minimum | Policy | Maximum |
|---|---|---|---|
| 1. Domestic stocks | 30% | 40% | 50% |
| 2. Foreign stocks | 13 | 18 | 23 |
| 3. High-yield fixed income | 0 | 2 | 4 |
|  | 45% | 60% | 70% |
| 4. Real estate | 4% | 7% | 10% |
| 5. Venture capital | 8 | 12 | 16 |
| 6. Commodities | 3 | 6 | 9 |
|  | 20% | 25% | 30% |
| 7. Domestic bonds | 10% | 15% | 25% |
| 8. Foreign bonds | 0 | 5 | 10 |
| 9. Cash equivalents | −10 | −5 | 20 |
|  | 10% | 15% | 35% |

SOURCE: Harvard Management Company, Inc. Used with permission.

negative insight could result in reduction to 30 percent. In no case, however, would the weight for domestic stocks be decreased below the minimum range of 30 percent or increased to more than the maximum range of 50 percent. By comparison, modification of the asset mix for illiquid assets such as real estate and venture capital is more difficult and more costly. As a practical matter, the weights for such assets are changed primarily by changing the pace of new commitments over an extended period.

## Implementing the Valuation Decision

Financial institutions currently stress three approaches to implementation. While the implementation in the "full portfolio" remains most widely used, two other approaches—"swing portfolio" and "overlay"—offer important advantages in specialized applications.

**Full Portfolio.**    An active asset allocation program may be implemented by buying and selling stocks or bonds within the full portfolio. As an example, Table 3-9 shows a $1 billion policy portfolio consisting of 50 percent stocks, 40 percent bonds, and 10 percent cash. As the table indicates, the portfolio manager could change the stock ratio from an overweighting of stocks by 10 percentage points to a 10-point underweighting by selling $200 million worth of stocks and buying $200 million worth of bonds. This method has the advantage of simplicity but also offers significant disadvantages in terms of trading costs. On the positive side, it requires no formal structure and involves transactions in securities familiar to all portfolio managers and investment committees. Offsetting negatives relate to commissions and the cost of market impact. These costs, which are almost always significantly higher than for transactions in futures, impose a heavy burden on performance.

Transactions in the full portfolio may also generate problems concerning the selection of stocks and bonds to buy or to sell. For a fund with a sufficiently large investment in index funds, the decision is straightforward. Any choice of issues, as determined by statistical sampling techniques, is appropriate as long as the portfolio continues to match the specified index within

**Table 3-9.** Full Portfolio Implementation

|  | % | $ millions |
|---|---|---|
| **Policy Portfolio:** | | |
| Stocks | 50% | $ 500 |
| Bonds | 40 | 400 |
| Cash | 10 | 100 |
|  | 100% | $1000 |
| **Current Allocation:** | | |
| Stocks | 60% | $ 600 |
| Bonds | 30 | 300 |
| Cash | 10 | 100 |
|  | 100% | $1000 |
| **Target Allocation:** | | |
| Stocks | 40% | $ 400 |
| Bonds | 50 | 500 |
| Cash | 10 | 100 |
|  | 100% | $1000 |
| **Required Transaction:** | | |
| Stocks | −20% | $−200 |
| Bonds | +20 | +200 |
| Cash | 0 | 0 |
|  | 0% | $ 0 |

SOURCE: Harvard Management Company, Inc. Used with permission.

prescribed limits. The decision becomes much more difficult, however, if the fund is managed externally by a number of active managers. Should a manager striving to outperform his or her benchmark (such as the S&P 500) be forced to sell (disrupting the stock selection process) because of an active asset allocation decision made by someone else? How will the transaction costs be allocated among the external managers and the active asset allocation program? Will the external managers be able to manage effectively against their benchmarks with frequent cash flow in and out of their accounts?

**Swing Portfolio.** Establishment of a swing portfolio provides an alternative framework for the operation of active asset allocation. To illustrate, Table 3-10 divides the portfolio shown in Table 3-9 into two segments. The core segment ($700 million) maintains asset allocation as determined by policy. The swing portfolio ($300 million) provides for implementation of the active asset allocation program. Table 3-10, which confines all transactions to the swing portfolio, shows the same shift in asset mix for the total portfolio as implemented in Table 3-9. The key advantage of the swing-portfolio approach to active asset allocation is the complete independence of the core portfolio. The assets in the core portfolio may be allocated to external managers without distorting their efforts with frequent inflows or outflows of cash. Separation of the swing portfolio from the remainder of the fund assets also permits closer control of the program of active asset allocation. All transactions

**Table 3-10.** Swing Portfolio

| | Core | | Swing | | Total | |
|---|---|---|---|---|---|---|
| | % | $ millions | % | $ millions | % | $ millions |
| **Policy Portfolio:** | | | | | | |
| Stocks | 50% | $350 | 50% | $150 | 50% | $ 500 |
| Bonds | 40 | 280 | 40 | 120 | 40 | 400 |
| Cash | 10 | 70 | 10 | 30 | 10 | 100 |
| | 100% | $700 | 100% | $300 | 100% | $1000 |
| **Current Allocation:** | | | | | | |
| Stocks | 50% | $350 | 83% | $250 | 60% | $ 600 |
| Bonds | 40 | 280 | 7 | 20 | 30 | 300 |
| Cash | 10 | 70 | 10 | 30 | 10 | 100 |
| | 100% | $700 | 100% | $300 | 100% | $1000 |
| **Target Allocation:** | | | | | | |
| Stocks | 50% | $350 | 17% | $ 50 | 40% | $ 400 |
| Bonds | 40 | 280 | 73 | 220 | 50 | 500 |
| Cash | 10 | 70 | 10 | 30 | 10 | 100 |
| | 100% | $700 | 100% | $300 | 100% | $1000 |

SOURCE: Harvard Management Company, Inc. Used with permission.

related to active asset allocation are absorbed by the swing portfolio, thereby facilitating performance measurement. At the same
time, the manager of the swing portfolio is free to transact in
futures contracts or other derivatives which permit significant
savings in transaction costs.

The shifts in asset mix within the swing portfolio appear more
aggressive than if the shift is compared to the much larger full
portfolio. Note that the proportion of stocks in the swing portfolio
in Table 3-10 declines from 83 to 17 percent, a net reduction of 66
percentage points. The comparable reduction for the full portfolio,
from 60 to 40 percent, amounts to 20 percentage points. Although
focus on the much larger change in the asset mix of the swing
portfolio may create concern among committee members, it highlights the specific decisions relating to active asset allocation.

**Overlay.**    A third alternative is to overlay the full portfolio with
positions in stock or bond futures. The asset mix of the full portfolio corresponds to the weights in the policy plan. Active asset allocation then buys or sells futures in order effectively to change the
asset mix. Overlay shares with the swing portfolio the important
advantage of low transaction costs. The use of futures minimizes
transaction costs and clearly separates transaction costs generated
by active asset allocation from those incurred for other purposes.
Overlay also offers an additional advantage, since it permits nearly all fund assets to be distributed to external managers. Futures
require little cash advance—typically less than 5 percent for an
S&P 500 contract. Consequently, overlay permits nearly all the
assets that would be allocated to a swing portfolio to be allocated
to external managers.

### Controlling Risk through
### Rebalancing

The objective of portfolio rebalancing is to compensate for differing rates of change in the market values of the assets which
comprise an investment portfolio. As mentioned earlier in this
chapter, the policy portfolio is typically rebalanced monthly or
quarterly. Since the managed portfolio will be measured against

the policy portfolio, it too must be rebalanced at the same intervals. By way of example, consider the policy portfolio shown in Tables 3-9 and 3-10. It consists of 50 percent stocks, 40 percent bonds, and 10 percent cash. Suppose that over a 1-month interval the market value of stocks increases by 10 percent while the overall value of the remainder of the portfolio (bonds and cash) remains unchanged. If the active manager began the month weighted identically to the policy portfolio, the weight for stocks in the managed portfolio will rise to 52.4 percent by the end of the month. Unless the manager sells an appropriate amount of stocks and distributes the proceeds as required over the remainder of the portfolio, stocks will be overweighted by 2.4 percent.

Note how the rebalancing schedule interacts with the active decision. Assume that the manager starts the month with a neutral weighting and the market drops by 15 percent over the next 10 days. The manager then decides that stocks are too cheap and the active percentage should be increased from 50 to 52 percent. Since relative market-price changes have effectively reduced the weight of stocks in both policy and actively managed portfolios to 46 percent, the increase to 52 percent in the managed portfolio represents a temporary overweighting of 6 percentage points. At month end, the rebalancing of the policy portfolio will restore the equity standard to 50 percent. Assuming no further changes in asset values over the month nor any further change in the actively managed equity percentage, the effective overweighting of the managed portfolio at that time narrows to 2 percent.

## Measuring the Success of Active Asset Allocation

Measurement of the value added by active asset allocation derives from comparison of the performance of the managed portfolio with that of the policy plan. Many institutional funds analyze performance in a format similar to that shown in Table 3-11. The total value added, as summarized in the upper part of

**Table 3-11.** Performance Attribution (Rate of Return)

|  | Compound annual rate | | 1 year | 6 months | 3 months |
|---|---|---|---|---|---|
|  | 5 years | 3 years |  |  |  |
| Actual portfolio | 12.6% | 10.5% | 7.9% | 3.6% | −3.2% |
| Policy portfolio | 11.4 | 9.6 | 8.4 | 3.8 | −2.8 |
|    Value-added | 1.2% | 0.9% | −0.5% | −0.2% | −0.4% |
| Performance attribution |  |  |  |  |  |
|   A. Active asset allocation | 0.8% | 0.5% | −0.3% | −0.3% | −0.3% |
|   B. Active management within asset class | 0.4 | 0.4 | −0.2 | 0.1 | −0.1 |
|      Total value-added | 1.2% | 0.9% | −0.5% | −0.2% | −0.4% |

SOURCE: Harvard Management Company, Inc. Used with permission.

the table, includes the results of active management from all sources. The lower section of the table differentiates between the sources of the performance. To calculate the value added from active asset allocation, the first step is to multiply the weightings for each asset group by the performance for the appropriate benchmark. Total performance for actively managed asset allocation equals the sum of the weighted performance of the individual asset groups. Total performance for the policy portfolio, using the standard policy weightings and the same benchmark indexes, reflects a similar calculation. The value added from active asset allocation is the difference between the performance of the two portfolios.

While the numbers in Table 3-11 are hypothetical, the scale is realistic. In a highly efficient market, there are many analysts and investment managers looking for misvaluations among asset classes. As a result, competition is intense. An investment program that outperforms a well-diversified policy portfolio by 1 to 1.5 percentage points per year, on average over an extended period, must be considered a success.

# Appendix 3-1
# Adjustments to Historical
# Returns*

## Converting the Past into the Future

There is no shortage of apparently sensible adjustments one could make to the historical return numbers in order to convert them into best-estimate forward-looking expectations. Indeed, our listing of adjustment candidates got so long that we decided to categorize possible adjustments into a four-level hierarchy. This hierarchy recognizes the reality and legitimacy of both objective and subjective elements in telling the best possible capital markets prospects story.

## Four Levels of Legitimate Adjustments to Historical Returns

### Level 1: Current Yield Curve-Based Adjustments

- These adjustments replace the average historical Treasury bonds/bills yield curve with the actual yield curve today, and use the current inflation rate as the starting inflation rate;

- Return prospects are thus generated based on an eventual convergence with the history-derived real rate of return on T-bills, bond maturity premium structure, and equity risk premiums...but these numbers now reflect the possibility of near-term divergence from long-term historical experience in real bond and bill returns...and also the possibility of long-term prospective inflation diverging from long-term historical inflation experience...and hence the possibility of nominal capital markets returns also deviating from long-term historical experience.

*This appendix is reprinted from the *Ambachtsheer Letter*, December 2, 1988, by permission of Keith P. Ambachtsheer & Associates, Inc.

## Level 2: Apparent Biases-in-History Adjustments

- Interest rates were pegged at artificially low levels through the 1940s into the early 1950s (for example, T-bill yields averaged 0.53 percent over the 1941–1950 period, while the inflation rate averaged 5.91 percent)...while we don't know what yields would have obtained in a free market environment over this period, they would almost certainly have been higher than observed, leading to an upward adjustment of possibly 0.5 percent to the historical 0.5 percent real interest rate;

- The pronounced upward trend in inflation and nominal interest rates over the 1926 to 1987 period (e.g., long Treasury yields started at 4.5 percent and ended at 9.1 percent) produced systematic capital losses to an investment policy of maintaining a long bond portfolio, estimated by Arnott-Sorenson at 0.8 percent per annum; this annual capital loss is an estimate of the amount by which the historical long bond maturity premium of 0.8 percent should be adjusted upward if the effect of that trend is to be removed;

- The systematic rise in the per dollar of dividend price of common stocks (i.e., the overall dividend yield fell from 5.6 to 3.5 percent over the 62-year period) produced an annual capital gain estimated by Arnott-Sorenson coincidentally the same as the annual bond capital loss: 0.8 percent, which then becomes an estimate by how much the equity risk premiums should be adjusted downward if the effect of that trend is to be removed.

## Level 3: "We're Not Just Anywhere in History" Adjustments

- Sharpe points out that the collective risk tolerance of capital markets participants is reasonably related to the value of capital assets per head...collective risk tolerance rises as that ratio improves (potentially reducing required maturity, default, and equity risk premiums) and falls as the capital assets/person ratio deteriorates (potentially raising these premiums); if today (a) the ratio is still relatively high and (b) the return covariance structure doesn't embody an abnormally high degree of risk, the implication is that current premium values should be below their historical averages;

- Bernstein points out that capital markets participants are real people with real memories; prolonged bad experiences with a particular asset produces prolonged periods of time where that asset class is 'marked down' by investors; the implication is that the prolonged bout of terrible bond results of the 1970s and early 1980s might still be impacting bond yields even today;

- A third possible adjustment in this category would recognize that the long-term historical averages embody a number of reasonably distinct eras with distinctly different capital markets and inflation experience: which one of these eras are the 1990s most likely (and least likely) to resemble?...to the degree we assign probabilities to the actual 1990s experience different from the historical frequency of that experience, adjustments to history-neutral return expectations could result.

### Level 4: "The World Is a Different Place" Adjustments

- The 1990s environment in which capital markets must function has dimensions to it where history might be of little use; the current savings/investments–exports/imports disequilibrium of the U.S. economy might top a list of such dimensions, with the apparent recapitalization of Corporate America under way for some time now, and the globalization and integration of capital markets possibly second and third in importance; ignoring these three dimensions in fashioning best-estimate capital markets prospects today seems to us as inappropriate in such an endeavor as ignoring historical capital markets experience itself; serious asset allocators must be prepared to contemplate adjusting history-neutral return expectations for these without-precedent factors, even in the absence of a historical security blanket;

- Not only must new capital asset demand-related phenomena be monitored; there is a supply side too; capital assets are supplied as part of the economic growth process; ultimately, their collective return must approximate the rate of economic growth they help generate; different-from-history economic growth prospects demand different-from-history capital market return prospects.

- The absence of comparable historical 1926–1987 numbers for real estate, venture capital, and foreign investments does not justify ignoring these asset classes for pension funds; whatever results are available, together with our understanding of the risk/return characteristics, should be used to graft return prospects for these asset classes on to the expectations set for bills, bonds, and stocks.

## Appendix 3-2
## How to Extract
## Consensus Views from
## Market Prices

An alternative method of deriving capital market assumptions extracts consensus estimates from market prices. These estimates, serving as inputs to an optimization model, aim to identify the policy portfolio which provides the optimum expected return for the designated level of risk. The approach earlier described in Chap. 3, pursuing the same objective, develops independent estimates for each input—expected return and risk for each asset group, and correlations of returns between asset groups. While this approach is widely used, the alternative presented below offers the advantage of greater internal consistency. The starting point, reversing the usual operation of the optimization model, is an estimate of the allocation of assets in the market portfolio. The market portfolio reflects the combined judgment of the investor consensus—provided the market is efficient and investors share the same objectives. While such assumptions are subject to important qualifications, the market portfolio provides a consistent standard for derivation of the

inputs necessary for optimization. The following comments*
address identification of inputs for the major asset groups likely
to be held in a large tax-exempt fund.

## Consensus Approach Strives to Minimize Subjectivity

The consensus approach strives to minimize subjectivity in
establishing the series of asset-allocation plans from which a
policy plan is chosen. It uses probability analysis to focus policy
asset allocation only on those portfolios included on the efficient
frontier. As indicated previously, policy asset allocation is efficient when it offers maximum expected return for a given level
of risk or minimum risk for a given level of expected return.
Many other policy plans for asset allocation are possible, but
they are ruled out because they are not efficient; they would
require the plan sponsor to accept less expected return than
could be achieved for the given level of risk.

Our purpose here is to address the principles underlying the
construction of an efficiently diversified policy plan for asset
allocation. Although the technical details are ordinarily provided by an outside consultant, plan sponsor executives with oversight responsibility for pension investments need to understand
the process to appreciate the critical role of policy asset allocation—and also to recognize its limitations. An understanding of
the conceptual framework is also necessary for the pension officer with direct responsibility for the assessment of the qualifications of candidates for the consultant's assignment.

## Optimization of Return

Calculation of the set of portfolios that makes up an efficient frontier is a standard statistical exercise that optimizes expected return

---

*These comments are reprinted from Walter R. Good and Douglas A. Love,
*Managing Pension Assets: Pension Finance and Corporate Goals*, McGraw-Hill, New
York, 1990, pp. 89–95. Reproduced by permission.

relative to risk. It requires three inputs for each asset category: (1) expected average rate of return, (2) variability of return, and (3) data relating to diversifiability (correlation between the returns of each pair of assets available for inclusion in the portfolio). The expected return is an estimate of total return, including both current income and capital appreciation. The other two inputs—the variability of return and correlations between returns—bear on the riskiness of the portfolio.

In sharp contrast to inputs to investment strategy, inputs to the policy optimization aim to represent the *consensus* views of investors as already reflected in current market prices. The goal of policy is to exclude individual judgments in order to control risk. The probable error in consensus expectations is quantifiable, using capital market theory supported by a widely accepted library of supporting research. By way of comparison, individual views of the investment outlook may defy conventional wisdom and still turn out to be very right, but there is no objective basis for advance assessment of their risks. Individual judgments are therefore the proper role of investment strategy rather than investment policy, since strategy risks can be controlled by limiting the role of strategy.

Two assumptions are critical to the establishment of investment policy. First, current market prices are the best estimate of value. Second, expected return is related to perceived risk.

**Current Market Price Is the Best Estimate of Value.** For the purpose of establishing investment policy, the consensus view is regarded as the best measure of current value in the light of currently available information. Although the consensus is made up of many disparate points of view, erroneous conclusions that are based on inadequate information or poor judgment tend to offset each other. Consequently, the current consensus view is reflected in current market prices, provided they are established in highly competitive public markets where material information is readily accessible to all participants. Consensus views may change substantially—and often do—as new information becomes available.

**Expected Return Is Related to Perceived Risk.** A second

policy assumption is that investors are risk-averse. They will hold an investment only when the expected return is sufficient to compensate for the associated risk. They will therefore price securities in the marketplace so that perceived higher risk is accompanied by higher expected return.

*Expected Return Depends on Nondiversifiable Risk.* The risk of significance to investors is the risk that cannot be diversified away (nondiversifiable risk). To the extent correlation of returns between asset groups is less than perfect, partially offsetting fluctuations for the individual asset groups eliminate some of the risk for the total portfolio. Therefore, in a competitive market, only nondiversifiable risk can expect to receive positive returns, on the average.

*Nondiversifiable Risk Reflects the Market Portfolio.* Nondiversifiable risk contributed by a particular asset in a portfolio depends not only on the correlation of returns with other portfolio assets but also on the proportion of the asset in the portfolio. For the consensus of investors, the relevant portfolio is their aggregate holdings, usually described as the *market portfolio.* As the proportion of an asset in the market portfolio increases, if other things are equal, it becomes more difficult to limit risk through diversification with other portfolio assets. As a result, the investor must be offered a higher expected return to induce holding the asset.

## Measurement of Risk

Risk is measured by the variability of returns, usually from month to month over an extended period (such as 5 years). Common experience suggests that a record of wide variations in returns implies a high degree of risk in forecasting future returns, while relatively stable past returns indicate low risk. In highly efficient markets, such as U.S. markets for the most widely traded stocks and bonds, an analysis of historical variability of returns has been shown to provide useful forecasts of future variability. The widely used statistical measure of the variability of returns is the standard deviation, which quantifies the probability that future returns will deviate by a given amount from the expected average returns over the specified time horizon.

### Benchmark Expected Returns

Expected return is derived in several different ways, depending on the asset group. The benchmark returns, used as reference points for estimating the returns of other assets, are those for Treasury bills and the S&P 500.

**Treasury Bills.**  The return on short-term Treasury bills (usually 30 days or 3 months) is generally accepted as a proxy for the risk-free rate. No security can have a higher credit rating than a Treasury obligation, and the very short maturity almost eliminates any risk due to changes in interest rates. As the minimum-risk investment, the return on Treasury bills also serves as the benchmark for calibrating the "excess" returns for other asset groups. Since the reason for holding other more risky assets is to achieve returns in excess of the risk-free rate, policy planning focuses on expected returns in excess of those for Treasury bills. (By definition, the excess return for Treasury bills is zero.)

**S&P 500.**  The excess return for the S&P 500, representing the predominant segment of the domestic equity market, is derived from long-term historical averages. Since investors attempt to avoid unnecessary risk, they will buy stocks only as long as the expected excess return is more attractive relative to the perceived risk. Similarly, they will sell stocks to the extent the expected return from stocks is inadequate relative to the risk. Thus, in highly competitive public markets, the continuing transactions of investors with conflicting views tend to price stocks so that the consensus view of expected excess return is equal to the return required to compensate investors for the level of risk represented by owning a share of the market. The actual excess return for any given year may turn out to be far different than expected by investors at the outset, since new information will continually result in reassessment of the investment outlook. Over a period of many years, nevertheless, the average of the excess returns actually achieved is likely to approach the average of the excess returns that had been expected. Based on this reasoning, the average of historical *excess* returns—subject to possible modification for demonstrated change in the level of risk—provides the best estimate of the consensus view of the expected excess return for the S&P 500. Policy studies generally use an expected excess return for the S&P 500 of about 5 to 7 percent.

**Bond Market.** The expected return for bonds is derived from comparison of nondiversifiable risk for the bond market with that for the S&P 500. Bonds are often represented by a comprehensive market index such as the Shearson Lehman Hutton Government-Corporate Bond Index. The risk demonstrated by bonds is usually greater than that for short Treasury bills but less than that for the S&P 500. Because bond returns do not correlate perfectly with returns for stocks or other asset groups, part of the risk relating to bonds can be diversified away. Given an estimate of the proportion of bonds in the market portfolio and the correlation of bonds with other component asset groups, a standard statistical program permits calculation of the bond risk that cannot be eliminated through diversification. Bonds will be bought by investors, acting in their own self-interest, until prices have been bid to levels where the trade-off of expected excess return to nondiversifiable risk is the same as that for stocks. Consequently, it is the measurement of the nondiversifiable risk relating to bonds that is the clue to the consensus view of expected excess return. For policy planning, the excess return on long-term Treasury bonds is usually estimated in the area of 1.5 to 3 percent.

## Estimating Correlations of Returns

Although correlations may be deduced from market history, they may also require application of judgment. For example, the correlation between returns for stocks and bonds over the previous 5 years, in the absence of contrary information, constitutes a useful forecast of correlation for the years ahead. Yet history has also shown that correlations can change dramatically as the economic environment undergoes fundamental change. During the first two decades after World War II, returns for bonds and stocks were largely independent of each other. In the deflation of the 1930s, in contrast, returns for high-quality bonds were negatively correlated with those for stocks, and in the last two decades the returns demonstrated a large positive correlation. As changes in the environment become an issue, judgment necessarily enters into the process of estimating correlations of returns.

## Major Components of
## Traditional Asset Groups

Diversification of the policy plan is facilitated by recognition that the traditional risky asset groups—stocks and bonds—are themselves composed of subgroups with less-than-perfect correlation of returns. The S&P 500, as a reflection of the stock market, is itself inadequate since it represents only about two-thirds of the market value of domestic common stocks traded in public markets. A separate equity group—described here as the non-S&P 500—therefore warrants a place in the policy plan. Similarly, in the area of fixed income, long bonds are frequently viewed as separate from intermediates. The fixed-income market may be represented by the Shearson Lehman Hutton Government-Corporate Bond Index, which aims to weight by market value the population of publicly traded taxable issues with maturities in excess of 1 year. For planning asset allocation, data is available separately for two major segments divided by maturity: (1) 1 to 10 years and (2) 10 years and over.

For these and other possible major segments of traditional asset groups—both common stock and fixed income—their characteristics can be estimated in much the same way as indicated for the total bond market. Measures of variability and correlation of returns, applied to estimates of the composition of the relevant market portfolio, determine the risk that cannot be diversified away. Comparison of their nondiversifiable risk with that for the S&P 500 provides the basis for estimating the expected return relative to the S&P 500.

## Nontraditional Assets

Pension funds have increasingly invested in nontraditional assets in recent years. Traditional investments have focused mainly on large-company stocks, bonds, and cash equivalents, which are widely traded in highly competitive domestic markets. As suggested previously, the record of market prices for these traditional investments provides generally comparable evidence of nondiversifiable risk and correlations of returns necessary to estimate expected returns. The nontraditional assets of possible interest to pension funds constitute a long list, but the most important are real estate, international investments, and venture capital. For such asset groups, the market data necessary to derive consensus expectations are either absent or less than fully comparable with data for traditional asset categories.

For nontraditional assets—reflecting sparse historical data—inputs for expected returns, risks, and correlations require the use of analogy combined with a degree of judgment. Subjective judgment can be minimized, however, by a conscious effort to eliminate from consideration subjective opinions about the prospective investment environment. While estimates for nontraditional assets will still be influenced by greater subjectivity than those for traditional asset types, the effect on the policy asset plan is limited to the extent that these asset groups are candidates for a smaller part of the total plan. It is not unusual for the maximum policy percentage for real estate, for example, to be limited to 10 or 15 percent of the policy plan. In a similar way, policy constraints may be established for international investments and for venture capital. Because the estimates of consensus expectations for nontraditional assets are subject to greater uncertainties than those for traditional investments, such constraints are necessary. Even with such constraints, however, optimization still requires estimated characteristics for nontraditional asset groups. This information is necessary not only to establish the allocation of the asset within the range permitted by the constraints but also to allow for the interaction of these assets with other assets.

**Real Estate.** Real estate provides the most prominent example of an asset group that requires extensive judgments about risk, correlations of return, and its proportion in the market portfolio. Data for the variability of returns for real estate funds notoriously understate risk, since reported variability is heavily distorted by use of appraisal data rather than actual transaction data. Real estate appraisals are based on a number of factors other than market prices because comparable market prices are frequently unavailable. Since each unit of real estate is unique, moreover, the appraiser must use discretion when applying prices established in another transaction to a particular property under review. The result is that appraisal values tend to be considerably more stable than stock or bond prices, which reflect actual transactions in highly liquid markets.

A review of the fluctuations in the value of real estate transactions over a wide variety of historical periods suggests that the risks in holding high-quality real estate may be similar to the risks associated with high-quality stocks as represented by the S&P 500. In a similar way, judgments may be made about correlations of returns with major asset groups. There have been periods like the 1930s when returns from real estate correlated positively with stocks, but in the 1970s the correlation turned negative for a substantial period. A judgment is required to determine the influences that are likely to bear on their correlation in the years ahead. An even more difficult judgment is to determine the proportion of real estate in the market portfolio that should be available to pension funds. As explained previously, the proportion of the asset in the market portfolio, the correlation of returns with other asset groups, and a measure of the variability of returns are all necessary to estimate the consensus view of expected returns.

**International Investments.**   For international investments, market data for stocks and bonds may be similar to that for domestic markets, but the resulting consensus estimates are not wholly comparable even under the best of circumstances. Among the most important reasons are various barriers to the free flow of capital, including taxes levied on foreign investors, and the much higher transaction costs incurred in foreign markets. As stated above, the arbitrary limitation on the proportion of international investments in the policy plan is warranted.

**Venture Capital.**   Data on venture capital returns are particularly unreliable, in part because there is no ongoing publicly traded market in these investments and also because the history of the industry is relatively short. Most of the data that we have seen is compiled with a heavy bias in favor of marketing venture capital partnerships; it is hardly useful as the basis for planning policy. One approach is to view venture capital as a segment of the market for very small capitalization stocks (for which data are available). Venture capital returns are highly dependent on the market for initial public offerings, since financial success for the venture capital partnership is ordinarily determined by the prices achieved as the individual ventures reach the stage when they can be offered to the public. When markets for the very small capitalization stocks are doing well, as they did from 1974 to 1983, the record of venture capital investments is also extraordinary. When very small capitalization stocks performed poorly in the 1969–1974 period, the venture capital business also encountered hard times.

# Reference

1. Reprinted with permission from *Improving the Investment Decision Process: Quantitative Assistance for the Practitioner and for the Firm* (Homewood, IL: Dow Jones–Irwin, 1984, p. 60), The Institute of Chartered Financial Analysts, Charlottesville, VA.

# PART 2

# Adapting Active Management to a Highly Efficient Stock Market

# 4
# Exploiting Information Embedded in Stock Prices

## Highly Efficient Market as Storehouse of Information

### Uncovering Opportunity for Active Asset Allocation

A highly efficient stock market provides a framework for market valuation that avoids the extremes associated with the two widely familiar concepts discussed in Chaps. 1 and 2. The assumption of an *inefficient, irrational market,* which underlies traditional active management, is too open-ended. Active decision makers operating in this framework cannot systematically make use of the current market price as an input to the decision process because they reject a rational relationship between price and value. The model of a *completely efficient market,* based on simplified textbook assumptions, is too rigid. It eliminates any possibility of active management, excluding the opportunity to gain advantage through exploiting the considerable information embedded in stock prices. *Recognition that the stock market is highly efficient*—but not completely efficient—permits active managers to reorder the way they operate. The highly efficient market, in contrast to the inefficient market, identifies market price as a storehouse of information to be exploited by the active decision maker. Unlike the completely efficient market, it does not eliminate the opportunity for active management.

The purpose of this chapter is to explain how recognition that the stock market is highly efficient facilitates active asset allocation. At any point, the price of the stock market 1 year hence may be stated as the sum of two components: (1) the current market price and (2) the 1-year change in price. A highly efficient stock market implies that the best estimate of value is, *with one qualification,* the current market price. The qualification concerns a small amount of information already available but not yet discounted by market prices. The goal of active asset allocation, as we envision it, is to identify and analyze such information. To the extent this goal is accomplished, the odds tilt in favor of an advantageous assessment of the likely change in market price. We present Figs. 4-1 through 4-4 to portray graphically our point of view.

Figure 4-1 illustrates the relationship between information and market price in a highly efficient stock market. The disparate views of investors, reflecting varying interpretations of currently available information, translate into consensus market prices. The lower section of the bar in Fig. 4-1 represents the "old" information which, at any point, is already reflected in the current market price. The remaining two sections focus on information which will change market prices over the coming year. "Slow" information, available for varying periods during the year ahead before becoming fully discounted, constitutes the middle section. At any point, a portion of this slow information is already available, while the remainder soon will become available. Only "fast" information qualifies for the upper section. As it becomes available, it will be discounted too rapidly to serve as a resource for active management.

Fully discounted old information (the large lower section) includes both publicly available facts and the consensus expecta-

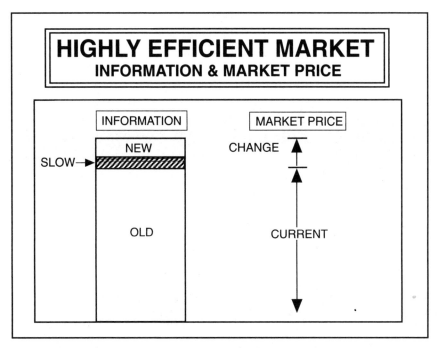

**Figure 4-1.** The relationship between information and market price in a highly efficient stock market.

tions that they generate. An example of a significant fact is last year's earnings, or even better, the earnings record for the past 25 years. A highly efficient market implies that such information is already built into the current level of stock prices. For example, suppose earnings over the last 25 years had been each year only half of what they actually were. Under these circumstances, the stock market would be much lower today than it actually is. An example of expectations already largely in the market is the near-term earnings outlook. Many stock market decisions reflect agonizing appraisal of the earnings outlook for the year ahead. Yet, as indicated in Chap. 7, such near-term earnings forecasts, in themselves, are unlikely to provide much help. The 1-year earnings forecast is to a very large extent already reflected in market prices, since economic visibility over the coming year is much clearer than for more extended periods.

The upper section of the bar represents new information which provides no opportunity for active management because it is so quickly reflected in stock prices. This rapid adjustment of stock prices to new information is a central characteristic of a highly efficient market. The evolving earnings outlook, to extend our earlier example, serves as an illustration. At any point, stock prices already reflect in large measure prospects for the coming year. As the year unfolds, investor visibility concerning the outlook for earnings will be correspondingly extended. Through an ongoing process, the level of stock prices will continually adapt to the changing estimates, usually at least 6 months and often as much as a year ahead. Adjustments of market price to new information are so rapid that even a hair-trigger response to the earnings implications for the year ahead offers active management, on average, no measurable advantage. As shown in Chap. 7, accurate advance knowledge of the earnings outlook for the S&P 500 over the year ahead in itself would provide little help to active management.

### Distinguishing between Fast and Slow Information

Old information will play a role in driving future stock prices but only to the extent that it is slow information. The thin margin of slow information represented by the middle section of Fig. 4-1 creates opportunity for enterprising active management. Because the implications of slow information are not readily apparent, market prices do not immediately discount their significance. Jack Treynor, addressing the distinction between slow and fast information, defines fast investment ideas as "...those whose implications are straightforward and obvious, take relatively little special expertise to evaluate, and consequently travel quickly..." In contrast, slow ideas are "those that require reflection, judgment, special expertise, etc. for their evaluation, and consequently travel slowly." Treynor adds that "...actual investment ideas lie along a continuous spectrum between these two polar extremes, but we can avoid some circumlocution by focusing on the extremes."[1] Note that the *processing* of information may translate into slow information individual items that otherwise would not qualify.

Recognition that the stock market is highly efficient facilitates analysis of slow information before it becomes thoroughly discounted by market prices. The first step is to distinguish between slow information and the much larger array of information already stored in current market prices. Proponents of the completely efficient market make no attempt to exploit this opportunity because, philosophically, they have ruled out the possibility of active management. Traditional active managers also encounter a philosophical constraint. They are burdened by their rejection of current market price as a rational source of information.

## How Much Slow Information?

Figure 4-1 allocates 85 percent of the bar to the old information already discounted in the current market price. This division of the bar is based on the relationship between the current market price and the 1-year price change in prospect. The precise percentage is arbitrary, since it necessarily changes from one year to the next. Our estimate, nevertheless, is generally consistent with both the concept of a highly efficient market and the market record of recent years. As new information becomes available over a 1-year time horizon, it is most unlikely to outweigh the influence of information accumulated over many past years and already discounted by market prices. This qualitative judgment is reinforced by the historical record. Data for the S&P 500 since 1955 indicate the market-price change in any one year has ranged from +38 percent to –30 percent. The median absolute change of 15 percent corresponds approximately to the division of the bar in Fig. 4-1.

Of the information driving the 1-year price change, how much should Fig. 4-1 allocate to slow information? It depends in part on the decision maker's identification of slow information. In any event, the answer cannot be exact, and the proportion changes from year to year. Based on our work as described in Chap. 6, about one-fourth the price change in any one year, on average, may reflect slow information. The middle section of the bar corresponds to this estimate. Part of the slow information is already available as old information but, unlike old information in the lower section, has not yet been discounted. Other slow information, still to become available, will also move market prices as it is discounted within the 1-year time horizon assumed by the graph. The middle section of the bar corresponds to the combined estimate covering both categories of slow information.

## Defining the Area of Critical Difference

The shading of this middle section of the bar underscores its critical significance to active asset allocation. Given the concept of a highly efficient market, a narrow band of old information which has not yet been discounted—slow information—is the only area where the active manager can gain advantage. In contrast, the information allocated to the lower section is already discounted by market prices. Similarly, the information in the upper section, although not yet discounted by the market, makes no contribution to the active decision process. Forecasts of such information may sometimes be correct and other times just plain wrong, but there is no net advantage.

By way of perspective, Fig. 4-2 portrays the relationship of information and market price as seen under the assumption of a completely efficient market. Figure 4-2 duplicates Fig. 4-1 in one important respect. The division of the bar between old information supporting current market price and other information driving the 1-year price change remains the same. The difference between the two bar charts is the absence in Fig. 4-2 of the shaded middle section. A completely efficient market rules out the possibility of the slow information necessary to gain advantage in anticipating future market price changes.

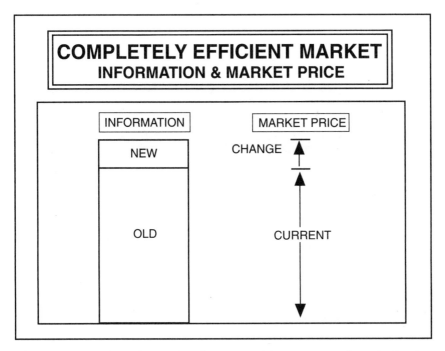

**Figure 4-2.** The relationship between information and market price under the assumption of a completely efficient stock market.

Similarly, Fig. 4-3 is constructed from the vantage point of traditional active management. As pointed out in Chap. 1, traditional active managers view stock prices as often irrational. Consequently, the division of the bar between old information represented by the current market price and other relevant information becomes inapplicable. Since an inefficient, irrational market leaves little room for identifying information already in the market, traditional active managers look elsewhere for inputs to stock market valuation. They select and analyze such inputs from the many sources of available information without reference to the information discounted by the current market price. The current market price enters the decision process at the

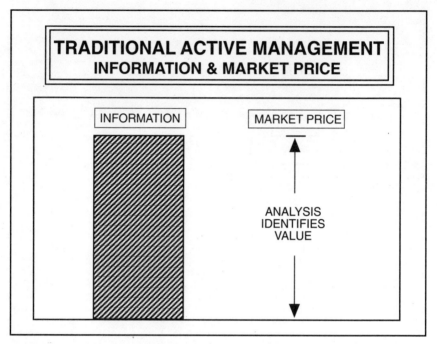

**Figure 4-3.** The relationship between information and market price from the vantage point of traditional active management.

very end, when, in relation to the estimated value, it serves as a measure of mispricing.

Figure 4-4, combining the three bar charts in a single frame, highlights the potential advantage for an active decision process that recognizes that the stock market is highly—but not completely—efficient. The critical differences between the three bars are the variations in the extent of the shaded area. *For the proponents of a completely efficient market,* there is no shaded area, because the opportunity for active management does not exist. *Traditional active management,* at the other extreme, is confronted with an extremely ambitious task. Shading extends over the entire bar, since the active decision process does not systematically make use of the relationship between current market price and already discounted information. *An active decision process, based on the principles of a highly efficient market,* in contrast, is

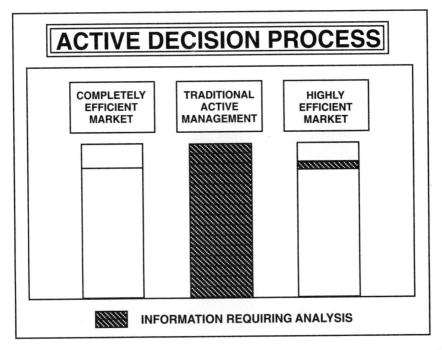

**Figure 4-4.** For the active decision process, information requiring analysis depends on stock market efficiency.

able to concentrate on the limited area of slow information represented by the much more narrow shaded area.

## Opening the Storehouse Door

### Making Use of Slow Information

If the stock market is a storehouse of information, how can active asset allocation benefit? The distinction between fast and slow information, as suggested earlier in this chapter, provides the clue. In a highly efficient market, slow information, as it translates into upward or downward pressure on market prices over the weeks or months ahead, will add to or subtract from the market price. The best estimate of value, therefore, consists of the sum of two quantities. By far the largest component of the estimate is the current market price, an input to the decision process readily available with perfect accuracy. The other component is the likely impact of the slow information on market price. Assessment of slow information constitutes the major challenge confronting active asset allocation.

Designation of current market price as the point of departure for valuing the stock market turns upside down the traditional view of the active decision process. As discussed in Chap. 1, traditional active management, forcefully warning against the irrationality of the stock market, determines current market value independently of the changing level of stock prices. For example, a sudden rise in stock prices, in the absence of a revision in estimated current value for other reasons, would automatically reduce the attractiveness of the stock market. The decision process presented in this book, in contrast, views the stock market as highly efficient. In this framework, it is dangerous to dismiss change in stock prices as simply evidence of irrationality. A better assumption, even if less than perfect, recognizes that stock prices move up and down for good reason. Acceptance of this rule—as a general description of how the stock market works—radically reshapes the decision process. Change in market price in itself no longer automatically changes the relationship between current market price and estimated current value. The attractiveness of the stock market may change but not simply because the current market price changes. The answer depends on the analysis of slow information.

### Defining the Time Horizon

The definition of slow information is sensitive to the time horizon required to impact market prices. If the time horizon is extremely short—hours or even a few days—market prices discount information too rapidly for it to be useful for our purposes. Under such circumstances, the information is more appropriately described as "fast" or "borderline fast." Over a much longer time horizon—beyond the next 6 to 12 months—the contribution of slow information to overall market-price change may well be dwarfed by other factors. The initially identified slow information, moreover, becomes increasingly vulnerable to revision, or even reversal, as the time horizon lengthens. In general, we look for slow information which will be discounted by the stock market within a year at most, and, preferably, within a considerably shorter period.

## Stressing the
## Underlying Logic

In our studies relating to the valuation of the stock market, two factors combine to contribute to the obscurity of slow information. First, no single item of slow information, viewed individually, is decisive in terms of its market impact. Given the powerful financial incentives afforded by the publicly traded financial markets, investors would quickly convert slow information into fast information if such opportunities could be easily identified. Second, combinations of items of slow information do not readily reveal their significance, since they require an understanding of how to add them up. Basic multiple regression analysis looks for linear relationships, but the relationships that we are seeking do not conform to a linear model.

In our efforts to detect slow information, we accord priority to the underlying logic. Understanding how the stock market works suggests where to look. Multiple regression analysis plays an important but secondary role. It is important because it can identify correlations consistent with the underlying logic. Its role is secondary to the underlying logic, nevertheless, because correlations do not prove cause and effect. Appendix 4-1 summarizes the limitations of decision models that rely primarily on "black-box" statistical analysis. A further test, as well as the ultimate goal, is the outcome achieved in real-time operations. Favorable results are necessary but, in themselves, are hardly sufficient to determine the choice of a decision process. An operating record never extends long enough to eliminate the possibility that chance explains favorable results. Appendix 4-2, quoting a recent analysis of data compiled by a leading investment consultant, again documents the fragility of past performance as the primary guide to future performance. To develop a decision process for active asset allocation in a highly efficient market, we therefore bring together three considerations. The underlying logic takes precedence, but we look for statistical confirmation over past history and continuing support in real-time operations.

# Explaining the Reluctance of Active Management

## Identifying the Barriers

In view of the potential advantages, why haven't active managers more aggressively reshaped the active decision process to exploit the concept of a highly efficient stock market? They have adapted in various ways to changing competitive pressures associated with passive management, as discussed in Chap. 2. Much less emphasis has been directed to the systematic use of the market itself as a fundamental information source. An active decision process, taking advantage of opportunities presented by a highly efficient market, aims to avoid futile reappraisal of information already in the market. Equally important, the current market price becomes available as a storehouse of information to be coordinated with slow information not yet fully discounted. In short, the task of active management is simplified and the probability of success is improved. The lack of momentum in this direction, in our judgment, reflects several imposing barriers that are only beginning to weaken.

## Conflicting Philosophies Create Deep Divisions

An extremely important barrier has been the deep division between traditional active management and the proponents of the efficient market hypothesis. Active managers earn their living—sometimes an extraordinarily high income—by convincing clients that they have gained and will gain advantage over the publicly traded securities markets. The efficient market hypothesis, in its strong form, takes the position that active managers do not add value to client portfolios. What is worse, according to this view, they subtract from client wealth through the cost of unnecessary transactions, inflated management fees, and incremental risk. From the introduction of the efficient market hypothesis in the late 1960s, the battle lines were drawn, separating the hard-liners on the efficient market from the practitioners of active management.

The resulting tensions have hardly been conducive to an open-minded effort on the part of either active management or proponents of the efficient market to find anything of use in each other's point of view. Active managers have often been more involved in defending against the threats arising from the efficient market hypothesis than considering its possible usefulness as a source of information. Hard-liners on the efficient market, most often situated in academic institutions, frequently have been all too ready to dismiss active management as futile. They have not been concerned, for the most part, with market prices as an ongoing source of information for the active decision process.

## Practical Experience
## Confronts Probability Analysis

Even with the best of intentions on both sides, there are other barriers to overcome. For people who have grown up within the framework of traditional active management, the idea of an efficient market is counterintuitive and appears distinctly out of step with their practical experience. Hard-liners on the efficient market, meanwhile, rely heavily on probability analysis. For the most part, their perspective differs markedly from the client orientation of the professional investment manager.

Traditional active managers, as discussed in Chap. 1, follow the "common-sense" approach. It is the same logic that any sensible business executive or consumer would use in day-to-day negotiations for real goods and services. They attempt to determine the value of the item independently of the offered price. They reflect a basic tenet of the free enterprise system, that buyers and sellers are adversaries, each attempting to take maximum advantage of the other. To many active managers, the idea that the market price might be a better estimate of value than a calculation based on broadly inclusive analysis of all relevant factors seems "just plain nuts."

Hard-line supporters of the efficient market hypothesis, convinced of the futility of active management, lack incentive to focus on ways to utilize market prices to contribute to the active decision process. Professor Robert S. Hamada,* speaking from the vantage point of the Graduate School of Business at the University of Chicago, underscores the chasm that he sees separating proponents of the efficient market and practitioners of traditional active management:

> There exist now very sophisticated statistical and econometric techniques using well accepted sampling and statistical theory, as well as large data bases on easily accessible and cheap computer systems. This research is incorporated in hundreds of "studies," worthy of that name, which have appeared in highly technical journals in the past decade. Unfortunately, it is not easy to translate these subtle results into catchy phrases for the lay person. Concepts resulting from these studies, such as an "efficient" stock market, random walks, and risk-expected return relations like the capital asset pricing model have permeated the popular press, but without a full understanding and description of the subtleties involved in their meaning....Are (stocks) predictable in a systematic way, other than compensating for the greater risk? All the early tests seemed to indicate that they are not; for if they are others would have noticed them, acted on this systematic relation, and, by so doing, would have removed it. As in all scientific research, when the tools (econometrics, computers, data bases) get more sophisticated, fine tuning occurs and currently not understood anomalies are discovered. And science goes on.[2]

*At the time, Professor of Finance and Director of the Center for Research in Security Prices; appointed Dean, Graduate School of Business, 1993.

## Assessing the
## Marketing Barrier

Marketing to clients represents a further barrier for an investment approach that depends on subtle distinctions to break new ground. Marketing specialists for investment firms place considerable weight on the rule, "Keep it simple." In general, their initial marketing presentation to the fund manager, assuming that they can get in the door, is limited to an hour or less. During this time, they both listen to the concerns of the prospect and cover a number of standard questions, such as the assets under management, the client list, and the experience and qualifications of the key people. Consequently, the time available to explore new and challenging concepts is, at best, limited. Prospects willing to pursue the subject at greater length in a subsequent meeting must allow for a further constraint. They must attain sufficient command of the subject matter to defend it before a higher level of management or an investment committee.

In short, the application of the efficient market hypothesis to active management is hardly the ideal theme for a marketing campaign. The efficient market hypothesis in itself, with the underlying mathematical support, is not necessarily an easy subject. In its extreme form, however, it can be condensed to a simple answer: the market price is the best estimate. The concept of a highly efficient market is more complex, since it shares many of the characteristics of the completely efficient market but is not exactly the same. The critical question, as explained in Chap. 2, concerns how it is different. The next step—to integrate a highly efficient market with active management—adds to the confusion. Discussion of this topic does not fit neatly into the established framework for either active or passive management.

## Need for a Fresh Perspective

Another barrier, at least as it applies to market valuation, is the absence of a clearly defined exposition of the process at work. Active managers have made many adaptations of the active decision process to the concept of a highly efficient market, including the use of index funds and other forms of passive management. In addition, a number of active management decisions accord a certain amount of weight, albeit in an unstructured way, to information embedded in stock prices. What has been missing, however, is a clear description of the systematic approach based on a coherent philosophical infrastructure. To delineate a thin margin of opportunity, as shown in Fig. 4-1, does not explain either how to identify it or how to make use of it. The explanation requires a great deal more support than a vague reference to "market inefficiencies." For investment managers in general, the assumption that "our decision process" addresses "market inefficiencies" becomes increasingly plausible during an extended period of favorable performance. In the absence of a more persuasive explanation, however, the market-inefficiencies argument is likely to prove fragile when performance deteriorates.

By way of example, Fig. 4-5 compares the cumulative total returns for small-capitalization stocks with those for large-capitalization stocks, as measured by the S&P 500. The Wilshire 4500, consisting of the issues in the Wilshire 5000 less those in the S&P 500, represents small-capitalization issues. For each of the two panels, we calibrate each total-return index so that the beginning point is 100. Panel A covers the 9 years ended 1983, when small-capitalization stocks rather consistently achieved the better returns. Over this period, portfolio managers who characteristically selected issues from the pool of small-capitalization stocks frequently attributed favorable portfolio performance to "inefficiencies" in this market. They argued that the professional investment community studied these issues much less intensively than those of General Electric, Exxon, and other large-capitalization issues. According to this view, skillful investment managers who bought and sold small-capitalization issues were able to reap the benefits of stock selection in irrational markets, much as envisioned by traditional investment management and described in Chap. 1. Panel B, covering the 9 years 1984 to 1992, underscores the dramatic change in market environment after midyear 1983. Portfolios concentrating on

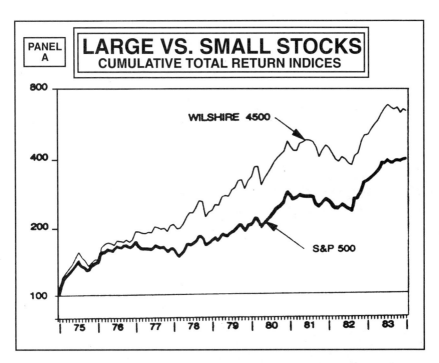

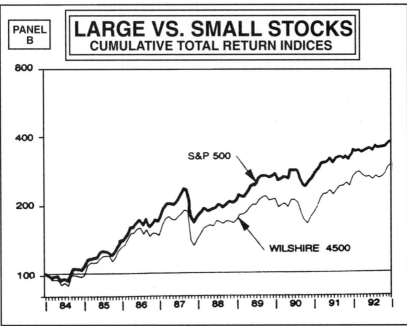

**Figure 4-5.** Comparison of the cumulative total returns for small-capitalization stocks with those for large-capitalization stocks (*a*) covering the years 1975 to 1983 and (*b*) 1984 to 1992. (*Source: Standard & Poor's Corporation and Wilshire Associates, Inc.*)

small-capitalization stocks have generally underperformed the broad market indexes over this more recent period. For so many portfolios, the case for "market inefficiencies" simply disappeared when the population of small-capitalization stocks no longer provided favorable performance comparisons with the broader market averages.

How can we recognize an approach to active asset allocation which is likely to exploit the opportunities presented by a highly efficient stock market over a wide range of changing market environments? This book aims to provide a clearly defined road map, and, to this end, addresses the key questions: How can information already discounted by stock prices be inferred? How can such information be combined in the active decision process with other information, not yet discounted, to improve chances of success? The previous chapters outline the conflicting assumptions underlying traditional active management and the efficient market hypothesis. The current chapter highlights the advantages to be gained from coordination of the active decision process with the concept of a highly, but not completely, efficient market. The remainder of the book, building on this foundation, presents a practical approach to active asset allocation.

## Appendix 4-1
## Confusing Correlation
## with Causation

Fischer Black, now partner, Goldman, Sachs & Co., was professor of finance at the Sloan School of Management, Massachusetts Institute of Technology, when he offered the following observations concerning econometric models:[3]

In the simplest case, the economic variables of interest obey a joint normal distribution. For any given values of some of the variables, each of the others follows a normal distribution. Many of the problems one encounters in trying to make sense of economic data come from the many ways in which the distribution of the variables can be other than joint normal. The most basic problem, though, is present even when all the variables are random and obey a joint normal distribution. That problem is the problem of relating correlation and causation.*

We will assume, in what follows, that all variables obey a joint normal distribution. The problem of relating correlation and causation is even more difficult in more complex cases, but it is so serious in the simplest case that we do not need to look at the complex cases.

In general, one can analyze data in two ways.† A "descriptive analysis" involves summarizing the data in various ways and developing methods for predicting, using purely statistical tools, future values of some of the variables. When the variables obey a joint normal distribution, the data can be summarized using the mean or average level of each variable, the standard deviation or variability of each variable, and the correlations among all pairs of variables. I use the word "correlation" as shorthand for such a summary.

A "structural analysis" involves searching for economic relations among the variables, partly in order to predict how the variables would change if various actions were taken by individuals, firms, or governments. A structural analysis or analysis of the economic relations among the variables is really an analysis of the causal relations among the variables.‡ We want to

---

*John W. Pratt and Robert Schlaifer ("On the Nature and Discovery of Structure," August 1981) discuss this problem too. Their abstract starts as follows: "We inquire into the conditions under which nonexperimental data reveal effects of a kind revealed by randomized experiments and relevant to decisions, although we define effects without regard to either. We argue that the general linear model as usually presented by statisticians fails to distinguish between effects and regression coefficients."

†The econometric texts I have found most helpful are Carl F. Christ, *Econometric Models and Methods* (New York: Wiley, 1966); E. Malinvaud, *Statistical Methods of Econometrics* (Amsterdam: North-Holland, 1966), Mrs. A. Silvey, trans.; Eric A Hanushek and John E. Jackson, *Statistical Methods for Social Scientists* (New York: Academic Press, 1977); and Edward E. Leamer, *Specification Searches* (New York: Wiley, 1978).

‡There is literature within econometrics that aims to test for causation in a narrower sense. See, for example, Christopher A. Sims, "Money, Income, and Causality," *American Economic Review*, September 1972, pp. 540–552. For a critical review of this literature, and a technical definition of causality, see C. W. J. Granger, "Testing for Causality: A Personal Viewpoint," *Journal of Economic Dynamics and Control*, November 1980, pp. 329–352.

know what the effects of an individual's, firm's or government's action will be. In this article, an "econometric model" means a model used for structural analysis. Thus, an econometric model is a model of "causation."

One of the basic principles of econometrics is "correlation does not imply causation." There is general agreement on this point when it is stated this way. The problem is that almost every attempt to develop an econometric model seems to make use of correlations in subtle ways to imply causation. Since an econometric model is by definition a causal model, and since regression coefficients are closely related to partial correlation coefficients, the use of regressions to develop or refine an econometric model usually amounts to interpreting correlation as implying causation.

If we are to learn about economics from data, we must make causal inferences. I have done several studies in which I try to infer causality from data.* But standard econometric methods do not in themselves allow us to make such inferences. People who do econometric studies often go to great lengths to bring other information that will tell about causation.†

I believe, though, that people have almost always failed in their attempts to derive causes from data. In one way or another, often subtle, they have confused correlation with causation. This confusion is covered up by the use of language that avoids

---

*See Fischer Black, Michael C. Jensen and Myron Scholes, "The Capital Asset Pricing Model: Some Empirical Tests," in Michael C. Jensen, ed., *Studies in the Theory of Capital Markets* (New York: Praeger, 1972), pp. 79–121; Black and Scholes, "The Effects of Dividend Yield and Dividend Policy on Common Stock Prices and Returns," *Journal of Financial Economics,* May, 1974, pp. 1–22; and Black, "Studies of Stock Price Volatility Changes," *Proceedings of the 1976 Meetings of the American Statistical Association, Business and Economic Statistics Section,* pp. 177–181.

†Leamer (*Specification Searches*) writes in part about what people do when they search for the econometric model that best fits the data. This can mean searching for causes, or searching for the best statistical model for the data. He emphasizes the search for the best statistical model. Thomas J. Sargent ("Interpreting Economic Time Series," *Journal of Political Economy,* April 1981, pp. 213–248) outlines some of what must be done to derive causal implications correctly.

the word "cause" and its derivatives. People often use "determine," "influence" and "predict," instead of "cause." They use "exogenous," "predetermined" and "independent" instead of "causal." They use "endogenous" and "dependent" instead of "resulting." They use "structure" instead of "causal relations."

In physics, or chemistry, or engineering, we use experiments to find out about causes. In economics, experiments are rarely done. But perhaps if we realized how little we can learn from correlations, we would do more experiments.

# Appendix 4-2
# Past Performance as
# Guide to the Future

A recent paper[4] issued by the Brookings Institution (and from which the following material is reprinted) included an analysis of performance data for pension funds compiled by the SEI Corporation, a large consulting firm. Although these authors question the value of active management, they are surprised to find that future performance, to a degree, correlates with past performance. Nevertheless, their work, like that of many other studies completed over the years, shows that the correlation is, at best, weak.

### Consistency of a Manager's
### Performance over Time

While our results suggest quite clearly that the average or the median fund manager does not add value during our sample period, some funds in some years show superior performance. Is this superior performance just a matter of luck, or is there some consistency over time in achieving good results? If we find that there is no consistency over time, we can make the stronger statement that not only do pension funds on average fail to add value, but that the same is true for just about all of them. If, on the other hand, we find some consistency, then some money managers have actually delivered value even if most have not.

At the very least, it may make sense for a sponsor committed to active management to put substantial weight on past performance when choosing a manager. In this section we address the issue of consistency. We primarily use the performance database, although we briefly look at the search database as well. As before, we look at the equity portion of the funds in the sample.

To check for consistency over time, we divide funds into quartiles based on performance over some period of time. Then we check whether funds manage to stay in their performance quartile over the subsequent period, particularly in the case of the best performance quartile. Put differently, we are asking whether the transition matrix between performance quartiles has diagonal entries above 25 percent. In addition, we are interested in knowing the performance difference in the follow-up period between this period's best and worst performers. We look at the annual, biannual, and triennial performance windows. We also look at transition matrices within investment styles since the relevant measures of consistency might be within a style rather than for all the funds combined.

Results on the triennial frequency are by far the strongest, both for pension funds as a whole and for individual styles (Table 4-1). There is very clear consistency. Diagonal entries of the transition matrix are typically above 30 percent. In expectation, the gain from investing in winners relative to losers is 2.1 percent per year for funds as a whole. A test for the difference of future returns between past returns quartiles 1 and 4 has a $t$-statistic of 7.4; the test for differences between past performance quartiles (1,2) versus (3,4) has a $t$-statistic of 6.1. These test statistics are no doubt a bit high because the assumption of independence across funds is violated.

Taken together, our results support the notion that some managers are more skillful than others in achieving superior investment performance. They also suggest that allocating money among money managers in response to past performance might be a worthwhile task for the sponsors. The results also weakly suggest that longer horizon performance evaluations might be preferred.

We must present these results with two caveats. First, because

**Table 4-1.** Equity Fund Performance over Time Using Quartile Rankings of Past Three-Year Performance to Predict Future Three-Year Performance[a]

| Investment style | | 1[b] | 2[b] | 3[b] | 4[b] | Return over past three-year period[c] | Return over future three-year period[c] |
|---|---|---|---|---|---|---|---|
| All | | | | | | | |
| (Top) | 1 | 37 | 29 | 20 | 13 | 24.3 | 15.9 |
| | 2 | 20 | 26 | 29 | 25 | 19.3 | 14.6 |
| | 3 | 19 | 24 | 30 | 26 | 16.1 | 14.5 |
| (Bottom) | 4 | 23 | 21 | 20 | 35 | 10.3 | 13.8 |
| Growth | | | | | | | |
| | 1 | 37 | 28 | 21 | 14 | 23.1 | 15.6 |
| | 2 | 20 | 27 | 29 | 24 | 17.8 | 14.5 |
| | 3 | 19 | 27 | 29 | 24 | 15.0 | 14.1 |
| | 4 | 25 | 19 | 21 | 35 | 9.0 | 13.3 |
| Yield | | | | | | | |
| | 1 | 30 | 23 | 23 | 23 | 25.6 | 15.2 |
| | 2 | 31 | 33 | 28 | 9 | 22.3 | 15.8 |
| | 3 | 17 | 24 | 29 | 29 | 18.8 | 14.4 |
| | 4 | 20 | 21 | 21 | 38 | 13.9 | 14.3 |
| Value | | | | | | | |
| | 1 | 33 | 25 | 25 | 16 | 24.2 | 15.6 |
| | 2 | 28 | 25 | 22 | 24 | 20.1 | 15.0 |
| | 3 | 16 | 25 | 32 | 26 | 16.9 | 14.6 |
| | 4 | 22 | 24 | 20 | 34 | 11.0 | 14.0 |

a. Performance database excluding cash portfolio. Too few observations prevented us from doing these calculations for the style "Other."

b. Data in these columns show transition probabilities for movement from a given past three-year performance quartile into various three-year performance quartiles.

c. Equally-weighted annual returns for all funds ranking in a given quartile based on past three-year performance.

there is a bias toward survival of the better funds, we may be overestimating the degree of consistency of performance over time.[5] Second, because we have results only for a relatively short period of time, we cannot be certain that the best performing funds in the first subperiod were not just lucky in the second subperiod due to the fortuitous success of a correlated set of investment strategies that they each employed. Although we made sure that consistency of performance over the sample period was not just the consequence of the performance of our four investment styles over this period, it could be the consequence of certain other strategies over both subperiods.

Our results do not imply that the best money managers selected in this way can be expected to beat a passive investment strategy since the expected returns net of management fees even for these good managers appear to be below the *S&P 500* returns. Our evidence suggests that by using three years of past performance data and choosing a manager in the top quartile, one can expect to beat the average manager by approximately 100 basis points. But recall that over our sample period the average manager underperforms the *S&P 500* by 130 basis points, and this does not even include 50 basis points of extra management fees.* Of course, we make no claim that we have searched for the optimal rule for using past data to pick managers. Perhaps the optimal filter rule can select a manager whose performance net of fees is superior to that of a passive indexing strategy—a subject for a more thorough future study.

---

*An alternative approach here would be to compare the second subperiod returns of the first subperiod top performers directly to the *S&P 500* returns. If we do that we find that the top performers average 15.9 percent; the *S&P 500* return is 15.4 percent. But this does not include approximately 50 basis points in extra management fees, which when included would put the two strategies about even. Moreover, the problem with this approach is that it gives a biased view of the performance of the better pension funds since pension funds do uniformly better in the second subperiod (1986–88 or 1987–89) than in the first subperiod (1983–85 or 1984–86), Hence, all pension funds, not just the best ones, look better when focusing on the second subperiod returns. We believe that the proper approach is to estimate the gain to picking a top performer separately and then to combine this information with performance data on the average fund for the entire sample period.

# References

1. Jack Treynor, "Long Term Investing," *Financial Analysts Journal,* May–June 1976, pp. 56–57.
2. Robert S. Hamada, *Chicago, the Long View,* University of Chicago Graduate School of Business brochure, 1983, pp. 2–3.
3. Fischer Black, "The Trouble with Econometric Models," *Financial Analysts Journal,* March–April 1982.
4. Joseph Lakonishik, Andrei Shleifer, and Robert W. Vishny, "The Structure and Performance of the Money Management Industry," *Brookings Papers on Economic Activity,* Brookings Institution, Washington, D.C., 1992, pp. 356–357, 359, 361–363.
5. Stephen Brown and others, "Survivorship Bias in Performance Studies," Working Paper, Stern School of Business, New York University, 1991.

# 5

# Three Key Factors
# Drive Stock Prices

## Confronting the Problem

### Tracking Too Much
### Information

What does a tiny fish swimming in a remote segment of a vast
ocean have to do with the stock market? The answer to this
question, at least most of the time, is, "Not much." In 1973, however, the usual abundant supply of anchovies disappeared from
the coast of Peru, greatly restricting an important source of live-
stock feed in South American markets. This mysterious development coincided with the onset of a shortage of world meat
supplies, exacerbating inflationary pressures on food prices in
the United States. The spike in food prices accompanied the oil
embargo by the Organization of Petroleum Exporting Countries
(OPEC) and strong growth of business activity in the industrial
world. Contemporary investment analysts therefore included
the failure of the Peruvian anchovy harvest among the noteworthy factors that contributed to the severe inflation and accompanying disruption of the financial markets in the period 1973 to
1974.

While stock market analysts seldom focus on the flow of
anchovies in South American waters, this fragment of history
illustrates the potentially wide range of significant influences on
the financial markets. At any point, scores of factors materially
shape investors' attitudes toward stock prices. The primary list

of shakers and movers of the financial markets may change, moreover, as changes in the investment environment periodically bring forth new candidates.

   To cite a more recent example, *The Wall Street Journal* displayed a headline on September 17, 1990, stating that the "Stock Market Is Dancing to Oil's Tune." The article introduced by this headline pointed out that the Dow Jones Industrial Average "has moved counter to oil prices in 22 of 30 trading days" since the Iraqi invasion of Kuwait. "On the days when the predominant pattern didn't hold," the report continued, "changes in both the industrial average and oil prices were mainly small." Figure 5-1 shows a clearly negative correlation between oil prices and the S&P 500 over the second half of 1990. This tight relationship was bound to disappear—and it did—as soon as the special reasons for the volatility in the oil markets subsided in early 1991.

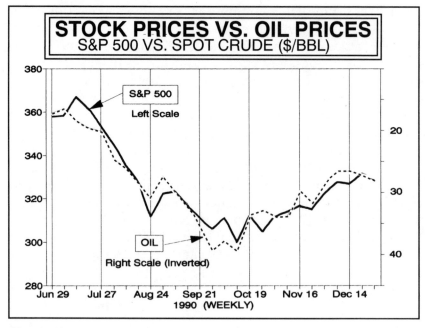

**Figure 5-1.**  A negative correlation between oil prices and the S&P 500 persisted over the second half of 1990.

The price of oil, although a major influence on financial markets during a period of uncertain outlook for oil supplies, has ordinarily been overshadowed by other influences. In the late 1980s, both stock and fixed-income markets displayed special sensitivity to the monthly report on unemployment and jobs creation. For a time in the mid-1980s, it was the monthly report on the foreign trade deficit that routinely seemed to move the financial markets. Particularly in the earlier part of the decade, the weekly report of the money supply achieved a special status as the critical news which could periodically unsettle the stock market. The list of examples could go on and on.

## How Does It All Add Up?

Traditionally, active investment managers have prided themselves on regularly tracking the wide range of factors that can significantly affect stock prices. A prominent investment manager, by way of example, has routinely distributed to its institutional clients each month several pages listing scores of items bearing on the valuation of the stock market. Each item is marked with a color: green for positive, yellow for caution, and red for negative. The same color code, shown on the first page, conveys the firm's current conclusion on stock prices.

But how does it all add up? Suppose, at a particular point in time, 50 percent of the many factors expected to influence stock prices in an important way rate as favorable and only 20 percent appear clearly unfavorable. Compilation of such a list leads to several further questions. Does the list include all the significant factors? Are the factors properly classified as favorable or unfavorable? Should the factors be equally weighted? Or, for example, might a minority of negative factors outweigh the favorable factors, supporting a negative conclusion?

## Relying Uncritically on Performance Measures

The traditional answer, which relies on the "good judgment" of the investment decision maker, too often depends on uncritical acceptance of a performance record. Within this framework, good investment judgment operates in some unexplained way. It allows the decision maker to recognize the relative importance of the scores of economic and financial developments and to come up with the right answer more times than not. Appraisal of the quality of the decision process requires, at best, hard, time-consuming effort—and in the end may still lead to uncertain conclusions. The outcome, in contrast, can be readily measured, with the results summarized in a performance ranking or other simple statistic. Consequently, the assessment of the decision process too often reflects the result which the decision maker happens to achieve, rather than the logic of the decision process itself. The danger of primary reliance on the performance record is its vulnerability to sudden change. Even a completely random decision process may register, purely through chance, impressive results for varying periods of time. In the absence of a superior decision process, an extremely favorable record likely reflects high volatility, which means the downside may become as alarming as the upside was impressive.

The performance record as a measure of investment skill is particularly fragile in the assessment of active asset allocation. For the stock market, there may be only three or four major turning points over a decade. The performance record is highly dependent on a very small number of major decisions, opening the door for chance to play a particularly large role. Consequently, *a good performance record is a necessary, but not sufficient, condition for the choice of a method of valuing the stock market.*

## Focusing on What Is Critical

### Defining Three Key Factors

To make use of information already embedded in stock prices, our approach to active asset allocation focuses on the three key factors that drive stock prices. Although an almost limitless range of information determines stock prices, a highly efficient market, as discussed in the previous chapter, implies that most of this information is already discounted. Information that is not yet discounted becomes significant only to the extent, when discounted, it changes investor perceptions of the three key factors. This chapter identifies these three key factors and shows how they relate to each other in the constant-growth model. It also explains the fundamental difference between our approach, which uses current market price as the point of departure in a highly efficient stock market, and the dividend-discount model. The latter, to the extent it assesses market value without regard for current market price, operates within the philosophical framework of traditional active management.

## Key Factor 1: Assessing Competition from Interest Rates

In examining the key factors that drive stock prices, we begin with the fixed-income market. What determines the market value of a relatively risk-free investment, such as a Treasury security? Suppose a Treasury bond, issued without provision for call prior to maturity, carries an 8 percent coupon. As of now, it matures in exactly 20 years. Given a face value of 100, how much is the bond worth? The only requirement for answering this question is information concerning interest rates. Figure 5-2 traces the value of the bond for various levels of interest rates that have prevailed since World War II. Based on yield to maturity of 2 percent (close to the postwar low), the current market value of the bond would be 198. At the other extreme, the postwar high of about 14 percent would result in a current market value of only 60.

The sensitivity of the Treasury bond to changing interest rates would be even greater for longer maturities.* Figure 5-3, holding the initial yield to maturity at 8 percent, relates changes in interest rates to maturity. It plots the effect of a 100-basis-point reduction in interest rates on prices of bonds with varying

---

*Duration, which also takes into account differences in the schedule of interest payments, is a more comprehensive measure of sensitivity to changes in interest rates. For the present purpose, the simpler concept of maturity illustrates our point.

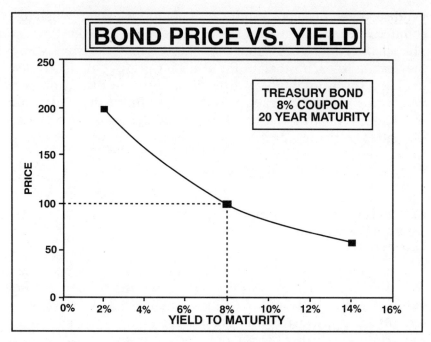

**Figure 5-2.** Tracing the value of a long bond for various levels of interest rates that have prevailed since World War II.

maturities. The longer the maturity, the greater is the impact on market price for any given yield to maturity. A bond with 20 years maturity and a yield of 8 percent would experience 75 percent of the maximum possible impact from a given change in interest rates. The percentage would rise to 87 and 94 percent for 30- and 40-year maturities, respectively.*

*Other things equal,* the stock market would be even more sensitive to changes in interest rates than the 30- and 40-year bonds shown in Fig. 5-3. The reason is the absence of a maturity limit for the stock market together with the extreme "other-things-equal" assumption, which implies no changes in other factors

---

*A bond with an infinite maturity, with an 8 percent coupon rate, and discounted at 8 percent is valued at 100. If the discount rate declines to 7 percent, the price of the bond will rise by 14 percent to 114 so that the yield to maturity will equal 7 percent. The value of a bond is determined by the sum of the present values for both future coupon payments and the principal to be repaid at maturity.

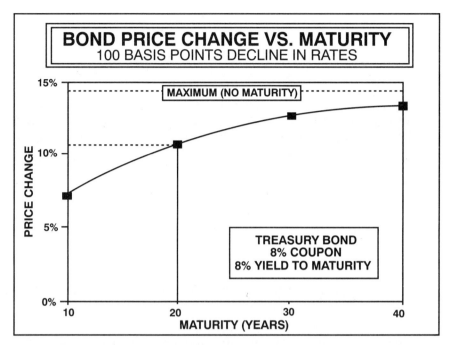

**Figure 5-3.** Plotting the effect on price of a 100-basis-point reduction in interest rates for Treasury bonds of varying maturities.

bearing on stock prices. (For purposes of comparison, think of the stock market as a single issue represented by an S&P 500 index fund.) In recent years, moreover, the low dividend yield for stocks, usually ranging between 3 and 4 percent compared to 7 to 9 percent for long-term Treasury bonds, has added to the leverage of changing interest rates on stock prices. The lower current yield for stocks relative to bonds means that a larger proportion of the present value depends on income deferred well into the future and is therefore subject to a longer period of discounting.

As a practical matter, *other things are not equal.* Interest rates may reflect, in varying degree, change in inflation expectations as well as in real rates. For example, a massive move in long-term rates over several years will almost certainly depend in large part on changing views of long-term inflation. Broad influences other than interest rates, meanwhile, also repeatedly bear on stock prices. A given change in interest rates may accompany a greater or smaller change in stock prices than in bond prices—or even a change in the opposite direction. The greater turbulence in the fixed-income markets beginning in the mid-1960s, nevertheless, has increased the role of interest-rate change in assessing the outlook for stock prices. By way of example, the correlation of returns between the S&P 500 and long Treasury bonds averaged more than 0.3 in the 1980s. (Perfect correlation is 1.0.) In contrast, the comparable figure for 1960 to 1964 was about –0.1, indicating a slightly negative correlation.

### Key Factor 2: How Market Prices Anticipate Dividend Growth

Suppose that the Treasury bond selected for purposes of illustration in the previous section is modified to make it more like the stock market. Assume two changes. First, the Treasury bond, like the stock market, no longer is subject to a maturity limit. Interest payments will continue into the indefinite future. Second, the coupon on the bond will rise at a specified annual rate. Investor confidence in the projected coupon rate, now rising rather than stable, will remain as high as previously, since, in our example, payment remains subject to the full faith and credit of the United States government. The interest rate used to determine the value of the stream of rising coupon payments, since it requires no allowance for risk, continues as before at 8 percent. Figure 5-4 shows the effect on the value of the bond of varying rates of growth in the coupon rate. With no increase in the coupon rate, the value remains at 100. Were the coupon to grow at 3 percent annually, the present value would rise to 160. A growth rate of 6 percent for the coupon would result in a rise to 400.

The purpose of Fig. 5-4 is to demonstrate the powerful effect on the stock market of a change in the long-term rate of dividend growth *as perceived by the consensus of investors.* In this example, the rising coupon rate substitutes for dividend growth. Change in the expected rate of dividend growth, like change in interest rates, ranks among the key factors driving stock prices. Interest rates measure competition from the principal alterna-

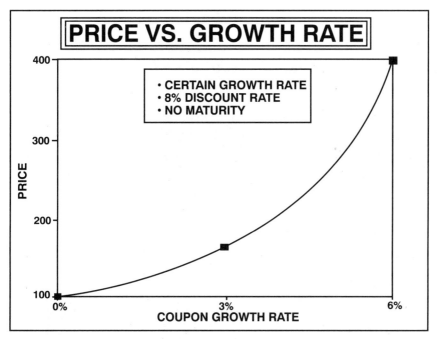

**Figure 5-4.** The effect on bond price if the coupon were to grow at various guaranteed rates.

tive to investment in stocks, while current and future dividend payments constitute the financial benefit accruing to stockholders in the aggregate. Individual shareholders may profit from the sale of a stock at an elevated price, but only because the purchasers expect benefits that will either accrue to them or appeal, in turn, to subsequent purchasers. While a company with a publicly traded stock may be liquidated in whole or part, limited activity of this sort does not materially alter this overview of the role of expected future dividends in establishing the value of the stock market.

## Key Factor 3: How Investor Confidence Impacts Valuation

Our hypothetical examples utilizing a Treasury bond have thus far ignored the influence of investor confidence on stock prices.

Figures 5-2 and 5-4 could accurately relate an interest rate or dividend-growth rate to market value because other factors were held constant. Complete certainty concerning the outlook for both interest rates and dividend growth would be sufficient to establish the value of the stock market. Because of the uncertainties associated with the outlook for both dividend growth and interest rates, investor confidence strongly influences the pricing of stocks.

Suppose the investor consensus expects dividends to grow at a rate of 6 percent annually, but the outlook is far from certain. The Treasury does not guarantee the projection of 6 percent growth—nor can anyone else. Meanwhile, investors as a group are risk-averse, which means they prefer a sure thing to something less certain. Investors will not pay as much for a dollar of dividends *expected* some years in the future as for the *certain* payment of the same dollar amount of interest on a Treasury security at the same future date. The same principle applies to interest rates, since fixed-income investments compete with common stocks for the allocation of portfolio funds. Uncertainty toward the outlook for interest rates translates into uncertainty concerning the value of the dividend stream anticipated for the stock market.

Of particular interest to active asset allocation is the change in investor confidence. It is necessary to distinguish, for example, between a change in the consensus estimate of dividend growth and a change in investor confidence concerning the estimate. Either change may take place independently of the other, both may operate to move stock prices in the same direction, or each may operate at least partially to offset the other. Figure 5-5 shows how a change in investor confidence affects the pricing of the stock market, other things equal. The graph compares price (vertical scale) with discount rate (horizontal scale). The discount rate ranges from 8 to 14 percent, reflecting varying levels of investor confidence concerning the expected dividend-growth rate of 6 percent. The first point plotted at the extreme left of Fig. 5-5 is the same—and based on the same assumptions—as the last point at the far right in Fig. 5-4. Comparison of Figs. 5-4 and 5-5 shows that a one-percentage-point increase in the discount rate, resulting from deterioration of investor confi-

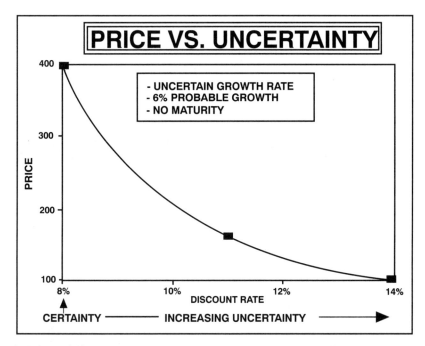

**Figure 5-5.** How a change in investor confidence affects the pricing of the stock market.

dence, exactly offsets an equal increase in the coupon-growth rate (in the hypothetical bond example) or the dividend-growth rate (for the stock market).

## Tying Together the Three Key Factors

### Targeting Present Value

Now that we have identified the three key factors (business outlook, interest rates, and investor confidence), we refer to the Gordon-Shapiro model[1] to show how they relate to each other. Identification of the three key factors serves to define the information required for the active decision process. Disappearance of anchovies off the coast of Peru, wide fluctuations in oil prices, or any of the many other influences on the stock market mentioned earlier in the chapter are significant only if they shape the investor consensus for one or more of the three key factors. The Gordon-Shapiro model, based on a constant-growth assumption, translates estimates of the three key factors into valuation of the stock market.

The starting point for the Gordon-Shapiro analysis is the concept of present value. For the stock market, the current value is the sum of the present values for all future dividend payments. Only two kinds of information are required to determine the current price level: (1) the dividends per share for each year into the long-range future and (2) the discount rate to be applied to the dividends received each year. Take as an example the S&P 500 on July 1, 1960. With benefit of hindsight, we are able to use for purposes of illustration the actual dividend payments over the subsequent 30 years. To simplify calculations, assume that all companies pay total dividends for the year on June 30. For the discount rate, we select 10 percent, which approximates the average rate of return (compounded) for stocks since 1926.

Figure 5-6 compares the dividend stream from 1961 to 1990 with the present value of each year's dividend. The payment of $2.02 in 1961, after discounting at an annual rate of 10 percent, resulted in a present value of $1.84 as of July 1, 1960. The payment of $12.10 in 1990, subject to a much larger discount, was worth $0.69 in 1960. The net present value of payments from 1961 to 1990 amounted to $33.

The present value of the S&P 500 on June 30, 1960, also includes allowance for the expected value of dividends after 1990. Since the dividend growth from 1961 to 1990 averaged 6.4 percent annually, we have arbitrarily projected gains for all future years at this rate. Based on the initial discount rate of 10 percent, the present value in 1960 of all the dividends after 1990 would amount to $20. Based on the arbitrary assumptions used here, the present value of the stock market on June 30, 1960, would have been $33 + $20 = 53. (We omit the dollar sign, as is the practice in quoting market prices.) The calculated value compares with the actual price of close to 57 recorded on the same date.

There is no reason that the two prices should be the same,

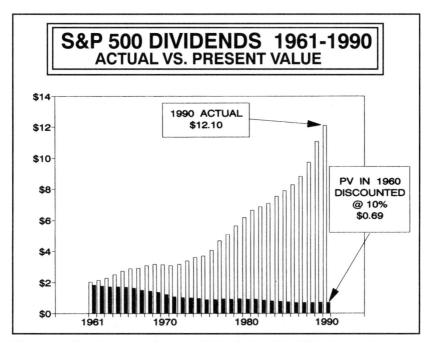

**S&P 500 DIVIDENDS 1961-1990**
**ACTUAL VS. PRESENT VALUE**

**Figure 5-6.** Present value in 1960 of the S&P 500 dividend stream over the period 1961 to 1990.

since our assumptions almost certainly differ from those of the consensus of investors on the valuation date. Contemporary expectations for dividend increases, which could not anticipate the surge of inflation in the following decades, had to be lower than actually materialized. The assumption for the discount rate in mid-1960 also would change over the measurement period. The same inflationary pressures which translated into nominally higher dividend increases also resulted in a higher discount rate over much of the period to date.

### How the Constant-Growth Assumption Simplifies Valuation

The constant-growth model greatly simplifies the present-value approach. Since we know the current dividend rate, a constant-growth rate indicates the precise payment for each year into the very long range future. Under this assumption, the tedious calculation illustrated in Fig. 5-6 reduces to the simple formula shown below:

$$P = \frac{D}{K - G}$$

where $P$ = price of stock market
$D$ = dividend payment over coming year
$K$ = discount rate
$G$ = dividend-growth rate

The Gordon-Shapiro model, because it substitutes constant growth for uneven growth, provides an approximation of the present value of the actual dividend payments. The constant-growth assumption in the Gordon-Shapiro model will result in a higher value than the present value of actual dividends if dividend growth in the early years is less than the compound average rate assumed for the longer-term. The result is just the reverse if dividend growth in the early years exceeds the compound growth rate.

By way of illustration, we use the Gordon-Shapiro formula to rework our present-value calculation. The beginning dividend is $2.02, exactly the same as previously. The discount rate remains at 10 percent. It is no longer necessary to calculate separately the present value of the dividend for each year into the future. We simply substitute a growth rate of 6.4 percent, since this number coincides with the average compound growth from 1961 to 1990 and also with the assumption used for years subsequent to 1990. The result is a price of 56, as shown below:

$$P = \frac{2.02}{0.100 - 0.064} = 56$$

The price of 56, based on the Gordon-Shapiro model, is 6 percent higher than the price of 53 based on the alternative present-value approach. The only difference in the two calculations concerns dividends paid 1961 to 1990. The Gordon-Shapiro model

.assumes a constant growth rate for this period of 6.4 percent. The present-value approach recognizes that the compound growth rate over these 30 years averaged 6.4 percent, but takes into account the actual payment in each year. Growth accelerated considerably in the second half of the period. From 1961 to 1975, the compound growth rate averaged 4.4 percent. Over the subsequent 15 years 1976 to 1990, the compound-growth rate averaged about 8.3 percent.

## Three Key Factors at Work in the Constant-Growth Model

The Gordon-Shapiro model, as well as the present-value calculation, relies on the three key factors that drive stock prices. The discount rate consists of two parts. One part is the *pure* interest rate, or *risk-free* rate. The other part is the allowance for risk, or the *risk premium*. The risk premium is that part of the discount rate which compensates the investor for uncertainty concerning the outcome. The Gordon-Shapiro model specifically includes the dividend-growth rate. The present-value calculation indirectly allows for the dividend-growth rate, since the total value is a function of the changing dividend payment year by year. To recognize the two parts of the discount rate, the Gordon-Shapiro model may be rewritten as follows:

$$P = \frac{D}{I + k - G}$$

where $I$ = the risk-free rate
$k$ = the risk premium.

Note that the technical terms referring to the three key factors in the constant-growth model correspond in a general way to the more familiar traditional terms. The left column of Table 5-1 lists traditional terms. The middle column shows the technical terms which define more rigorously the components of the Gordon-Shapiro model. The column on the right specifies the symbols in the Gordon-Shapiro model.

**Table 5-1.** Symbols Used in the Gordon-Shapiro Model

| Traditional | Technical | Symbol |
|---|---|---|
| Interest rates | Risk-free rate | $I$ |
| Investor confidence | Risk premium | $k$ |
| Business outlook | Dividend-growth rate | $G$ |

# How the DDM
# Goes Astray

## Operating in the Framework
## of Traditional Active
## Management

We differentiate our approach to active asset allocation from the
various versions of tactical asset allocation (TAA) based on the
dividend-discount model (DDM). The DDM is a term commonly
used to describe the constant-growth model presented by
Gordon and Shapiro and discussed earlier in this chapter. The
goal of TAA is the same as that for our approach to active asset
allocation, but the underlying philosophy and implementation
differ fundamentally. Practitioners of TAA have developed various methods to estimate the three required inputs. The standard
approach, nevertheless, operates within the philosophical
framework of traditional active management, determining the
value of the stock market without reference to the information
embedded in stock prices.

## DDM in Operation

To illustrate the practical implications, we select the following
estimates developed as of year end 1989 to serve as required
inputs. Since the choice of *risk-free rate* is almost always a long-
term bond—which could range from a Treasury security to a
high-grade industrial-bond index—our example selects a 30-

year Treasury bond. To allow for the *risk premium* (relative to the 30-year Treasury bond), we use 2 percent. The yield of any selected bond already allows for a risk premium related to maturity or quality. Even Treasury bonds are not risk-free, and high-grade industrials are priced at a discount to Treasuries to compensate for additional risk relating to possible default of either interest payments or repayment of principal. Stocks require a further increment in the risk premium because of the uncertainties relating to future dividend growth. We project *dividend growth* at 6.3 percent annually. For the purposes of this example, we assume that the year-end 1989 price of the long Treasury bonds is consistent with a future rate of inflation of 5.0 percent annually. We add an additional 1.3 percentage points to reflect the average relationship between inflation and dividend growth over the then-available historical record from 1927 to 1989.

We applied the inputs as listed above to the standard DDM model at year end 1989. The yield to maturity for the 30-year Treasury bond was then 8.0 percent. Dividend payments for the S&P 500 over the four quarters of 1990 were estimated at $12.20. This information, combined with the assumptions for the risk premium and dividend-growth rate as listed above, provides an estimated current value for the S&P 500 of 330 (compared to the then-current price of 353).

$$P = \frac{12.20}{0.080 + 0.020 - 0.063} = 330$$

## What's Wrong with This Answer?

Since the S&P 500 ended 1990 at 330, the DDM at first glance may seem to offer an amazingly effective tool for valuing the stock market. It is based on sound theory—the constant-growth model. It is simple, requiring only estimates of the three key factors that drive stock prices. Assuming the inputs can be applied consistently, it provides a quantitative discipline insulated from the emotional influences associated with either bear markets or bull markets.

While these claims are generally valid, they do not address the fundamental problems associated with the DDM. First, the calculated price is highly sensitive to relatively small errors in estimates of one or more of the three key factors. Second, estimates of dividend-growth rate and risk premium, which are highly subjective, are prone to large errors. Such errors may be partially offsetting, or they may reinforce each other. Third, results are disproportionately driven by changes in bond yields. The only changes in the three key factors available on a daily basis are for interest rates. We discuss each of these points in the following sections.

## Magnifying Small Errors

Figure 5-7 traces the sensitivity of the DDM to changes in the inputs. In our example, the DDM calculated the price of the S&P 500 at 330. Other things equal, a 100-basis-point increase in the risk premium or reduction in the dividend-growth rate would drop the calculated market price by 21 percent. If both happened together, the estimated market price would decline by 35 percent. Even a net error of only 50 basis points would distort the market price estimate by 12 percent. As shown by the graph, the percentage errors would be even larger on the upside.

## Estimating Investor
## Perception of Dividend Growth

A second problem in developing estimates for the DDM relates to the long-term rate of dividend growth. Prospects for the next 6 to 12 months reflect declarations to date as well as recent earnings achievements and the operating results indicated for the near-term. What is needed for the DDM, however, is much more ambitious. The DDM requires the views of the investor consensus concerning the average compound rate of dividend growth many years beyond the next year. Depending on the methodology, the range of possibilities is wide.

**Differing Answers from Historical Data.**     Figure 5-8 suggests the problems in projecting long-term dividend growth from

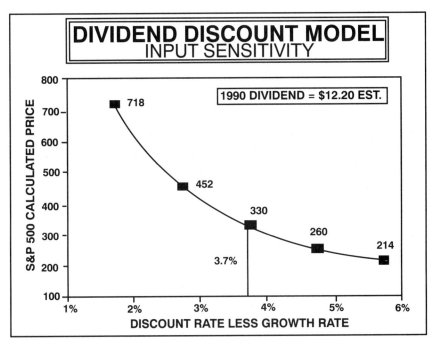

**Figure 5-7.**  Tracing the sensitivity of the dividend-discount model (DDM) to changes in the inputs.

historical data. Should the estimate, which looks decades into the future, reflect the available record of the S&P 500 over the 66 years 1927 to 1992? Over that time interval, dividend growth has averaged 4.5 percent at a compound annual rate. Would the compound rate of 5.6 percent over the 40-year period 1953 to 1992 provide a better measure? The compound rate for the past 20 years, 1973 to 1992, argues for a still higher figure, since it amounted to 7.1 percent.

**Inflation-Based Approach.**  Another method would tie dividend growth to inflation. Over the 66 years 1927 to 1992, the annual rate of dividend growth has averaged about 1.2 percentage points higher than the inflation rate. The stability of this relationship is brought into question by wide variations that have persisted over extended periods. Figure 5-9 shows that the difference by

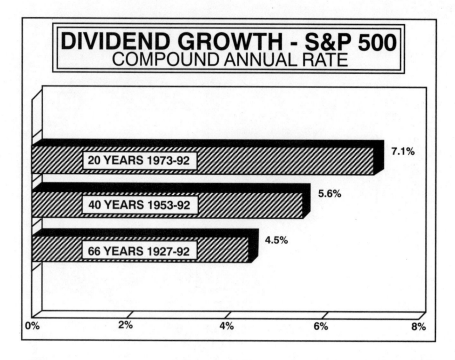

**Figure 5-8.** Alternative measures of historical dividend growth for the S&P 500. (*Source:* The Analysts Handbook *issued by Standard & Poor's Corporation.*)

*decades* has ranged from +3.1 to –2.4 percentage points. The inflation-based approach, moreover, requires a projection of inflation itself. As suggested by the volatility of the bond market in recent years, the inflation outlook is subject to frequent surprises. To a degree, errors in dividend-growth projections resulting from unanticipated changes in the rate of inflation are offset by similar changes in bond yields. Yet, the relationship between bond yields and various measures of inflation is far from stable.

**Pattern of Dividend Growth Makes a Difference.**    Another problem concerning dividend-growth projections relates to the pattern of dividend growth. Table 5-2 presents three projections of dividend growth. For perspective, projection *B* repeats the assumptions underlying the DDM calculation shown on page 133. The current dividend is $12.20 in each case. The compound annual

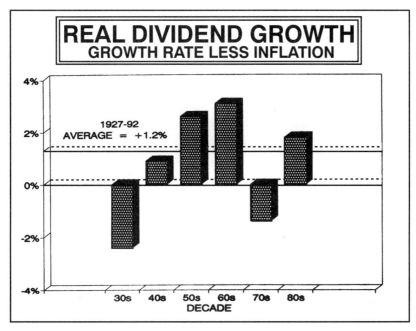

**Figure 5-9.** Variations in the compound annual rate of real dividend growth (nominal growth rate less rate of inflation) for the S&P 500 over successive decades. (*Source:* The Analysts Handbook *issued by Standard & Poor's Corporation.*)

rate after the first 5 years is also the same in each case—6.3 percent—but the 5-year rate of annual dividend growth differs as shown. The present value indicated in the far right-hand column is based on a discount rate of 10.0 percent. Even though the dividend-growth rates after 5 years, as well as the discount rates, are identical, the present value for projection *A* is 40 percent greater than for projection *C*.

To allow for wide variation in rate of dividend growth, such as shown in Table 5-2, requires an extremely high standard of business forecasting. As outlined in Chap. 7, most economists share considerable agreement concerning the outlook for the next 6 to 12 months, but economic visibility fades rapidly by the second year ahead. An erroneous assessment of the dividend-growth pattern for even 2 or 3 years could introduce considerable distortion in the results.

**Table 5-2.** Annual Rate of Dividend Growth

|   | First 5 years, % | After 5 years, % | Present value at 10.0% |
|---|---|---|---|
| A | 10.3 | 6.3 | 390 |
| B | 6.3 | 6.3 | 330 |
| C | 2.3 | 6.3 | 278 |

## Assessing the Risk Premium

The risk premium is elusive, even in hindsight. While investors may not project future dividend growth with much assurance, they are at least able to measure what it has been in the past. The magnitude of the risk premium over past periods, in contrast, cannot be directly measured.

The standard method for inferring the risk premium requires analysis of the long-term record. The starting point is an assumption that investors in the aggregate operate rationally in an efficient market. They price stocks at the beginning of each year to reflect their expectations concerning the return in excess of the risk-free rate (excess return). For this purpose, the risk-free rate is usually represented by the return on short Treasury bills. Because economic visibility is limited, new information becoming available during the year will require revisions in the outlook. Consequently, the excess return for the stock market over any given year will differ—sometimes a great deal—from the consensus expectations of investors at the beginning of the year. Time narrows these differences. Over an extended period of years, differences between actual and expected excess returns in one direction will tend to offset differences in the other direction. The long-term average of actual excess returns therefore provides an estimate of the risk premium. By this method, the risk premium for the S&P 500 over the period 1926 to 1992 amounted to 6.4 percent, based on the compound annual rate of excess return over the entire 67-year span. Although this approximation of the risk premium is useful for certain purposes, it is far from precise. There are two reasons for this: sampling error and change in the risk premium.

**Sampling Error.** The sum of the differences between actual and expected excess returns depends to a degree on the time period covered by the sample. Differences between the actual and expected excess returns during the period of the sample are most unlikely to offset each other completely. Even if the risk premium were stable over the entire past history of the S&P 500, a sampling error remains. The estimate of the risk premium would change, because of the sampling error, as the years included in the sample change. Figure 5-10 traces the fluctuations in average excess return for consecutive 20-year periods ended 1945 to 1992. Note that average excess returns over 20-year periods ranged from 15.3 to 0.6 percent. Other things equal, the average for the entire 67-year period of 6.4 percent qualifies as a better estimate of the current risk premium than an estimate based on a shorter period. The wide variation in results over the 20-year periods, nevertheless, provides a graphic reminder that the long-term estimate itself may be subject to significant sampling error.

**Change in the Risk Premium.** Most applications of the DDM assume that the current risk premium is lower than indicated by the 67-year record. Investors base this adjustment on a perception that the stock market is less risky today than indicated by the data since 1926, which include the extreme bear markets prior to World War II. While there is good reason to recognize a significant reduction in stock market risk since the 1930s, the quantitative adjustment for the change cannot be accomplished with much precision. A widely accepted method for making this adjustment reflects the changing variability of returns over time. In a highly efficient market, there is a logical relationship between variability and risk. The price of short-term Treasury bills is highly stable because the risk is extremely small. As the maturity of Treasury issues lengthens, the risk increases and so does the variability. Returns on industrial bonds demonstrate yet greater risk and variability, while stocks are still more risky and more variable than bonds.

Figure 5-11, which provides perspective on the changing vari-

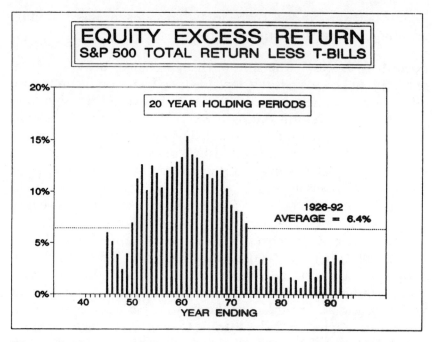

**Figure 5-10.** Tracing the fluctuations in the compound annual rate of excess return for the S&P 500 over consecutive 20-year periods ended 1945 to 1992. (*Source: Stocks, Bonds, Bills, and Inflation 1993 Yearbook, Ibbotson Associates, Chicago, annually updates the work by Roger G. Ibbotson and Rex A. Sinquefield. Used with permission. All rights reserved.*)

ability of the S&P 500 since 1926, underscores the practical difficulty in translating such data into adjustments in the risk premium. The vertical scale shows the average standard deviation (statistical measure used to gauge the variability of investment returns) over prior 20-year periods. It has ranged from a low of 12 percent in the 20 years ended 1968 to a high of 30 percent for the period ended 1946. For the last 20 years ended 1992, it amounted to 16 percent. Should the risk premium be based on the average since 1926, ignoring the substantial change in variability over the period? Should adjustment be made for the decline in variability, as indicated by the record for the most recent 20 years? Or should adjustment be based on a shorter period, such as 5 or 10 years? In practice, the error in making such adjustments in the risk premium is likely to be significant.

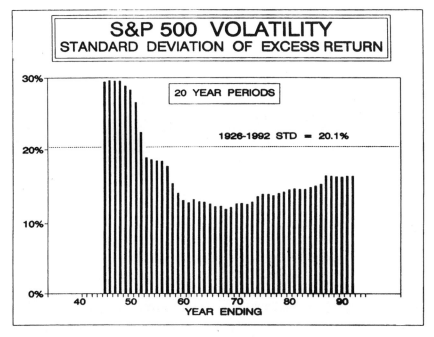

**Figure 5-11.** A perspective on the changing variability of the excess return of the S&P 500, as measured by standard deviation, over all 20-year periods ended 1945 to 1992. (*Source:* Stocks, Bonds, Bills, and Inflation 1993 Yearbook, *Ibbotson Associates, Chicago, annually updates the work by Roger G. Ibbotson and Rex A. Sinquefield. Used with permission. All rights reserved.*)

## Why DDM Reflects
## Interest-Rate Bias

The DDM is particularly sensitive to the interest-rate input. A selected long bond yield, rather than a short Treasury bill yield, usually represents the risk-free rate in the DDM. The choice reflects the extended maturity of the long bond, since valuation of the stock market, ideally, requires an estimate of the long-term, risk-free rate. Changes in bond yields, reported in the daily newspaper to two decimal places, can hardly be ignored. If bond yields move by 25 basis points (one-fourth percentage point) in a month, as they frequently have in recent years, the change immediately shows up in the DDM valuation of the stock market. No similar mechanism exists for tracking the other estimated inputs to the DDM. Estimates of dividend growth, with their orientation to the very long term, are revised much less frequently. Even if the dividend projection is adjusted for revisions over the next few years, dividend-growth estimates are much less flexible than bond yields. Estimates of the risk premium are especially sticky. For some versions of the DDM, a constant, based on long-range historical experience, represents the risk premium. Where adjustments in the risk premium reflect changes in variability of stock prices, comparisons are likely to be based on 5-year moving averages, which change only very gradually. Other methods, such as those using option prices, are likely to provide more frequent adjustments but not necessarily more acceptable results.

Ease of securing the data does not mean that the bond yield is a wholly adequate input for the purposes of the DDM. Although the best example of a risk-free rate is the yield on a very short Treasury bill, the short maturity is a disadvantage in valuing the stock market, which looks far beyond the current year. The futures markets in Treasury bills, for example, show how investors' expectations over a more extended period can vary from the current rate. The long bond yield, although preferable to the short Treasury bill yield as an input to the DDM, also fails to meet the specific definition of the risk-free rate required by the DDM. Even if the bond is a Treasury issue, its yield is not the same as the risk-free rate. Investors price a long-term bond to allow for the risk-free rate plus a risk premium. For a Treasury bond, the risk premium relates to the maturity of the issue. For an industrial bond, an additional risk premium is included to allow for default risk. As a result, the bond-yield input to the DDM, despite accurate reporting of the current quotation, may also contribute to significant error in the valuation of the stock market.

The degree of interest-rate bias demonstrated by the DDM depends in substantial degree on the changing volatility of bond yields. Figure 5-12 traces the record since 1926. It is no accident that the DDM achieved acceptance in the 1970s and 1980s when

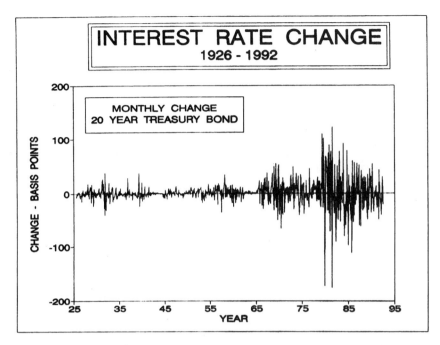

**Figure 5-12.** Estimated monthly change in yield to maturity for a 20-year Treasury bond. (*Source:* Stocks, Bonds, Bills, and Inflation 1993 Yearbook, *Ibbotson Associates, Chicago, annually updates the work by Roger G. Ibbotson and Rex A. Sinquefield. Used with permission. All rights reserved.*)

the volatility of interest rates became a critical issue for the stock market. Interest rates, however, are only one of the three key factors that drive stock prices. A danger is that the DDM becomes irrelevant during periods when interest rates do not dominate pricing of the stock market.

# Reference

1. Myron J. Gordon and E. Shapiro, "Capital Equipment Analysis: The Required Rate of Profit," *Management Science* 3:102–110, October 1956.

# 6
# Identifying
# Cause and Effect

## Focusing on Change
## Rather Than Level

### Deriving a Dynamic Model

This chapter traces the development of our decision process for active asset allocation from the logic summarized in Chaps. 1 to 5. As the initial step, this first section describes conversion of the constant-growth model of the stock market from a static version, as discussed in the previous chapter, to a dynamic model. While the static version attempts to evaluate market-price *level*, the dynamic model addresses market-price *change*. A second section discusses the framework for selection of three measures of potential change which serve as inputs to the model. A final section concerns the need for weighting of these measures and how weighting translates into decision rules.

Although our model of the stock market shares common roots with the DDM, it differs fundamentally in both structure and operation. A *highly efficient* market implies a *highly rational* relationship between current market price and information currently available to investors. Acceptance of this principle permits a critical distinction concerning the information important to investors. At any point, many items of information bear on market price, as illustrated in Chap. 5, and their interrelationships may be complex. For example, the relationship of market price to any one causal factor (say, a rise in the rate of inflation, a decline in the foreign exchange value of the dollar, or growth of the money supply) will likely change depending on the changing role of other factors. How can the investment decision maker simplify efforts to organize and evaluate the vast amount of relevant information? To this end, we use the current market price—which already discounts most of the information which investors worry about—as our point of departure. As a result, we are able to shift attention from the extremely wide range of information bearing on the *level* of the stock market to the thin margin of information likely to bring about a *change* in market price.

### Three Key Factors Explain Yield Change

The comparison shown below highlights the difference between our model and the traditional efforts which attempt to estimate the market level. The first line reproduces the constant-growth model as employed in our example of the DDM in Chap. 5. It can be described as the *static* version, since it views the stock market in equilibrium at a point in time. To solve for price ($P$) requires individual estimates of the level for each of the three key factors. The second line restates the constant-growth model to reflect change. (The symbol $\Delta$ indicates change.) This restated model is therefore appropriately described as the *dynamic* version. To solve for change in price ($\Delta P$) requires individual measures of the change in each of the three factors. The dynamic model derives mathematically from the static model, as outlined in App. 6-1.

Static
$$P = \frac{D}{I + k - G}$$

Dynamic
$$\frac{\Delta P}{P} = \frac{\Delta D}{D} - \frac{\Delta I}{Y} - \frac{\Delta k}{Y} + \frac{\Delta G}{Y}$$

where $P$ = price
$\quad\quad D$ = dividend
$\quad\quad I$ = risk-free rate
$\quad\quad k$ = risk premium
$\quad\quad G$ = dividend-growth rate
$\quad\quad Y$ = yield

Figure 6-1 graphically traces the flow of information through the dynamic model. The objective, as shown at the top of the diagram, is to estimate the change in the price of the stock market. We assume a time horizon of 1 year, since information relating to much shorter periods is likely to be already discounted and information over much longer periods is usually too far in the future. As shown on the second line, the market-price

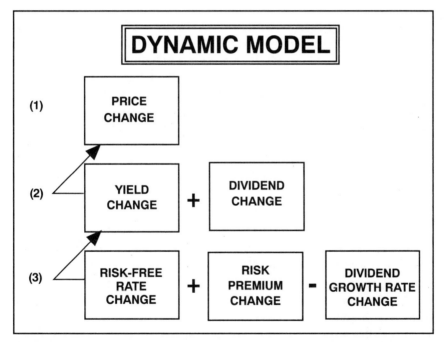

**Figure 6-1.** How the dynamic model relates market-price change to change in the three key factors.

change amounts to the sum of the price changes due to (1) dividend change and (2) yield change. The third line of the diagram represents the three key factors which determine yield change. As explained in App. 6-1 (Eq. 6-8), the yield change for the stock market depends on changes in three broad factors: the expected dividend-growth rate into the long-range future, the long-term risk-free rate, and the risk premium. Commonly used terms which, in an approximate way, refer to the same key factors are business outlook, interest rates, and investor confidence.

## How Yield Change Overwhelms Dividend Change

For the dynamic model, the critical issue affecting market-price change over a 1-year period is clearly the yield change. At least since the early years after World War II, year-to-year dividend changes have moved in a relatively narrow range. At any point, moreover, market price already discounts that part of the change for the year ahead already anticipated by the investor consensus. *Unexpected* change in dividend payments, independent of yield change, seldom accounts for more than two or three percentage points of the 1-year change in market price. In contrast, the stock market yield may move over a wide range, sometimes by as much as 100 basis points (one percentage point) or more within a 1-year period. A one-percentage-point change in yield would account for about a 20 to 35 percent change in market price, depending on the beginning yield. Since the three key factors identified here determine dividend yield, they also constitute the key factors that drive stock prices.

Figure 6-2 underscores the relationship of yield change to market-price change over 1955 to 1991. Panel A compares dividend change to market-price change. The horizontal dispersion of the data points indicates almost no discernible relationship over a 1-year time horizon between dividend change and market-price change. Panel B, which compares yield change (yield change over the year ahead divided by current yield 1 year ahead) with market-price change, stands in sharp contrast. The

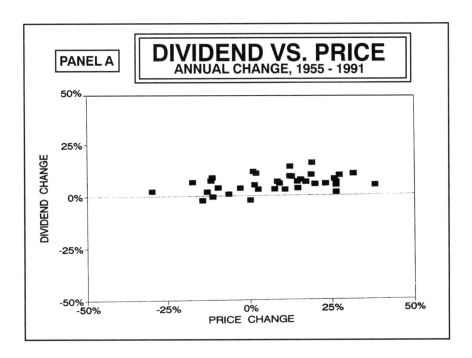

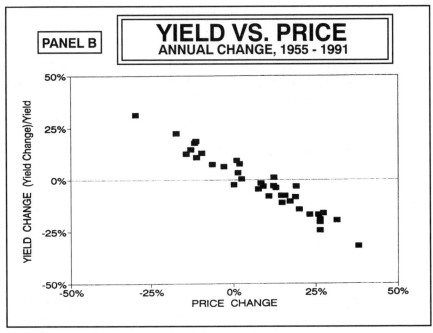

**Figure 6-2.** Annual market-price change over 1955 to 1991 related to (a) dividend change and (b) yield change. (*Source:* The Analysts Handbook *issued by Standard & Poor's Corporation.*)

data display a clearly defined downward slope, indicating a rather tight negative correlation between yield change and market-price change. A standard statistical measure shows that 94 percent of the variance in market price over this period is explained by yield change. Only 18 percent of market-price variance can be attributed to dividend change. The two variance calculations add to moderately more than 100 percent because of a limited degree of covariance.

## Comparing Earlier Periods with Recent Decades

We separate the earlier years, 1927 to 1954, from the period beginning 1955 because of important changes in economic and financial conditions between the two periods. Available data for the S&P 500 (and its predecessor indexes which included fewer issues) extend back to the base year 1926. The earlier years included the extreme economic dislocations and the highly volatile stock prices of the 1930s. They also reflected the impact of World War II and the Korean hostilities, together with accompanying price controls, rationing, and excess profits taxes. The last 3 or 4 decades appear more representative of the contemporary stock market environment than the earlier history. Economic activity has proceeded at a steadier pace. Despite protracted military involvement in Vietnam, the national economy has operated since the mid-1950s without the wartime regulations that characterized earlier hostilities. Inflation and episodes of volatile interest rates, meanwhile, have become more prominent problems.

As explanation for market-price change, the dominant role of yield change depends on the continuation of the broad economic framework since the mid-1950s. Figure 6-3 shows the same comparisons as in Fig. 6-2 but for the earlier period. Over 1927 to 1954, dividend increases and decreases, reflecting the instability of the business environment, were much more extreme than they have been subsequently. Over these years, the variation in market price reflected both dividend change and yield change

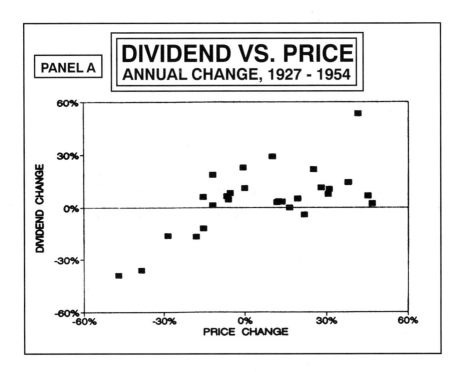

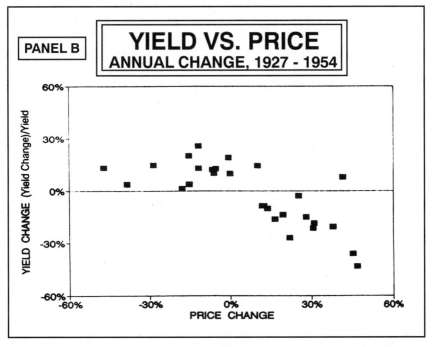

**Figure 6-3.** Annual market-price change over 1927 to 1954 related to (*a*) dividend change and (*b*) yield change. (*Source*: The Analysts Handbook *issued by Standard & Poor's Corporation.*)

in more nearly equal proportions. Figure 6-4 compares the variability of yield change with that for dividend change over the two periods. As measured by the standard deviation, variability of market price over the entire 65 years from 1927 to 1991 was 20 percent, reflecting a considerably higher figure of about 25 percent for 1927 to 1954 and less than 16 percent for 1955 to 1991. The variability of the yield change declined from 18 percent in the earlier period to 14 percent for the more recent period. In contrast, the variability of year-to-year dividend change over the same interval dropped from 18 to 4 percent. The much steadier pattern of dividend change in the more recent period accounts for most of the difference in market-price variability over the two periods.

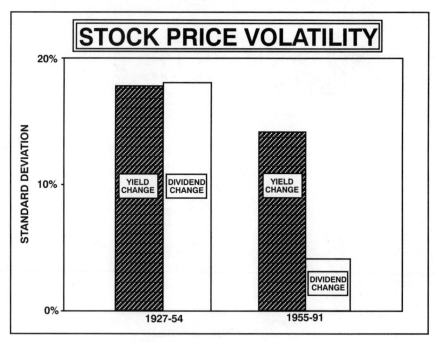

**Figure 6-4.** Comparing the variability of yield change with that for dividend change over 1927 to 1954 and 1955 to 1991.

# Selecting Model Inputs

## Identifying the Three
## Prime Variables

With the dynamic model in place, the next challenge is to identify the appropriate inputs. We distinguish between the *three prime variables,* which serve as inputs to our model, and the *three key factors,* which drive stock prices but are hidden from view. The key factors, as clearly defined in the constant-growth model, are the very long term constant-growth assumptions which summarize the collective views of the investor consensus. If accurately quantified, they would fully explain the current level of stock prices, but no investor is able to measure them. The prime variables, in contrast, derive in each case from publicly available information. They provide clues (although not *proportional* measures) to change in the key factors. Identification of a prime variable depends, first, on a logical relationship with one or more of the key factors that drive stock prices and, second, on a test of statistical significance. Table 6-1 lists each prime variable classified according to the key factor to which it is most closely related.

For each of the prime variables, validation follows a three-step process. First, we apply historical simulation to likely alternatives. For this exercise, we assume advance knowledge of still-to-be-reported data—such as dividend payments or short-

**Table 6-1.** Prime Variables Related to Key Factors

| Key factor | Prime variable |
|---|---|
| Business outlook (dividend-growth rate) | Acceleration/deceleration dividend growth (second year ahead vs. coming year) |
| Interest rates (risk-free rate) | Change in Treasury bill yield (coming year vs. prior year) |
| Investor confidence (risk premium) | Price/earnings ratio (four-quarter trailing earnings) |

term interest rates—and test our concept in the context of the scaling. (We explain *scaling* in the final section of this chapter.) Multiple-regression analysis provides evidence of the contribution of various alternative inputs to explaining market-price change. Since historical simulation benefits from hindsight advantage, the immediate purpose is to identify past relationships rather than to demonstrate forecasting advantage. Second, we operate in real time (beginning more than a decade ago), substituting objective estimates for the hindsight advantage which characterizes the historical simulation. The scaling remains the same, but our focus shifts to measures that qualify as slow information. As defined in Chap. 4, a thin margin of slow information—which market prices do not immediately discount—provides the only opportunity available to active management. Third, we apply simple decision rules to the three prime variables, which serve as the core of our model. Since these decision rules respond to the same issues as scaling, they generate the same broad pattern of market valuations, as documented in Chap. 10. The following comments explain the information included in each prime variable.

## Assessing the Business Outlook

The business outlook is central to the valuation of the stock market because it relates to the stream of dividends that investors expect to receive into the long-range future. Consensus expectations, already discounted by market prices, heavily reflect the past record as well as the rather well-defined indications for dividend payments over the *first year ahead.* As the coming year unfolds, the investment consensus concerning the future dividend stream will define with increasing accuracy the outlook for the cash dividend payment over the *second year ahead.* To the extent this new information differs from expectations embedded in market prices, it will influence the long-term consensus view of the dividend-growth rate. Note that year-to-year changes in dividend payments for a broad stock index sum up the combined influence of many factors, including the rate of business activity, the level of profitability, and the condition of corporate balance sheets. Chapter 7, looking specifically at the economic variables which shape the business outlook, outlines the advantage of focusing on dividend change rather than earnings change. By way of perspective, Fig. 6-5 traces the varying rate of change (second year ahead) for S&P 500 dividends over the period 1927 to 1991.

Absent the hindsight advantage available to historical simulation, real-time operations require objective estimates of dividend growth for each of the next 2 years. For an objective measure of the likely *dividend change over the next four quarters,* we turn to the indicated dividend rate (IDR). The IDR, reported weekly in *Standard & Poor's Outlook* and *Barron's,* adjusts for dividend declarations that have not yet been translated into full-year dividend payments. As shown in Chap. 7, the rate of dividend payments implied by dividends declared but not yet paid provides an

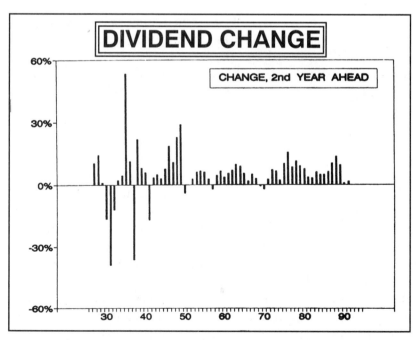

**Figure 6-5.** Tracing the rate of change for S&P 500 dividends, second year ahead, over 1927 to 1991. (*Source*: The Analysts Handbook issued by *Standard & Poor's Corporation*.)

objective estimate for dividend growth over the year ahead. The proxy for the rate of *dividend growth over the second four quarters ahead* may be derived from models of varying degrees of sophistication, but the formulation shown here is both simple and effective. It addresses the normalized rate of dividend growth, taking into account the level of inflation. This approach recognizes that both the long bond rate and the normalized rate of dividend growth incorporate consensus judgments concerning the prospective rate of inflation. The normal growth rate, as measured by the long-term historical average, approximates the yield for the long Treasury bond less 100 basis points. Since, as inflationary expectations rise, the upward trend in the rate of dividend growth tends to lag the rise in bond yields, both scaling and decision rules adjust accordingly.

## Tracking Interest Rates

To track interest rates, we compare the average yield in prospect for short Treasury bills over the coming four quarters with the average yield reported for the past four quarters. The short Treasury bill is widely accepted as an approximation of the risk-free rate but for a much shorter time horizon than required to value the stock market. Although bonds have the advantage of a longer maturity, their yields include allowance for risk. The bond risk premium, reflecting uncertainties relating to future interest rates or the changing outlook for the credit rating of the borrower, may vary significantly over time. Our work indicates that the best choice is the short Treasury bill yield—but averaged over a year rather than measured at a single point. Averaging Treasury bill yields over four quarters significantly moderates the day-to-day volatility associated with very short maturities. Figure 6-6, covering the 66 years from 1927 to 1992, traces the change in yield for 30-day Treasury bills (average yield for the current year less prior-year average yield). For real-time operations, as explained in Chap. 8, we derive the necessary data from the market for Treasury bill futures.

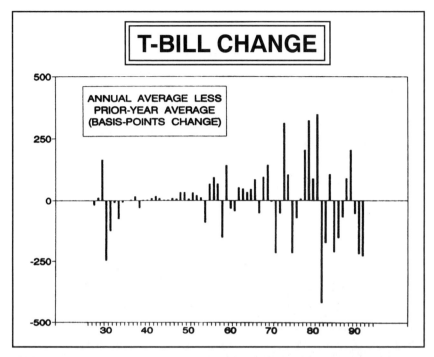

**Figure 6-6.** Tracing the change in yield for 30-day Treasury bills over 1927 to 1992. (*Source:* Stocks, Bonds, Bills, and Inflation 1993 Yearbook, *Ibbotson Associates, Chicago, annually updates the work by Roger G. Ibbotson and Rex A. Sinquefield. Used with permission. All rights reserved.*)

## Monitoring Investor Confidence

The price-earnings ratio (P/E) serves as the prime variable gauging investor confidence. For our purposes, it relates how much the investor consensus is willing to pay for four-quarter trailing earnings. Figure 6-7 plots P/Es for the S&P 500 at the beginning of each calendar year for 1927 to 1993. The critical issue is whether the confidence—or lack thereof—implied by the level of P/E is warranted. In a highly efficient market, P/Es

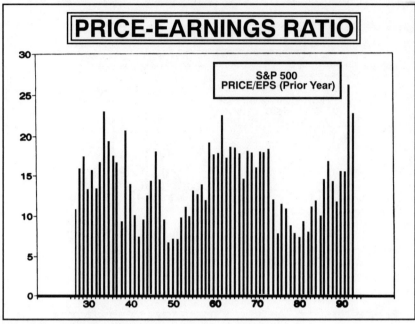

**Figure 6-7.** Plotting price-earnings ratios for the S&P 500 at the beginning of each year over 1927 to 1993. (*Source*: The Analysts Handbook *issued by Standard & Poor's Corporation.*)

are usually high or low for good reason. In Chap. 9, however, we present evidence concerning extremely high and low P/Es which supports the contrarian point of view. We infer the likelihood of change based on the tendency of P/Es for a broad market index to revert from an extreme position toward the mean. Eventually, confidence, as measured by the P/E, will return toward the mean, either because the anticipated events materialize or because the likelihood of their occurrence recedes. The challenge for the decision maker is to balance the high or low confidence implied by the price-earnings ratio against the other key factors that drive stock prices. Note that in real-time operations three quarters of the trailing four-quarter earnings have already been reported, but the final quarter requires an estimate. Chapter 9 explains why the final-quarter estimate, although at times wide of the mark, is unlikely to introduce a substantial

distortion in the P/E calculation. It also shows how a completely objective measure—reported earnings for the four quarters
ended 3 months earlier—may be substituted with much the
same results.

# Translating Scaling into Decision Rules

### Weighting the Prime Variables

Scaling addresses the weighting which the decision process
applies to each of the prime variables. Most investors would
agree that, other things equal, accelerating dividend growth,
declining interest rates, or low P/E would be positive for valuation of the stock market. The same logic, applied in reverse,
identifies decelerating dividend growth, rising interest rates, or
a high P/E as negatives. Although the prime variables routinely
provide such information, both positive and negative, they are
likely to contribute little to the decision process in the absence
of weighting. Because the stock market is highly efficient, they
seldom provide an unambiguously positive or negative pattern
across the board. The continuing challenge is how to weight
mixed signals of varying strength.

Weighting recognizes the relationship of each prime variable
to change in market price over a 1-year time horizon. Each of
the prime variables presents a comparison between two measures. One measure represents data widely available, well
understood, and already embedded in market prices. The other
measure relates to data likely to be embedded in market prices
1 year ahead. The difference between the two measures provides an estimate, when appropriately weighted, of prospective
market-price change. Table 6-2 organizes the three prime variables in this framework. The middle column lists the measures
associated with initial consensus expectations, while the right-
hand column represents information not yet fully discounted by
stock prices. A larger difference between any pair of measures
implies a larger impact on market valuation—but by how

**Table 6-2.** Components of Prime Variables in Real Time

|  | Already discounted | To be discounted |
|---|---|---|
| Dividend change (four-quarter average) | Annualized growth (implied by IDR*) | Normalized growth (derived from bond yield) |
| Treasury bill yield (four-quarter average) | Prior-year average (as reported) | Coming-year average (futures market) |
| Price/earnings ratio (trailing earnings) | Current (as reported) | Mean-reverting (from extremes) |

*Indicated dividend rate.

much? A constant weighting for each prime variable would imply market-price impact proportional to the difference. If such were the case, multiple-regression analysis (a statistical tool widely used in the development of computer models) could readily assign appropriate fixed weights to each prime variable. Unfortunately, fixed weights applied to variables bearing on market valuation neither explain well the past record nor work for long in real-time operations. For each variable, there are good reasons to expect the weighting to change as the circumstances change.

## Why Weightings Change

Among considerations which modify the weightings applied to the prime variables, two stand out. Weightings routinely take into account the extent of the difference between the information already discounted and that still to be discounted. Interest rates provide an illustration. A large swing in interest rates warrants lower weighting than a smaller change since it is more likely to be at least partially retraced. High volatility works in both directions. The overall significance to market valuation, while greater for the larger difference, is *not proportionally more significant*. Second, weightings allow for interrelationships between the prime variables as well as between prime variables and other economic measures. If dividends are depressed, for example, the probability of a return toward a more normal growth rate by the second year ahead strongly reflects the course of interest rates. Declining interest rates favor recovery of a depressed rate of dividend growth, while rising rates, under such circumstances, have rather regularly exerted a negative influence. Appendix 6-2 identifies two additional variables which supplement the three prime variables. While each of these measures add incrementally to our understanding of market-price change, their value is limited by high correlations with information already included in our decision process.

## Decision Rules Derive from Scaling

Decision rules, which establish the weights applied to each of the prime variables as circumstances change, serve as a simple method of scaling. We have made use of a computerized model both to experiment with alternative inputs in historical simulation and also to validate our findings in real-time operations. Following the logic outlined in Chaps. 1 to 5, the computerized model places the three prime variables at the core of the decision process. Scaling adjusts weighting of the prime variables to reflect the changing probabilities as circumstances change. Further study has shown that appropriate decision rules applied to the three prime variables accomplish, in an approximate way, the same goals. In essence, decision rules constitute a simplified method of scaling.

We present our *decision-rules* model in Chaps. 7 to 10. The main difference from the computerized model is the degree of refinement. The computerized model produces a spectrum of market valuations, ranging from overvaluation amounting to 20 percent or more to undervaluation of the same magnitude. The decision-rules model provides much the same information but with only three rankings: overvaluation, neutral valuation, and undervaluation. Like the computerized model, it addresses the primary purpose of active asset allocation, which is to respond unambiguously when it detects large overvaluation or under-valuation. Chapter 10, following discussion of each of the prime variables individually in Chaps. 7 to 9, shows how the prime variables interact to provide a measure of valuation. It also compares the valuations provided by the decision-rules model with the real-time record of the computerized model. Chapter 11 completes the decision process by spelling out the decision rules.

# Appendix 6-1
# Dynamic Model Derived
# from Static Model

Both the static and dynamic models relate market price ($P$) to dividend ($D$) and yield ($Y$). The dynamic model is the first derivative of the static model.

1. By definition

$$Y = \frac{D}{P} \tag{6-1}$$

2. Rearranging Eq. 6-1

$$P = \frac{D}{Y} \tag{6-2}$$

3. Solving Eq. 6-2 for incremental change

$$\Delta P = \frac{\Delta D}{Y} - \frac{\Delta Y \times D}{Y^2} \tag{6-3}$$

4. Dividing Eq. 6-3 by Eq. 6-2

$$\frac{\Delta P}{P} = \frac{\Delta D}{D} - \frac{\Delta Y}{Y} \tag{6-4}$$

5. Static (constant-growth) model

$$P = \frac{D}{I + k - G} \qquad \text{(6-5)}$$

where $I$ = risk-free rate
$k$ = risk premium
$G$ = dividend-growth rate

6. Rearranging Eq. 6-5

$$\frac{D}{P} = I + k - G \qquad \text{(6-6)}$$

7. Therefore,

$$Y = I + k - G \qquad \text{(6-7)}$$

8. Solving Eq. 6-7 for incremental change

$$\Delta Y = \Delta I + \Delta k - \Delta G \qquad \text{(6-8)}$$

9. Substituting Eq. 6-8 in Eq. 6-4

$$\frac{\Delta P}{P} = \frac{\Delta D}{D} - \frac{\Delta I + \Delta k - \Delta G}{Y} \qquad \text{(6-9)}$$

10. Dynamic (constant-growth) model (restatement of Eq. 6-9)

$$\frac{\Delta P}{P} = \frac{\Delta D}{D} - \frac{\Delta I}{Y} - \frac{\Delta k}{Y} + \frac{\Delta G}{Y} \qquad \text{(6-10)}$$

# Appendix 6-2
# Information Content in
# Other Economic Measures

The decision-rules model presented in this book derives from extensive real-time experience and back-testing for our computerized model. The computerized model offers greater flexibility for two reasons. First, it processes (with the aid of built-in probability analysis) the inputs to the decision process on a daily

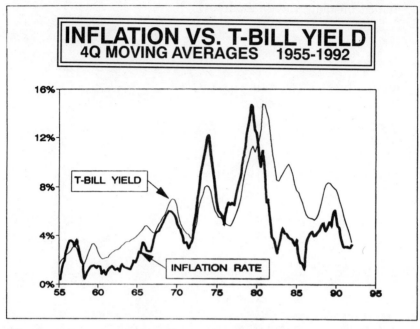

**Figure 6-8.** Comparing four-quarter moving averages for the rate of inflation and the yield on short Treasury bills over 1955 to 1992. (*Source*: Stocks, Bonds, Bills, and Inflation 1993 Yearbook, *Ibbotson Associates, Chicago, annually updates the work by Roger G. Ibbotson and Rex A. Sinquefield. Used with permission. All rights reserved.*)

basis. The aim is to distinguish day-to-day changes in overvaluation or undervaluation. Second, it includes two supplementary variables in addition to the three prime variables. One variable, as plotted in Fig. 6-8, compares the rate of inflation to the yield on short Treasury bills. The other, as shown in Fig. 6-9, looks at dividend yield in relation to the short Treasury bill yield. While each of the supplemental variables provides incremental information, the three prime variables constitute the backbone of each model. As demonstrated by comparisons over an extended period (Fig. 10-1), the decision-rules model serves as a less complex, widely accessible version of the computerized model.

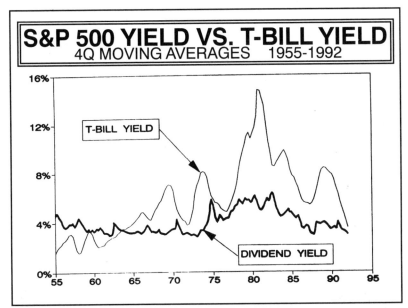

**Figure 6-9.** Comparing four-quarter moving averages for S&P 500 dividend yield and short Treasury bill yield over 1955 to 1992. (*Sources*: The Analysts Handbook *issued by Standard & Poor's Corporation*; Stocks, Bonds, Bills, and Inflation 1993 Yearbook, *Ibbotson Associates, Chicago, annually updates the work by Roger G. Ibbotson and Rex A. Sinquefield. Used with permission. All rights reserved.*)

# PART 3

## Understanding the Pitfalls and Opportunities

# 7

# How the Business Outlook Impacts Stock Prices

## Confronting the Dilemma

### How Earnings Frustrate Investors

In assessing the business outlook, investors have traditionally focused on earnings as the critical element. They look to earnings for insight concerning both future dividend payments and the internal investment necessary to support future growth. Active decisions to increase or to decrease exposure to the stock market have necessarily involved an assumption, explicit or implied, concerning earnings prospects. Yet, the link between stock prices and the business outlook is often a source of frustration for investors. Even a highly accurate forecast of earnings for the year ahead, in itself, offers little help in assessing the course of the stock market. In this chapter, we consider why this is so and what to do about it.

The attention accorded earnings reflects an enduring long-term relationship with stock prices. Figure 7-1 covers the 67 years of available data concerning earnings growth for the S&P 500. As shown by the graph, the gain for stock prices over the years 1926 to 1992 has been accompanied by similar increases for earnings and dividends. The least-squares method identifies

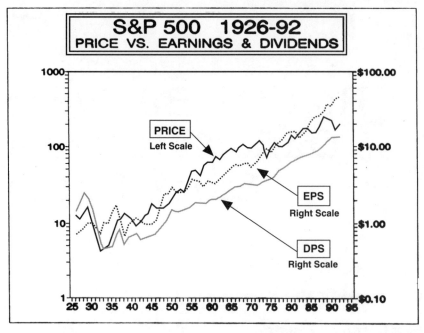

**Figure 7-1.** Comparing long-term trends for market price, earnings, and dividends of the S&P 500 over 1926 to 1992. (*Source*: The Analysts Handbook *issued by Standard & Poor's Corporation.*)

the trend for each series. By this measure, both stock prices and earnings have trended upward at a compound annual rate of 5.8 percent. The comparable rate for dividends is 5.0 percent.

## Market Significance Depends on Time Horizon

The historical relationship between stock prices and earnings is very different for the 1-year time horizon than for longer time intervals. Because economic visibility falls off rapidly beyond the next 6 to 12 months, estimates of overall corporate profits usually focus on approximately the year ahead. Other things equal, the outlook for lower earnings is widely regarded as a caution signal—a reason to cut back on stocks. An estimate of higher earnings, in contrast, generally adds to bullishness. The logic is intuitively appealing in view of the parallel long-term trends for earnings and stock prices, but it overlooks the way a highly efficient market works. As a guide to the stock market outlook over the coming year, a completely accurate assessment of earnings 1 year ahead would have been just plain wrong more often than not.

From 1927 to 1992, the S&P 500 moved contrary to the direction of earnings in 36 years and in the same direction as earnings in only 30 years. Panel A of Fig. 7-2 shows the direction of stock prices (up in 24 years and down in 17) when earnings rose. Panel B provides the same information concerning stock prices (up in 19 years and down in only 6) for years when earnings declined. The black areas of the two bar charts represent the number of years when stock prices and earnings moved in *opposite* directions. Note that the results summarized in Fig. 7-2

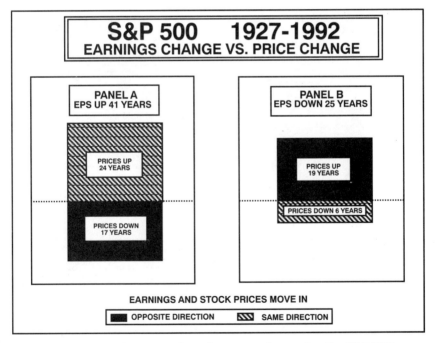

**Figure 7-2.** The direction of market-price change for the S&P 500 over 1927 to 1992 (*a*) when earnings rose and (*b*) when earnings declined. (*Source*: The Analysts Handbook *issued by* Standard & Poor's Corporation.)

are based on the assumption that the investment manager had access to a *perfect* forecast of earnings over the coming year. What would have happened if the allocation to stocks had depended on an earnings forecast that was much less accurate? Since even the completely accurate earnings forecast for the year ahead contains little useful information in projecting stock prices over the 1-year horizon, the introduction of random errors in these estimates would not change the probable outcome. Over a 1-year time horizon, stock prices are at least as likely to move contrary to earnings as in the same direction.

**How Long Is the Long Term?**

Figure 7-3 traces the relationship between changes in earnings and changes in stock prices over a wide spectrum of time hori-

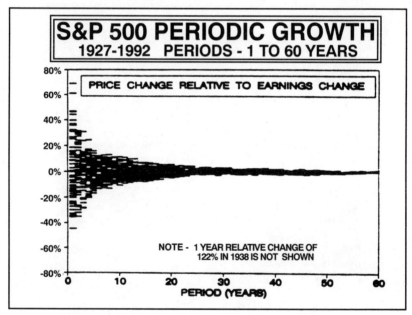

**Figure 7-3.** Compound annual rate of change of S&P 500 price relative to earnings over time horizons ranging from 1 to 60 years. (*Source:* The Analysts Handbook *issued by* Standard & Poor's Corporation.)

zons. The horizontal scale represents time, marking periods of 1 to 60 years during the 66 years ended 1992. The vertical scale measures the compound annual rate of change for stock prices *relative* to the comparable annual rate of change for earnings. Each data point indicates the disparity between the changes in market price and earnings for the time interval shown. For the 1-year time interval, there are 66 data points, spread widely in either direction above or below the zero line. The number of data points declines to 57 at the 10-year interval and continues to decrease as the time interval increases. For 60 years, almost the entire period for which comparisons are available, there are seven data points. As the time interval increases, the dispersion of the data points around the baseline narrows. The dispersion is by far the greatest over a 1-year time horizon. Note that at 10 years, however, the compound rate of change for market price may still vary from that for earnings by as much as 10 percent *annually.* Only after more than 50 years does the maximum dispersion narrow to a compound annual rate of less than 1 percent.

Historical relationships between earnings and market prices are consistent with the concept that active asset allocation operates in a highly efficient market. Investors are well aware of the fundamental importance of earnings and the long-term relationship between earnings and stock prices. Because investors are highly sensitive to earnings, stock prices rapidly adjust to the changing outlook as new information surfaces. At any point, stock prices have already rather thoroughly discounted consensus prospects for earnings over the year ahead. Advance information concerning earnings over a longer time horizon would clearly be useful, but economic visibility rapidly deteriorates with extension of the time horizon. As the year unfolds, the stock market will respond to new information, with surprises as likely in one direction as another. Most of the market-price response, however, will likely reflect the evolving consensus view of business more than 12 months ahead, revised expectations for interest rates, and changing investor confidence.

# What to Do: Focus on Dividends

## Why Dividends Rather Than Earnings?

Absent a crystal ball, how can this dilemma concerning stock prices and the business outlook be resolved? Our response focuses on analysis of dividend growth rather than forecast earnings. Traditional security analysis has focused on earnings rather than dividends for understandable reasons. Although corporate managements relate dividends to earnings, the dividend payout for any individual company may be influenced by many factors other than earnings progress. Our goal, nevertheless, is to assess the probable pattern of dividend growth from the first year ahead to the following year for the overall stock market. The argument in favor of focusing on dividends rather than earnings for this purpose rests on two key points: better-defined standard of measurement and the difference between a broad stock index and individual stocks.

**Better-Defined Standard of Measurement.**   Compared to earnings, dividend payments provide a more clearly defined standard of measurement. The dollars paid out as dividends, at any point, have the same value for all companies and all investors. Earnings, in contrast, are not only much more volatile from quarter to quarter, but their quality depends on how they are calculated. Reported earnings are shaped by a number of factors that may distort the assessment of both current earnings and future earning power. Within the choices provided by Generally Accepted Accounting Principles, earnings reflect assumptions made in the past—which may not have been accurate—as well as assumptions relating to an uncertain future. They may be calculated differently by two competing companies offering the same product lines, and the differences are likely to be greater if companies operate in very different industries. Earnings can be altered suddenly by implementation of a change set forth by the Financial Accounting Standards Board. They are almost always distorted by changing rates of inflation and are subject to write-offs that may not have been widely anticipated.

**Difference between a Broad Stock Index and Individual Stocks.** Investor emphasis on earnings rather than dividends, while warranted for the analysis of individual stocks, carries over to the valuation of the overall stock market, which presents a different set of characteristics in this regard. For individual companies, a wide range of circumstances peculiar to each company— and not necessarily indicative of the value of the company's stock—can influence the dividend payout. By way of example, consider just one factor: company growth prospects. At one extreme, a company's stock may warrant a very high price-earnings ratio as all earnings are plowed back to exploit extremely attractive growth opportunities. Consequently, there is no dividend—and no dividend growth. Another company, in contrast, may increase dividends sharply as a transition to higher payout ratio reflects recognition of diminishing growth opportunities. For a broadly based stock index, overall dividend payments tend to average out the many different factors which render dividends a misleading gauge for individual companies. At any point, the S&P 500 is certain to contain companies in a high-growth phase, where dividends do not keep pace, and other companies in the opposite situation. On balance, these specific company factors tend to offset each other from one period to another. Consequently, acceleration or deceleration in aggregate dividend growth is much more significant as a clue to changing valuation for a broadly based stock index than for individual issues.

## Comparing Correlations

Statistical analysis shows that prices for the broadly based stock indexes correlate at least as well with dividend-growth change as with earnings-growth change. Table 7-1 compares the *change* in stock prices over the *first* year ahead and the *change* in the dividend-growth rate over the *second* year ahead. The data cover the years 1955 to 1991, an extended period which avoids the severe dislocations resulting from World War II and the Korean hostilities as well as the depression of the 1930s. We focus on this period because it appears, in comparison with earlier periods, more representative of the broad economic framework in which the stock market currently operates. In 16 of the 37 years from 1955 to 1991, dividend growth accelerated in the second

**Table 7-1.** Dividend-Growth Change and Stock Prices, 1955 to 1991*

| Dividend-growth change (second-year ahead) | Number of years | S&P 500 Up | Down | % Up |
|---|---|---|---|---|
| More than +1% | 16 | 15 | 1 | 94 |
| +1% to –1% | 5 | 4 | 1 | 80 |
| Less than –1% | 16 | 8 | 8 | 50 |
| Total | 37 | 27 | 10 | 73 |

*Market-price change in year indicated compared to change in dividend-growth rate second year ahead.

year ahead by at least one percentage point. In 15 of these years, stock prices rose. When the change in dividend growth ranged from an acceleration of one percentage point to a deceleration of one percentage point, stock prices increased in 4 of the 5 years. Deceleration of dividend growth by more than one percentage point was accompanied by an increase in stock prices in only 8 of 16 years.

Table 7-2 displays comparable data relating the change in stock prices (first year ahead) to earnings changes (second year ahead). The left-hand column separates the yearly data into three segments, as in the previous table. The limits for each of the three groupings are necessarily wider, since earnings are

**Table 7-2.** Earnings-Growth Change and Stock Prices, 1955 to 1991.*

| Earnings-growth change (second-year ahead) | Number of years | S&P 500 Up | Down | % Up |
|---|---|---|---|---|
| More than +5% | 13 | 13 | 0 | 100 |
| +5% to –5% | 8 | 6 | 2 | 75 |
| Less than –5% | 16 | 8 | 8 | 50 |
| Total | 37 | 27 | 10 | 73 |

*Market-price change in year indicated compared to change in earnings-growth rate second year ahead.

more volatile than dividends. For the upper grouping, the results are much the same as for dividend growth in Table 7-1. Stock prices rose in each of the 13 years when earnings growth improved by five percentage points or more in the following year. Comparisons in the middle and lower groupings displayed much the same pattern as for dividend-growth change. More refined statistical techniques, however, relate the magnitude of change in stock prices to the magnitude of change in dividends or earnings. On this basis, the correlation of market-price change with dividend change is stronger than with earnings change.

## Objective Measures of Change in Dividend-Growth Rate

### Entering the "Side Door"

In order to develop a prime variable to monitor the business outlook, we enter the "side door" rather than the "front door." As shown in Table 7-1, advance identification of dividend growth for the second year ahead would be highly useful. The straightforward approach—which we describe as going through the front door—focuses specifically on estimates for dividends in each of the 2 years ahead. The side-door approach which we present here serves much the same purpose but offers important advantages. It is objective, easily understood, and readily available to anyone with access to the financial press.

The side-door approach focuses on the change in the consensus view of dividend growth rather than the individual estimates for the first and second years ahead. Two measures, viewed in relation to each other, provide an indication of the *potential* for acceleration or deceleration in the dividend-growth rate. One measure is the *indicated dividend rate* (IDR), which permits week-to-week tracking of the prospective rate of dividend payments for about 6 months ahead. Even though the full-year dividend rate ultimately may differ for reasons not yet apparent, the IDR provides a basis for appraisal of the current consensus view of near-term dividend growth. The other measure derives from *long bond yields* as currently quoted in the fixed-income market. It aims to assess the "normal" level of dividend growth, in light of current expectations for inflation, rather than to provide a specific estimate for the second year ahead. Whether dividend growth will likely move in the direction of this benchmark depends, in part, on the status of the other two prime variables.

## Understanding the Indicated Dividend Rate

Standard & Poor's Corporation compiles the IDR and reports it to investors in its publications (*Outlook,* issued weekly, and monthly supplements to *The Analysts Handbook*). As shown in Fig. 7-4, *Barron's,* a weekly financial magazine widely available at newsstands, also carries this information. Although separate data are available for the S&P 500 and S&P 400, our comments here will be directed to the broader index, the S&P 500.*

The IDR specifies the annual dividend payment based on the dividends declared to date. When a company declares a change in the quarterly dividend payment, the IDR assumes that this new rate is paid on an annual basis. The IDR also includes a change in prospective payments anticipated by the declaration of extra dividends. Because declarations of dividends lead payments, the IDR serves as a proxy for the dividend to be paid over the four quarters to end 6 months ahead. The following example provides an illustration: On June 30, 1989, the last reported four-quarter dividend payments (period ended March 30, 1989) amounted to $9.98. At that time, the IDR was $11.17. For the four quarters ended 6 months later (calendar year 1989) total dividend payments amounted to $11.05. The error amounted to 1.1 percent.

Figure 7-5 provides a broad historical perspective. It compares changes for two measures of dividend growth at the beginning

---

*Appendix 7-1 lists historical data for the IDR.

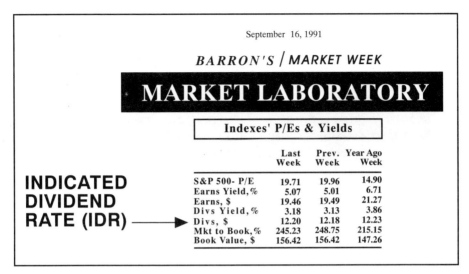

**Figure 7-4.** *Barron's,* as well as other publications, reports the indicated dividend rate to investors.

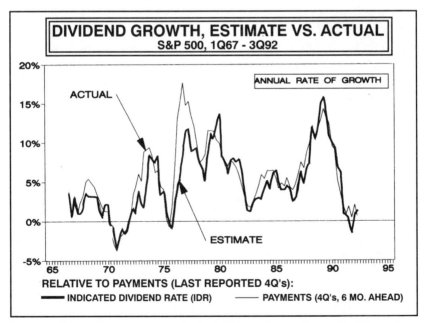

**Figure 7-5.** Comparing projected dividend growth derived from the indicated dividend rate with actual growth subsequently reported. (*Source:* The Analysts Handbook *issued by Standard & Poor's Corporation.*)

of each quarter from the first quarter of 1967 to the third quarter of 1992. The heavy line shows the percentage difference between the IDR and dividend payments for the last four quarters already reported. Dividend payments already reported at the beginning of each calendar quarter cover the four quarters ended 3 months earlier. The source of this information is the monthly supplement to *The Analysts Handbook,* issued by Standard & Poor's Corporation and available in many public libraries as well as by subscription. The lighter line traces the percentage difference between dividend payments as subsequently reported for the four quarters to end 6 months ahead and dividend payments for the same base period (four quarters ended 3 months earlier). Figure 7-5 shows both series, actual and IDR-derived, converted to annual rates of change. By way of illustration, the IDR at the beginning of 1990 was $11.55, 8.2 percent greater than the actual payments for the four quarters ended September 30, 1989, of $10.67. Since the IDR anticipates actual dividend payments over the year to end 6 months later, the percent increase applies to a 9-month period. The corresponding annualized growth rate, based on multiplying the 9-month rate of 8.2 percent by $\frac{4}{3}$, is 10.9 percent. The same adjustment applies to the record of the three-quarter change in actual dividend payments.

The annual rate of dividend growth implied by the IDR provides a base for assessing the likely change in the consensus view of dividend growth.* The IDR-derived estimate, which looks 6 months into the future, may diverge increasingly from the dividend-growth rate for the full year ahead as the year approaches its end. The critical issue, however, is not the precision of the estimate for the entire year. Rather, what matters is that this measure approximates the consensus view of the dividend-growth outlook from the current vantage point. The current market price discounts the current views of investors and will change as the investor consensus changes.

*Appendix 7-2 presents an alternative method of calculating the annualized rate of dividend growth implied by the IDR. It requires only the information regularly available in *Barron's.*

With the IDR-derived annualized rate of dividend growth as a base, prospects for acceleration or deceleration in the growth rate depend on two considerations. One consideration is the current normalized rate of dividend growth, given the level of inflation in prospect. Yield data for the fixed-income market provides a basis for tracking change in the rate of expected inflation. The other consideration is the presence of conditions, financial and otherwise, likely to move the rate of change in the direction of the normalized rate. To address this second consideration, Chap. 10 reviews the three prime variables in relation to each other.

## Estimating Normalized Dividend Growth

Since dividend growth tends to reflect the level of inflation, the normalized rate of dividend growth must be adjusted for this factor. The relevant rate of inflation in estimating future dividend growth is not what it has been, but, rather, what it will be. Official government figures trace the course of past inflation, but they tell little concerning expected inflation. A better measure is the fixed-income market, which adjusts rapidly to the changing consensus outlook for inflation. At the beginning of 1955, for example, long-term Treasury bonds were yielding less than 3 percent because investors anticipated little, if any, long-term inflation. Yields for similar issues in early 1990 were close to 9 percent. Under then-prevailing conditions, bond yields reflected renewed fears that inflation would soon creep upward from the 4 to 5 percent rate of the previous 3 years.

To make use of the relationship between normalized dividend growth and bond yields, we distinguish between the *current* rate of inflation and the *anticipated* rate. Dividend growth reflects the sum of two components, real growth of dividends and the current rate of inflation. Over the history of the S&P 500 (since 1926), real dividend growth, even though the dividend payout has lagged the growth of earnings on balance, has averaged a little more than 1 percent annually. To the extent the downward drift in the dividend payout has now leveled off, real dividend growth may creep upward—perhaps averaging as much as 2 percent annually into the long-range future. Our estimate of normalized real dividend growth, to reflect a range of 1 to 2 percent, is therefore 1.5 percent. Most estimates of long bond returns, meanwhile, range about 1.5 percent to 3.5 percent above the level of anticipated inflation. Historical comparisons since 1926 show the difference between bond returns and realized inflation to be at the lower end of this range. From the 1950s through the early 1980s, however, investors did not foresee the extent of eroding bond prices attributable to repeated upward revisions in inflation expectations. To allow for this factor, our single-point estimate of real bond returns is the midpoint of the 1.5 to 3.5 percent range, or 2.5 percent. The equation below incorporates the two single-point estimates. It derives normalized dividend growth (NDG) for the S&P 500 (consisting of real dividend growth plus anticipated inflation) from the yield to maturity $(Y_B)$ on a 20-year Treasury bond (real return plus anticipated inflation). The result is an estimate of NDG that is one percentage point less than the long bond return.

$$NDG = Y_B - 1\%$$

Our measure of NDG provides a basis for determining when current dividend growth, as viewed by the investor consensus, is weak and when it is strong. As bond yields respond in an approximate way to changing expectations for inflation, they do not necessarily forecast a parallel change in dividend growth. On the contrary, changes in bond yields and dividend-growth rates often diverge. The bond yield, however, directs attention to the current rate of dividend growth in relation to the changing level of anticipated inflation. Weak dividend growth, as defined here, is at least one percentage point less than NDG. Similarly, strong dividend growth is one percentage point or more in excess of NDG. If, for example, the current long bond yield is 8 percent, then NDG would equal 7 percent. Weak dividend growth would be less than 6 percent, and strong dividend growth would amount to more than 8 percent.

## Combining the Clues

Viewed in isolation, the prime variable relating to the business outlook provides little guidance concerning valuation of the stock market. Table 7-3 compares the difference between two measures, near-term dividend growth (NTDG) and NDG, with the subsequent four-quarter change in stock prices. Data are limited to the years 1967 to 1992 since dividend-growth comparisons based on the IDR are unavailable for earlier years. To expand the sample size, data include calculations made at the beginning of each calendar quarter. The three classifications of the dividend data shown in the table, however, do not in themselves shed much light on the likelihood of subsequent market-price change. The table classifies NTDG as weak when it lags NDG by one percentage point. Similarly, NTDG is strong if it exceeds NDG by more than one percentage point. The remaining data points, within one percentage point of NDG, make up the neutral category.

The prime variable relating to the business outlook becomes more meaningful in combination with the other two prime variables. In a highly efficient stock market, near-term forecasts of dividends as well as earnings are already largely discounted.

**Table 7-3.** Normalized versus Near-Term Dividend Growth, 1Q67 to 1Q92*

| Dividend growth (near-term) | Difference NDG – NTDG | Number quarters | S&P 500, 4Q change | | |
|---|---|---|---|---|---|
| | | | Up | Down | % Up |
| Weak | More than +1% | 67 | 48 | 19 | 72 |
| Neutral | +1% to –1% | 12 | 8 | 4 | 67 |
| Strong | Less than –1% | 22 | 15 | 7 | 68 |
| Total | | 101 | 71 | 30 | 70 |

*Market-price change over four-quarter period beginning in the quarter indicated compared to the difference between normalized dividend-growth rate (NDG) and near-term dividend-growth rate (NTDG). 1Q67 = first quarter of 1967, 4Q = four-quarter.

Asset allocation decisions based mainly on such information are likely to be counterproductive, adding to both transaction costs and risk without improving expected return. How stock market valuation can benefit from an overview of the three prime variables is the subject of Chap. 10. It brings together clues relating to the three key factors that drive stock prices. These clues include the analysis of dividend growth (as discussed in this chapter) in addition to the data concerning interest rates and investor confidence (presented in Chaps. 8 and 9).

## Appendix 7-1
## Indicated Dividend Rate:
## Historical Data

Standard & Poor's Corporation began publishing the IDR during 1966. Table 7-4 presents data for the beginning of each month since January 1967, as published by Standard & Poor's Corporation in the monthly supplements to *The Analysts Handbook*. Table 7-5 lists weekly data, as provided by *Barron's*, beginning with the issue dated January 4, 1988.

## Appendix 7-2
## Alternative Calculation of
## Dividend-Growth Rate

An alternative method of calculating the dividend-growth rate does not require information concerning reported dividend payments. The method previously described in this chapter compares the current IDR (secured from *Standard & Poor's Outlook* or from *Barron's*) with the last reported four-quarter dividend payment (available in the monthly supplement to *The Analysts Handbook*). The result of this comparison, appropriately annualized, serves as a proxy for the consensus view of the rate of dividend growth in prospect over the coming year. The alternative method, in contrast, compares the current IDR with the IDR 1 year previously. Only one information source is required, since *Barron's* regularly provides both items on a weekly basis. By way

**Table 7-4.** Indicated Dividend Rate, S&P 500, 1967 to 1992*

| Year | Jan. | Feb. | Mar. | Apr. | May | Jun. | Jul. | Aug. | Sep. | Oct. | Nov. | Dec. |
|------|------|------|------|------|------|------|------|------|------|------|------|------|
| 1967 | 2.91 | 2.92 | 2.92 | 2.94 | 2.92 | 2.93 | 2.92 | 2.92 | 2.93 | 2.92 | 2.93 | 2.94 |
| 1968 | 2.95 | 2.97 | 2.99 | 3.00 | 3.01 | 3.01 | 3.02 | 3.04 | 3.06 | 3.06 | 3.07 | 3.10 |
| 1969 | 3.10 | 3.11 | 3.14 | 3.14 | 3.15 | 3.14 | 3.15 | 3.15 | 3.15 | 3.14 | 3.17 | 3.20 |
| 1970 | 3.20 | 3.22 | 3.21 | 3.21 | 3.17 | 3.17 | 3.16 | 3.16 | 3.15 | 3.16 | 3.16 | 3.12 |
| 1971 | 3.10 | 3.10 | 3.09 | 3.08 | 3.09 | 3.09 | 3.09 | 3.08 | 3.07 | 3.06 | 3.06 | 3.07 |
| 1972 | 3.06 | 3.07 | 3.07 | 3.08 | 3.08 | 3.10 | 3.11 | 3.10 | 3.11 | 3.09 | 3.10 | 3.16 |
| 1973 | 3.17 | 3.18 | 3.19 | 3.20 | 3.21 | 3.20 | 3.21 | 3.26 | 3.30 | 3.33 | 3.35 | 3.47 |
| 1974 | 3.48 | 3.54 | 3.57 | 3.58 | 3.60 | 3.59 | 3.63 | 3.66 | 3.71 | 3.72 | 3.73 | 3.66 |
| 1975 | 3.68 | 3.70 | 3.68 | 3.70 | 3.68 | 3.68 | 3.72 | 3.72 | 3.70 | 3.71 | 3.70 | 3.68 |
| 1976 | 3.68 | 3.69 | 3.71 | 3.71 | 3.75 | 3.80 | 3.82 | 3.84 | 3.88 | 3.92 | 3.94 | 4.10 |
| 1977 | 4.11 | 4.17 | 4.36 | 4.40 | 4.46 | 4.52 | 4.56 | 4.64 | 4.63 | 4.65 | 4.65 | 4.75 |
| 1978 | 4.81 | 4.95 | 4.95 | 5.00 | 5.02 | 5.07 | 5.07 | 5.09 | 5.15 | 5.16 | 5.18 | 5.15 |
| 1979 | 5.21 | 5.28 | 5.35 | 5.39 | 5.50 | 5.60 | 5.64 | 5.65 | 5.69 | 5.76 | 5.82 | 5.92 |
| 1980 | 6.01 | 6.00 | 6.09 | 6.23 | 6.31 | 6.26 | 6.17 | 6.22 | 6.23 | 6.27 | 6.28 | 6.32 |
| 1981 | 6.34 | 6.38 | 6.45 | 6.52 | 6.55 | 6.58 | 6.66 | 6.68 | 6.72 | 6.75 | 6.83 | 6.82 |
| 1982 | 6.91 | 6.92 | 6.94 | 6.96 | 6.94 | 6.89 | 6.89 | 6.88 | 6.84 | 6.88 | 6.84 | 6.82 |
| 1983 | 6.91 | 6.89 | 6.95 | 6.99 | 6.99 | 7.05 | 7.06 | 7.06 | 7.10 | 7.10 | 7.12 | 7.11 |
| 1984 | 7.14 | 7.20 | 7.25 | 7.31 | 7.31 | 7.41 | 7.46 | 7.45 | 7.52 | 7.53 | 7.59 | 7.69 |
| 1985 | 7.72 | 7.77 | 7.80 | 7.90 | 7.91 | 7.93 | 7.95 | 7.96 | 7.96 | 7.97 | 7.99 | 8.06 |
| 1986 | 8.07 | 8.07 | 8.12 | 8.16 | 8.17 | 8.18 | 8.28 | 8.25 | 8.25 | 8.25 | 8.28 | 8.33 |
| 1987 | 8.40 | 8.42 | 8.52 | 8.52 | 8.67 | 8.70 | 8.74 | 8.68 | 8.84 | 8.82 | 8.94 | 9.02 |
| 1988 | 9.09 | 9.13 | 9.24 | 9.30 | 9.67 | 9.70 | 9.77 | 9.84 | 9.89 | 9.94 | 9.98 | 9.98 |
| 1989 | 10.27 | 10.43 | 10.68 | 10.81 | 10.97 | 11.12 | 11.17 | 11.30 | 11.38 | 11.41 | 11.52 | 11.58 |
| 1990 | 11.55 | 11.66 | 11.76 | 11.88 | 11.95 | 12.09 | 12.13 | 12.21 | 12.18 | 12.28 | 12.25 | 12.32 |
| 1991 | 12.40 | 12.40 | 12.20 | 12.20 | 12.19 | 12.21 | 12.18 | 12.17 | 12.17 | 12.18 | 12.12 | 12.13 |
| 1992 | 12.13 | 12.16 | 12.20 | 12.28 | 12.41 | 12.42 | 12.45 | 12.41 | 12.48 | 12.50 | 12.55 | 12.52 |

*Reported as of the beginning of the month.

SOURCE: Monthly supplement to *The Analysts Handbook,* issued by Standard & Poor's Corporation.

of example, the IDR on June 30, 1989, was $11.17 compared with $9.77 a year earlier, indicating an annual rate of dividend growth of 14.3 percent. The growth rate based on comparison of the current IDR with latest reported four-quarter dividend payments, as previously described, is 15.9 percent. Figure 7-6, comparing the annual rates of dividend growth calculated by the two methods over the period from the first quarter of 1968 through the first quarter of 1993, underscores the similarity of results.

**Table 7-5.** Indicated Dividend Rate, S&P 500, 1988 to 1992*

| Issue | IDR | Issue | IDR | Issue | IDR | Issue | IDR | Issue | IDR |
|---|---|---|---|---|---|---|---|---|---|
| 04-Jan-88 | 9.07 | 24-Oct-88 | 9.97 | 14-Aug-89 | 11.34 | 04-Jun-90 | 12.09 | 25-Mar-91 | 12.20 |
| 11-Jan-88 | 9.08 | 31-Oct-88 | 9.99 | 21-Aug-89 | 11.31 | 11-Jun-90 | 12.09 | 01-Apr-91 | 12.19 |
| 18-Jan-88 | 9.09 | 07-Nov-88 | 9.93 | 28-Aug-89 | 11.36 | 18-Jun-90 | 12.08 | 08-Apr-91 | 12.20 |
| 25-Jan-88 | 9.09 | 14-Nov-88 | 10.06 | 04-Sep-89 | 11.39 | 25-Jun-90 | 12.08 | 15-Apr-91 | 12.21 |
| 01-Feb-88 | 9.09 | 21-Nov-88 | 10.08 | 11-Sep-89 | 11.37 | 02-Jul-90 | 12.14 | 22-Apr-91 | 12.14 |
| 08-Feb-88 | 8.81 | 28-Nov-88 | 10.11 | 18-Sep-89 | 11.39 | 09-Jul-90 | 12.11 | 29-Apr-91 | 12.13 |
| 15-Feb-88 | 8.81 | 05-Dec-88 | 10.11 | 25-Sep-89 | 11.35 | 16-Jul-90 | 12.16 | 06-May-91 | 12.19 |
| 22-Feb-88 | 9.20 | 12-Dec-88 | 10.10 | 02-Oct-89 | 11.42 | 23-Jul-90 | 12.15 | 13-May-91 | 12.17 |
| 29-Feb-88 | 9.20 | 19-Dec-88 | 10.19 | 09-Oct-89 | 11.50 | 30-Jul-90 | 12.19 | 20-May-91 | 12.21 |
| 07-Mar-88 | 9.24 | 26-Dec-88 | 10.21 | 16-Oct-89 | 11.47 | 06-Aug-90 | 12.21 | 27-May-91 | 12.19 |
| 14-Mar-88 | 9.24 | 02-Jan-89 | 10.25 | 23-Oct-89 | 11.46 | 13-Aug-90 | 12.21 | 03-Jun-91 | 12.20 |
| 21-Mar-88 | 9.27 | 09-Jan-89 | 10.25 | 30-Oct-89 | 11.49 | 20-Aug-90 | 12.20 | 10-Jun-91 | 12.18 |
| 28-Mar-88 | 9.27 | 16-Jan-89 | 10.29 | 06-Nov-89 | 11.55 | 27-Aug-90 | 12.18 | 17-Jun-91 | 12.16 |
| 04-Apr-88 | 9.29 | 23-Jan-89 | 10.34 | 13-Nov-89 | 11.53 | 03-Sep-90 | 12.19 | 24-Jun-91 | 12.16 |
| 11-Apr-88 | 9.32 | 30-Jan-89 | 10.44 | 20-Nov-89 | 11.55 | 10-Sep-90 | 12.19 | 01-Jul-91 | 12.17 |
| 18-Apr-88 | 9.40 | 06-Feb-89 | 10.49 | 27-Nov-89 | 11.66 | 17-Sep-90 | 12.23 | 08-Jul-91 | 12.20 |
| 25-Apr-88 | 9.48 | 13-Feb-89 | 10.51 | 04-Dec-89 | 11.61 | 24-Sep-90 | 12.23 | 15-Jul-91 | 12.20 |
| 02-May-88 | 9.52 | 20-Feb-89 | 10.65 | 11-Dec-89 | 11.58 | 01-Oct-90 | 12.27 | 22-Jul-91 | 12.20 |
| 09-May-88 | 9.63 | 27-Feb-89 | 10.68 | 18-Dec-89 | 11.62 | 08-Oct-90 | 12.27 | 29-Jul-91 | 12.15 |
| 16-May-88 | 9.68 | 06-Mar-89 | 10.68 | 25-Dec-89 | 11.64 | 15-Oct-90 | 12.27 | 05-Aug-91 | 12.20 |
| 23-May-88 | 9.68 | 13-Mar-89 | 10.70 | 01-Jan-90 | 11.63 | 22-Oct-90 | 12.25 | 12-Aug-91 | 12.16 |
| 30-May-88 | 9.69 | 20-Mar-89 | 10.74 | 08-Jan-90 | 11.62 | 29-Oct-90 | 12.22 | 19-Aug-91 | 12.18 |
| 06-Jun-88 | 9.71 | 27-Mar-89 | 10.69 | 15-Jan-90 | 11.56 | 05-Nov-90 | 12.26 | 26-Aug-91 | 12.18 |
| 13-Jun-88 | 9.71 | 03-Apr-89 | 10.82 | 22-Jan-90 | 11.56 | 12-Nov-90 | 12.30 | 02-Sep-91 | 12.14 |
| 20-Jun-88 | 9.71 | 10-Apr-89 | 10.82 | 29-Jan-90 | 11.63 | 19-Nov-90 | 12.30 | 09-Sep-91 | 12.18 |
| 27-Jun-88 | 9.71 | 17-Apr-89 | 10.82 | 05-Feb-90 | 11.65 | 26-Nov-90 | 12.29 | 16-Sep-91 | 12.20 |
| 04-Jul-88 | 9.71 | 24-Apr-89 | 10.84 | 12-Feb-90 | 11.68 | 03-Dec-90 | 12.31 | 23-Sep-91 | 12.18 |
| 11-Jul-88 | 9.71 | 01-May-89 | 10.93 | 19-Feb-90 | 11.71 | 10-Dec-90 | 12.32 | 30-Sep-91 | 12.19 |
| 18-Jul-88 | 9.78 | 08-May-89 | 10.98 | 26-Feb-90 | 11.73 | 17-Dec-90 | 12.35 | 07-Oct-91 | 12.24 |
| 25-Jul-88 | 9.78 | 15-May-89 | 11.02 | 05-Mar-90 | 11.74 | 24-Dec-90 | 12.37 | 14-Oct-91 | 12.21 |
| 01-Aug-88 | 9.78 | 22-May-89 | 11.08 | 12-Mar-90 | 11.79 | 31-Dec-90 | 12.33 | 21-Oct-91 | 12.21 |
| 08-Aug-88 | 9.83 | 29-May-89 | 11.11 | 19-Mar-90 | 11.83 | 07-Jan-91 | 12.33 | 28-Oct-91 | 12.14 |
| 15-Aug-88 | 9.87 | 05-Jun-89 | 11.12 | 26-Mar-90 | 11.84 | 14-Jan-91 | 12.33 | 04-Nov-91 | 12.13 |
| 22-Aug-88 | 9.88 | 12-Jun-89 | 11.11 | 02-Apr-90 | 11.86 | 21-Jan-91 | 12.33 | 11-Nov-91 | 12.10 |
| 29-Aug-88 | 9.88 | 19-Jun-89 | 11.12 | 09-Apr-90 | 11.90 | 28-Jan-91 | 12.33 | 18-Nov-91 | 12.13 |
| 05-Sep-88 | 9.88 | 26-Jun-89 | 11.18 | 16-Apr-90 | 11.91 | 04-Feb-91 | 12.38 | 25-Nov-91 | 12.11 |
| 12-Sep-88 | 9.88 | 03-Jul-89 | 11.19 | 23-Apr-90 | 11.90 | 11-Feb-91 | 12.40 | 02-Dec-91 | 12.12 |
| 19-Sep-88 | 9.88 | 10-Jul-89 | 11.18 | 30-Apr-90 | 11.91 | 18-Feb-91 | 12.25 | 09-Dec-91 | 12.13 |
| 26-Sep-88 | 9.88 | 17-Jul-89 | 11.18 | 07-May-90 | 11.98 | 25-Feb-91 | 12.18 | 16-Dec-91 | 12.15 |
| 03-Oct-88 | 9.93 | 24-Jul-89 | 11.18 | 14-May-90 | 12.04 | 04-Mar-91 | 12.19 | 23-Dec-91 | 12.15 |
| 10-Oct-88 | 9.95 | 31-Jul-89 | 11.33 | 21-May-90 | 12.06 | 11-Mar-91 | 12.19 | 30-Dec-91 | 12.15 |
| 17-Oct-88 | 9.97 | 07-Aug-89 | 11.31 | 28-May-90 | 12.09 | 18-Mar-91 | 12.18 | 06-Jan-92 | 12.12 |

**Table 7-5.** Indicated Dividend Rate, S&P 500, 1988 to 1992* (*Continued*)

| Issue | IDR | Issue | IDR | Issue | IDR | Issue | IDR | Issue | IDR |
|---|---|---|---|---|---|---|---|---|---|
| 13-Jan-92 | 12.08 | 30-Mar-92 | 12.27 | 15-Jun-92 | 12.42 | 31-Aug-92 | 12.40 | 16-Nov-92 | 12.59 |
| 20-Jan-92 | 12.06 | 06-Apr-92 | 12.25 | 22-Jun-92 | 12.43 | 07-Sep-92 | 12.55 | 23-Nov-92 | 12.59 |
| 27-Jan-92 | 12.09 | 13-Apr-92 | 12.25 | 29-Jun-92 | 12.43 | 14-Sep-92 | 12.50 | 30-Nov-92 | 12.65 |
| 03-Feb-92 | 12.17 | 20-Apr-92 | 12.27 | 06-Jul-92 | 12.44 | 21-Sep-92 | 12.60 | 07-Dec-92 | 12.62 |
| 10-Feb-92 | 12.17 | 27-Apr-92 | 12.27 | 13-Jul-92 | 12.44 | 28-Sep-92 | 12.64 | 14-Dec-92 | 12.62 |
| 17-Feb-92 | 12.13 | 04-May-92 | 12.29 | 20-Jul-92 | 12.43 | 05-Oct-92 | 12.64 | 21-Dec-92 | 12.53 |
| 24-Feb-92 | 12.14 | 11-May-92 | 12.29 | 27-Jul-92 | 12.43 | 12-Oct-92 | 12.64 | 28-Dec-92 | 12.58 |
| 02-Mar-92 | 12.22 | 18-May-92 | 12.38 | 03-Aug-92 | 12.43 | 19-Oct-92 | 12.64 | | |
| 09-Mar-92 | 12.21 | 25-May-92 | 12.42 | 10-Aug-92 | 12.40 | 26-Oct-92 | 12.67 | | |
| 16-Mar-92 | 12.22 | 01-Jun-92 | 12.42 | 17-Aug-92 | 12.43 | 02-Nov-92 | 12.64 | | |
| 23-Mar-92 | 12.26 | 08-Jun-92 | 12.45 | 24-Aug-92 | 12.40 | 09-Nov-92 | 12.57 | | |

*As reported weekly.

SOURCE: *Barron's National Business and Financial Weekly.*

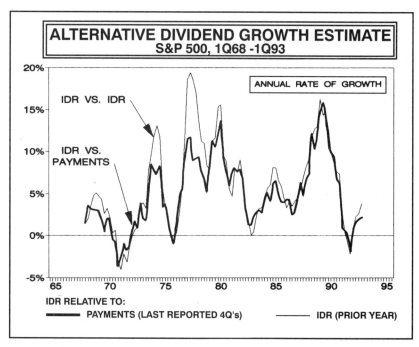

**Figure 7-6.** Comparing the annual rates of dividend growth by two methods: current IDR with last reported four-quarter dividend payment and current IDR with the IDR 1 year previously. (*Source:* The Analysts Handbook *issued by Standard & Poor's Corporation.*)

# 8

# Interest Rates as a Guide to Stock Prices

## Searching for the Risk-Free Rate

### Changing Investor Response

In the early years after World War II—prior to the mid-1960s—investors were unlikely to view the upward trend in interest rates as a threat to stock prices. To many observers, the course of stock prices during these early years appeared to be virtually independent of interest rates. Economic forecasts allowed for the influence of interest rates and credit conditions on business activity, earnings, and dividends. Given an economic framework, however, investors seldom identified interest rates as a separate determinant of stock market valuation. The attractiveness of stocks, for example, did not seem to depend on whether high-quality bond yields were 3 percent, as they were in the bear market of 1953, or 5 percent, the level which characterized the bull market of 1963 to 1965. The same creeping inflation that accounted for rising interest rates during these earlier postwar years also provided a widely accepted argument for buying stocks. Investors could see that as inflation eroded bond prices, it also supported *nominal* growth for both corporate earnings and dividend payments.

Beginning in 1966, the relationship between interest rates and stock prices changed dramatically. In that year, federal government financing of the rapidly escalating military requirements of the Vietnam War, along with continuing growth in spending for domestic programs, created a painful, though relatively brief, credit crunch. The sharply higher interest rates translated into a bear market in stocks even though business activity, while slowing, continued to grow. Since 1966, dynamic swings in interest rates have accompanied every major stock market decline and subsequent recovery.

Figures 8-1 and 8-2 graphically portray the changing relationship between stock prices and interest rates. Figure 8-1 compares data for two sharply contrasting 5-year periods. Panel A traces prices for the S&P 500 and 20-year Treasury bonds over 1961 to 1965. The purpose is to highlight the extremely limited influence of interest rates on stock prices in the early postwar years prior to the mid-1960s. Other 5-year periods during this time span show similar patterns. Panel B, drawn to the same scale as Panel A, reviews the same relationships for 1981 to 1985. It provides a particularly clear example of the greatly increased correlation between interest rates and stock prices since 1966. Figure 8-2, meanwhile, measures changing correlations over the period 1955 to 1992. Each data point reflects the correlation over the previous 60 months between monthly price changes for the S&P 500 and 20-year Treasury bonds. The scale measuring correlation ranges from +1.0, which means that bond and stock prices would always move proportionally in the same direction, to –1.0, which would mean they would always move proportionally in opposite directions. Note the marked change in the relationship beginning in 1966. Over the 60-month periods ended in years prior to 1966, the correlation was negative, as other influences overshadowed the limited influence of interest rates on stock prices. Subsequently—and coincident with sharply higher volatility for interest rates—a distinctly positive correlation has characterized each measurement period. The reduction in positive correlation for the 5-year periods ended October 1987 through September 1992 reflects the October 1987 stock market crash. At that time, as stock prices plunged, bond prices soared.

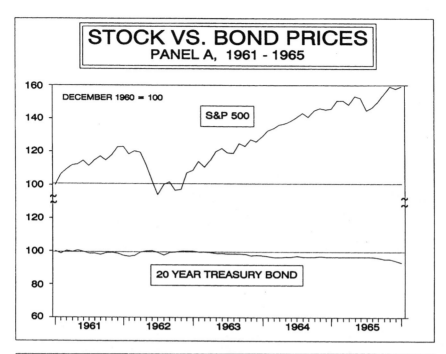

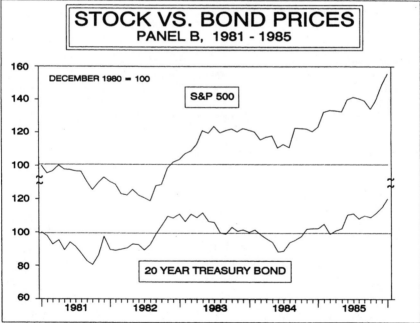

**Figure 8-1.** The sharply contrasting relationships between stock prices and bond prices (a) over 1961 to 1965 and (b) over 1981–1985. (*Source*: Stocks, Bonds, Bills, and Inflation 1993 Yearbook, *Ibbotson Associates, Chicago, annually updates the work by Roger G. Ibbotson and Rex A. Sinquefield. Used with permission. All rights reserved.*)

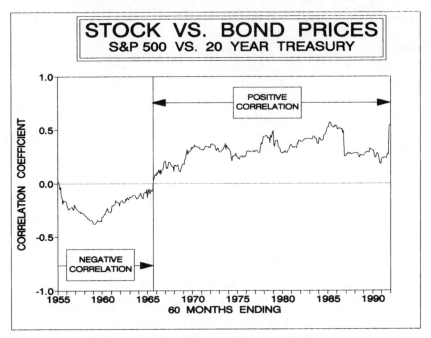

**Figure 8-2.** Tracing the changing correlation between stock prices and bond prices over 1955 to 1992. (*Source:* Stocks, Bonds, Bills, and Inflation 1993 Yearbook, *Ibbotson Associates, Chicago, annually updates the work by Roger G. Ibbotson and Rex A. Sinquefield. Used with permission. All rights reserved.*)

## Consider the Shortcomings

In looking for ways to measure the changing influence of interest rates on stock prices, we note the shortcomings of the various alternatives along the Treasury yield curve. Our analysis recognizes that the long-term risk-free rate, as assessed by the investor consensus and explained in Chap. 6, is hidden from view. It defies precise measurement, since no publicly quoted interest rate provides an adequate proxy. Consider how both short rates and long rates for Treasury securities differ from the risk-free rate incorporated in the pricing of the stock market.

**Treasury Bills.** The rate on *short* Treasury bills may differ greatly from the consensus view of the *long-term* risk-free rate. Treasury bill rates, reflecting very near term conditions in the credit markets, have fluctuated as much as 100 or 200 basis points in a single month. Investors are well aware that the volatility may represent temporary conditions. Large swings in one direction are often promptly followed by at least partial retracement. The stock market does not automatically react as if each swing in short-term rates were a change in the long-term risk-free rate. Day-to-day adjustments in Treasury bill yields contrast sharply with the relative stability which characterizes the long-term outlook for the consensus risk-free rate.

**Longer Maturities.** Bonds have the advantage of longer maturity, but their yields also include a changing allowance for risk. The advantage of the longer maturity is less than complete, since the bond maturity is shorter than that of the stock market. Volatility of long Treasury bond yields, although about half that of Treasury bill yields, is not the same as the volatility of the risk-free rate incorporated in the stock market discount rate. At the same time, bond yields reflect changing allowance for risk. For Treasury bonds, the risk premium reflects the possibility that interest rates may rise, resulting in capital loss. For industrial bonds—even very high grade bonds—the risk premium may also change as a result of company, industry, or general economic factors.

### Developing a Compromise Solution

In the absence of a single clear answer, a compromise provides a workable approach. The aim is to detect change in the consensus view of the risk-free rate. For this purpose, point-to-point measures of Treasury bill yields present an important disadvantage, since they can be heavily distorted by very short term fluctuations at either the beginning or the end of the period. Similar measures for long bond yields reflect changes in bond risk premiums, which may differ considerably from changes for equity risk premiums. By way of compromise, we average Treasury bill yields over a period to smooth volatility. More specifically, we compare 90-day Treasury bill yields over the coming four quarters with the same series for the past four quarters. To make use of this relationship, the investment decision maker requires continuing access to consensus estimates of future Treasury bill yields. We shall show later in this chapter how to derive such information from transactions in the futures markets.

**Change, Not Level.**   We stress that comparison of two four-quarter averages provides a measure of change, not level. There is no evidence that the long-term risk-free rate coincides with the yield on short Treasury bills, or, for that matter, with yields on long bonds or any other yield reported in the financial press. Because the relationship with the long-term risk-free rate is not stable, changes in Treasury bill yields are in themselves not an accurate indicator of changes in the underlying risk-free rate. It is reasonable to expect, nevertheless, that *substantial* change in the *average* Treasury bill yield from one year to the next would in some way bear on the consensus view of the risk-free rate.

**Already in the Market.**   The average Treasury bill yield for the past four quarters may be viewed as information "already in the market." The consensus view of the long-term risk-free rate does not adjust to each turn in Treasury bill yields. Investors recognize that Treasury bill yields are volatile. The increase today may be rapidly followed by reversal tomorrow—or perhaps the day after. Consequently, long-term assessment of the risk-free rate reflects an accumulation of information concerning the fixed-income markets. Consider the following comparison: It is one thing for Treasury bill yields to rise 50 basis points during a month but average for the year only 10 basis points higher than the previous year. It is something else for continuing fluctuations in Treasury bill yields to result in a rise in the average for the year of 50 basis points. The average rise over an extended period counts for more than the short-term fluctuation.

**Next Four Quarters.**   In a similar way, the unfolding record of interest-rate changes will influence investor attitudes over the coming year. A short-term turn in interest rates may in some small way affect the consensus view of the risk-free rate that applies to the valuation of common stocks. The cumulative impact over a year, however, is better defined by the average over the same period.

# Examining Historical Relationships

## Testing the Interest-Rate Prime Variable

Our historical review of the interest-rate prime variable involves two methods of developing the necessary data. We first examine the prime variable with the benefit of hindsight, relying on advance knowledge of actual changes in Treasury bill yields over successive four-quarter periods. To eliminate the benefit of hindsight, we then substitute contemporary consensus estimates.

## Benefiting from Hindsight

The comparison of changes in stock prices and interest rates, as displayed in Table 8-1, reflects advance knowledge of interest-rate data subsequently reported. For this purpose, the change in short rates is measured by the average yield for the 3-month Treasury bill, next four quarters less the last four quarters. The change in stock prices is represented by the change in the S&P 500 over the year ahead. Comparisons are made on the first day of each year, 1955 to 1992. The data are divided into three categories. The first category includes the 16 years when the *decline* in average Treasury bill yields, next four quarters less the last four quarters, exceeds 25 basis points. At the other extreme, a

**Table 8-1.** Change in Treasury Bill Yields and Stock Prices, 1955 to 1992

| 3-Month Treasury bill yields (next 4Q less last 4Q) | Number of years | S&P 500 | | % Up |
|---|---|---|---|---|
| | | Up | Down | |
| 1. Decline, more than 25 BP* | 16 | 14 | 2 | 88 |
| 2. +25 to −50 BP | 5 | 4 | 1 | 80 |
| 3. Rise, more than 50 BP | 17 | 10 | 7 | 59 |
| Total | 38 | 28 | 10 | 74 |

*BP = basis points.

third category brings together 17 years when the rise in Treasury bill yield *exceeds* 50 basis points. The middle category includes the remaining data, 5 years when the change in the four-quarter averages of Treasury bill yields amounts to either a small-to-moderate decline (not exceeding 25 basis points) or a limited rise (up to 50 basis points).

This historical simulation suggests the likelihood of a negative correlation between interest rates, as measured by the prime variable, and stock prices. The combined data (for years when interest rates declined and years when they rose) is more significant than either set viewed individually. Stock prices rose in 28 of the 38 years since 1955, an average of 74 percent. For the 16 years when interest rates declined significantly (by at least 25 basis points), stock prices advanced in 88 percent of the years. The favorable performance of stock prices in comparison with the 38-year average, although less than conclusive, is consistent with a negative correlation relative to changes in interest rates. Meanwhile, stock prices increased a below-average 59 percent of the years when interest rates rose significantly (by at least 50 basis points), providing further support for negative correlation. Overall, these comparisons indicate the likelihood of correlation but are not sufficient in themselves to meet rigorous tests of statistical significance.

The importance which we attach to the relationship between changes in stock prices and interest rates depends primarily on considerations other than the limited evidence shown in Table 8-1. Logically, as spelled out in Chap. 5, changes in interest rates affect the valuation of the stock market. Our real-time experience with the dynamic model, moreover, confirms a critical role for changes in interest rates in explaining changes in stock prices. The statistical relationship becomes more significant when multiple regression allows for the influence of other prime variables in addition to changing interest rates.

## Substituting Contemporary Consensus Estimates

Our decision process, in order to exploit the relationship between interest rates and stock prices, requires estimates of the outlook for short-term interest rates over the coming four quarters. Table 8-1 benefits from hindsight since it assumes advance knowledge concerning the course of interest rates. The challenge in real-time operations is to identify the estimate which best substitutes for such advance knowledge. To examine the inputs available to decision makers in day-to-day operations, we look to consensus estimates. Acceptance of the consensus as the best estimate assumes that the decision maker is unable to identify in advance the superior forecaster. A consensus estimate provides an objective measure of the outlook for interest rates, changing as the individual estimates which make up the consensus change. Although it may be wide of the mark, it is more reliable, on average, than the individual estimates which are included in the consensus. Individual estimates will at times provide better accuracy than the consensus and, at other times, larger error. On balance, however, the average error for the individual estimates will be larger than that for the consensus estimate.

We prefer, among the various alternatives for gauging the investor consensus, the futures market for Treasury bills. In the absence of quotations for Treasury bill futures, any one of several readily available surveys provides much the same information. We discuss the futures markets in the section immediately following. We then examine survey data compiled over more than 20 years by the *Washington Bond and Money Market Survey* (Washington, D.C.). Although the historical record is shorter, *Blue Chip Financial Forecasts* (Capitol Publications, Inc., Alexandria, Va.) provides another example of survey data secured from a large sample of highly qualified institutional forecasters.

**Treasury Bill Futures.**   The views of the many participants in the highly competitive public market for Treasury bill futures determine the daily price changes. Investors gain large rewards by taking the winning side of the market and incur severe financial penalties for the wrong forecast. They therefore translate as rapidly as possible their changing views of future interest rates into market action. Since the market-based estimates provided by futures contracts are updated each trading day, they are more sen-

THE WALL STREET JOURNAL TUESDAY, OCTOBER 1, 1991

## INTEREST RATE INSTRUMENTS

### FUTURES

TREASURY BILLS (IMM) - $1 mil.; pts. of 100%

| | Open | High | Low | Settle | Chg | Discount Settle | Chg | Open Interest |
|---|---|---|---|---|---|---|---|---|
| Dec | 94.93 | 94.94 | 94.92 | 94.93 + | .01 | 5.07 − | .01 | 28,490 |
| Mr92 | 94.98 | 95.01 | 94.98 | 95.01 + | .01 | 4.99 − | .01 | 17,439 |
| June | 94.88 | 94.89 | 94.86 | 94.87 + | .01 | 5.13 − | .01 | 1,241 |
| Sept | .... | .... | .... | 94.60 + | .06 | 5.40 − | .06 | 192 |

Est vol 2,401; vol Fri 3,781; open int 47,428, +501.

**Figure 8-3.** An example of the quotations for the Treasury bill futures. (*Source:* The Wall Street Journal, *October 1, 1991*.)

sitive at turning points than survey-derived estimates. Figure 8-3 provides an example of the quotations of the Treasury bill futures market appearing daily in *The Wall Street Journal* and weekly in *Barron's* (among other publications). For October 1, 1991, the contracts required for calculation of the four-quarter average mature during December 1991, and March, June, and September 1992. The specific maturity date during the final month of the quarter varies from one quarter to the next. Appendix 8-1 provides background information concerning short-term interest-rate futures contracts. Table 8-2 provides details of the calculation. The first-quarter figure is the average of the spot rate as of October 1, 1991, and the yield for the futures contract maturing in December 1991. Similarly, figures for each of the subsequent three quarters are determined by the average yield for futures contracts maturing approximately at the beginning and end of the quarter. The table combines these calculations to provide a four-quarter average yield of 5.11 percent.

Because the four-quarter average requires estimates for five different points in time, it is not highly dependent on any one of the inputs. The current spot rate and the estimate four quarters

**Table 8-2.** Average Treasury Bill Yield, Next Four
Quarters, derived from 3-Month Treasury Bill Futures

|  | Yield, % | Weight | Weight × Yield, % |
|---|---|---|---|
| Spot rate | | | |
| October 1, 1991 | 5.11 | 1 | 5.11 |
| Futures contracts | | | |
| December 1991 | 5.07 | 2 | 10.14 |
| March 1992 | 4.99 | 2 | 9.98 |
| June 1992 | 5.13 | 2 | 10.26 |
| September 1992 | 5.40 | 1 | 5.40 |
| Total | | 8 | 40.89 |
| Average yield (total/8) | | | 5.11 |

ahead each receive a weighting of one. The other three estimates, each representing both the beginning and the end of a
quarter, receive a weighting of two. The one or two estimates for
the dates farthest ahead may be less reliable than the others, but
the effect of error is limited by the weighting. The estimate for
four quarters ahead, for example, has a weighting of only ⅛. A
25-basis-point error in this one estimate would distort the four-
quarter average by three basis points. The same error in the
same direction for both the third and fourth quarters ahead,
reflecting an aggregate weighting of ⅜, would change the four-
quarter estimate by nine basis points.

**Surveys of Leading Decision Makers.** In order to review the
correlation of the interest-rate prime variable with stock prices, we
test it against stock market history. The contemporary consensus
estimates of interest rates required for this purpose are taken from
surveys of leading decision makers. Such surveys have been available for a much longer period than data provided by the futures
markets for Treasury bills. We conducted our own monthly survey
for several years, and various services continue to furnish such
data. For back-testing, a widely quoted survey provided by the
*Washington Bond & Money Market Report* (WB&MMR) is particularly useful because of its relatively long history. Earlier identified as
the *Goldsmith-Nagan Survey*, it is available for the beginning of

each calendar quarter since 1970. The WB&MMR surveys about 30 financial market analysts in the last month of each calendar quarter. The respondents, prior to the beginning of the quarter, provide point estimates for 3-month Treasury bill yields one and two quarters ahead.* Averages of these estimates serve as consensus estimates. Table 8-3, which follows the same format as Table 8-2, shows the calculation which represents the average of the coming four quarters. Since no estimates are available for the third and fourth quarters ahead, we assume that these estimates are the same as for the end of the second quarter ahead. To facilitate comparison, Table 8-3, based on WB&MMR survey information, begins at the same point as Table 8-2. Table 8-4 relates the estimated four-quarter change in Treasury bill yields to the subsequent change in stock prices. It parallels Table 8-1, based on reported Treasury bill yields. An important difference, however, is the time span. The survey estimates are available since 1970, while the reported data in Table 8-1 begin with 1955.

**Table 8-3.** Average Treasury Bill Yield, Next Four Quarters, derived from WB&MMR Survey Data

|  | Yield, % | Weight | Weight × Yield, % |
|---|---|---|---|
| Spot rate | | | |
| October 1, 1991 | 5.11 | 1 | 5.11 |
| Consensus estimates | | | |
| December 31, 1991 | 5.00 | 2 | 10.00 |
| March 31, 1992 | 5.21 | 5 | 26.05 |
| Total | | 8 | 41.16 |
| Average yield (total/8) | | | 5.15 |

*Appendix 8-2 lists estimates of future Treasury bill rates, as provided by the WB&MMR from 1970 to 1992.

**Table 8-4.** Change in Treasury Bill Yields and Stock
Prices, 1970 to 1992
WB&MMR Survey Data

| 3-Month Treasury bill yields (next 4Q less last 4Q) | Number of years | S&P 500 | | % Up |
|---|---|---|---|---|
| | | Up | Down | |
| 1. Decline, more than 25 BP* | 10 | 9 | 1 | 90 |
| 2. +25 to –50 BP | 5 | 3 | 2 | 60 |
| 3. Rise, more than 50 BP | 8 | 6 | 2 | 75 |
| Total | 23 | 18 | 5 | 78 |

*BP = basis points.

## Anticipating the Broad Pattern of Change

The survey estimates of four-quarter change in Treasury bill
yields have anticipated rather well the broad pattern of actual
changes which subsequently took place. Table 8-5 brings together the percentage comparisons from Tables 8-1 and 8-4. For the
most part, differences reflect the differing time spans covered by
the two sets of data. Errors in estimates relative to subsequently
reported results accounted for misspecification of the interest-
rate change for 3 of the 23 years covered by the data. Figure 8-4
measures consensus estimates of interest-rate change against
subsequently reported results. Panel A covers the 10 years when
the survey estimated a decline in four-quarter average yield by
more than 25 basis points. In each of these years, the actual
decline also exceeded 25 basis points. Similarly, estimated
increases in excess of 50 basis points in 8 years were validated
by actual results. For the 5 years when the estimated change
was in the middle category—between a decline of 25 basis
points and a rise of 50 basis points—the results were mixed. It
was in three of these years that misspecification of the interest-
rate change took place. For two of these years, the decline

**Table 8-5.** Change in Treasury Bill Yields and Stock Prices
WB&MMR Survey Data Compared with Reported Treasury Bill
Yields

| 3-Month Treasury bill yields (next 4Q less last 4Q) | No. of Years | | S&P 500: % up | |
|---|---|---|---|---|
| | Survey | Reported | Survey, % | Reported, % |
| 1. Decline, more than 25 BP* | 10 | 16 | 90 | 88 |
| 2. +25 to –50 BP | 5 | 5 | 60 | 80 |
| 3. Rise, more than 50 BP | 8 | 17 | 75 | 59 |
| Total | 23 | 38 | 78 | 74 |

*BP = basis points.

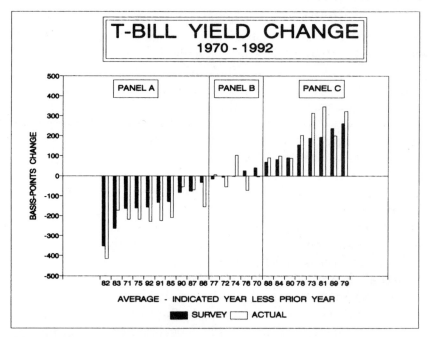

**Figure 8-4.** Comparing survey estimates of Treasury bill yield
change with actual change subsequently reported over the period 1970
to 1992. (*Source:* Washington Bond & Money Market Report *and
Ibbotson Associates.*)

exceeded 25 basis points, and, in one year, the rise was greater than 50 basis points. Three factors explain the extent of the correlation documented in Fig. 8-4:

**Over Half of the Required Information Was Already Reported.** The actual results for the last four quarters are a matter of record. In addition, the current spot price, which accounts for a weight of $\frac{1}{8}$ in the estimated average for the coming four quarters, is also available. Consequently, of the information incorporated in the two averages (last four quarters and next four quarters), items with a total weight of $\frac{9}{16}$ are already reported.

**Graduated Response Minimizes Significance of Estimate Errors.** The significance of errors in the estimates for the four quarters ahead are minimized as the difference between the past four quarters and the next four quarters widens. We identify the more extreme estimates of four-quarter yield change as a decline of at least 25 basis points or an increase of 50 basis points or more. Beyond these extremes—in either direction—estimate errors are less likely to provide wrong information concerning the direction of the four-quarter yield change.

**Consensus Estimates Control Error Better.** As pointed out previously, a consensus estimate controls error better, on average, than the individual estimates which underlie the consensus. Although it may turn out to be wide of the mark, it provides the best estimate, on average, in light of the information currently available.

**Balancing Interest Rates against Other Prime Variables**

Since three key factors account for the change in stock prices, the prime variable relating to interest rates requires consideration in the context of the other two prime variables. As suggested by Tables 8-1 and 8-4, there is reason to be skeptical of bearish views of the stock market when the outlook favors a significant drop in the four-quarter average of short rates (by at least 25 basis points). Other things equal, declining short-term rates render other investments more attractive, including both bonds and stocks. At the same time, declining interest rates provide stimulus to business activity, with favorable implications for earnings and dividends. The record, whether based on subsequently reported average yields or contemporary estimates, supports a negative correlation between changes in short rates and stock prices. The limited correlation presented in this chapter, nevertheless, underscores the need for a balanced view of stock market valuation. Chapter 10 measures prospects for interest rates against estimates relating to the other key factors that drive stock prices.

# Appendix 8-1
## Contract Specifications for Treasury Bill Futures*

| 3-Month U.S. Treasury Bill Futures | |
| --- | --- |
| Ticker symbol | TB |
| Contract size | $1,000,000 |
| Contract months | Mar., Jun., Sep., Dec. |
| Minimum price change | 0.01 = $25 |
| Price limit | None |
| Trading hours† (Chicago time) | 7:20 a.m.–2:00 p.m. (last day–10:00 a.m.) |
| Last day of trading | 9/20/89 12/12/90<br>12/13/89 3/06/91<br>3/07/90 6/26/91<br>6/27/90 9/18/91<br>9/19/90 12/11/91 |
| Delivery | Delivery shall be made on three successive business days. The first delivery day shall be the first day of the spot month on which a 13-week Treasury bill is issued and a 1-year Treasury bill has 13 weeks remaining to maturity.‡ |

*Contract specifications are subject to change. All matters pertaining to rules and specifications herein are made subject to and are superseded by official Chicago Mercantile Exchange rules. Current Chicago Mercantile Exchange rules should be consulted in all cases concerning contract specifications. Check with your broker to confirm this information.

†Trading will end at noon on the business day before a Chicago Mercantile Exchange (CME) holiday weekend and on any U.S. bank holiday that the CME is open.

‡The first delivery day is the day after the last trading day.

SOURCE: Chicago Mercantile Exchange, *Opportunities in Interest Rates* 1989, p. 14.

## Appendix 8-2
## Survey of Interest-Rate Expectations, 1970 to 1992

Table 8-6 compares the spot rate for 3-month Treasury bills at the beginning of each calendar quarter with contemporary consensus estimates for 3 and 6 months ahead. It covers the period from the first quarter of 1970 through the fourth quarter of 1992. We reproduce this data with permission of *Washington Bond and Money Market Report*, which compiled it from a continuing survey of a large number of leading interest-rate forecasters.

**Table 8-6.** Treasury Bill Rates (3-Month Discount), Survey Expectations, 1970 to 1992

| Quarter (beginning) | Spot rate* | 3 Months ahead | 6 Months ahead | Quarter (beginning) | Spot rate* | 3 Months ahead | 6 Months ahead |
|---|---|---|---|---|---|---|---|
| Jan-70 | 7.85 | 7.05 | 6.44 | Jul-75 | 6.00 | 5.89 | 6.23 |
| Apr-70 | 6.35 | 5.74 | 5.73 | Oct-75 | 6.41 | 6.86 | 6.96 |
| Jul-70 | 6.52 | 6.10 | 5.95 | Jan-76 | 5.20 | 5.73 | 6.10 |
| Oct-70 | 5.86 | 5.75 | 5.65 | Apr-76 | 4.87 | 5.38 | 5.73 |
| Jan-71 | 4.73 | 4.76 | 4.80 | Jul-76 | 5.35 | 5.63 | 6.13 |
| Apr-71 | 3.66 | 3.61 | 3.98 | Oct-76 | 5.10 | 5.43 | 5.75 |
| Jul-71 | 4.86 | 5.24 | 5.49 | Jan-77 | 4.33 | 4.61 | 4.96 |
| Oct-71 | 4.71 | 4.86 | 5.01 | Apr-77 | 4.60 | 5.00 | 5.43 |
| Jan-72 | 3.78 | 4.07 | 4.33 | Jul-77 | 5.01 | 5.35 | 5.65 |
| Apr-72 | 3.83 | 4.38 | 4.76 | Oct-77 | 6.12 | 6.19 | 6.30 |
| Jul-72 | 4.04 | 4.60 | 5.13 | Jan-78 | 6.19 | 6.32 | 6.60 |
| Oct-72 | 4.54 | 5.20 | 5.46 | Apr-78 | 6.24 | 6.56 | 6.78 |
| Jan-73 | 5.12 | 5.45 | 5.65 | Jul-78 | 7.01 | 7.38 | 7.42 |
| Apr-73 | 6.40 | 6.77 | 6.55 | Oct-78 | 8.20 | 8.51 | 8.38 |
| Jul-73 | 7.94 | 7.75 | 7.23 | Jan-79 | 9.27 | 9.58 | 9.35 |
| Oct-73 | 7.14 | 7.26 | 6.73 | Apr-79 | 9.60 | 9.60 | 9.46 |
| Jan-74 | 7.54 | 6.79 | 6.49 | Jul-79 | 8.94 | 8.92 | 8.59 |
| Apr-74 | 8.22 | 7.21 | 7.10 | Oct-79 | 10.69 | 10.00 | 9.27 |
| Jul-74 | 7.74 | 7.40 | 7.12 | Jan-80 | 11.90 | 11.42 | 10.38 |
| Oct-74 | 6.20 | 7.48 | 7.20 | Apr-80 | 14.97 | 14.30 | 12.60 |
| Jan-75 | 6.71 | 6.31 | 6.03 | Jul-80 | 7.70 | 6.48 | 6.81 |
| Apr-75 | 5.62 | 5.04 | 5.27 | Oct-80 | 11.34 | 10.16 | 9.73 |

**TABLE 8-6.** Treasury Bill Rates (3-Month Discount), Survey Expectations, 1970 to 1992 (*Continued*)

| Quarter (beginning) | Spot rate* | 3 Months ahead | 6 Months ahead | Quarter (beginning) | Spot rate* | 3 Months ahead | 6 Months ahead |
|---|---|---|---|---|---|---|---|
| Jan-81 | 14.50 | 12.87 | 12.11 | Jan-87 | 5.52 | 5.18 | 5.23 |
| Apr-81 | 13.00 | 11.43 | 11.89 | Apr-87 | 5.63 | 5.55 | 5.69 |
| Jul-81 | 14.05 | 13.05 | 13.26 | Jul-87 | 5.67 | 5.81 | 5.95 |
| Oct-81 | 14.46 | 14.17 | 13.04 | Oct-87 | 6.75 | 6.91 | 7.10 |
| Jan-82 | 11.32 | 10.10 | 10.86 | Jan-88 | 6.05 | 5.83 | 6.01 |
| Apr-82 | 13.18 | 11.58 | 12.60 | Apr-88 | 5.70 | 5.87 | 6.11 |
| Jul-82 | 13.08 | 12.49 | 12.11 | Jul-88 | 6.55 | 6.77 | 7.00 |
| Oct-82 | 7.40 | 8.03 | 8.31 | Oct-88 | 7.26 | 7.45 | 7.63 |
| Jan-83 | 7.89 | 7.36 | 7.74 | Jan-89 | 8.10 | 8.41 | 8.50 |
| Apr-83 | 8.64 | 8.38 | 8.41 | Apr-89 | 9.05 | 9.04 | 8.87 |
| Jul-83 | 9.03 | 8.76 | 8.77 | Jul-89 | 7.98 | 7.97 | 7.89 |
| Oct-83 | 8.70 | 8.84 | 8.89 | Oct-89 | 7.77 | 7.70 | 7.67 |
| Jan-84 | 8.95 | 9.28 | 9.34 | Jan-90 | 7.85 | 7.29 | 7.19 |
| Apr-84 | 9.71 | 9.93 | 9.96 | Apr-90 | 7.80 | 7.85 | 7.73 |
| Jul-84 | 9.99 | 10.34 | 10.68 | Jul-90 | 7.78 | 7.50 | 7.42 |
| Oct-84 | 10.21 | 10.48 | 10.97 | Oct-90 | 7.15 | 7.06 | 6.87 |
| Jan-85 | 7.85 | 8.02 | 8.40 | Jan-91 | 6.60 | 6.36 | 6.20 |
| Apr-85 | 8.16 | 8.80 | 8.87 | Apr-91 | 5.76 | 5.69 | 5.76 |
| Jul-85 | 6.76 | 7.22 | 7.55 | Jul-91 | 5.58 | 5.67 | 5.85 |
| Oct-85 | 6.93 | 7.46 | 7.70 | Oct-91 | 5.14 | 5.00 | 5.21 |
| Jan-86 | 7.27 | 7.06 | 7.19 | Jan-92 | 3.73 | 3.93 | 4.11 |
| Apr-86 | 6.36 | 6.37 | 6.54 | Apr-92 | 4.01 | 4.07 | 4.21 |
| Jul-86 | 6.11 | 6.28 | 6.50 | Jul-92 | 3.65 | 3.69 | 3.92 |
| Oct-86 | 5.24 | 5.24 | 5.35 | Oct-92 | 2.82 | 2.78 | 3.00 |

*Date of spot rate coincides with the date survey results were reported, generally within days of the beginning of the quarter.

SOURCE: *Washington Bond & Money Market Report*, formerly the Goldsmith-Nagan Survey.

# 9

# Gauging Investor Confidence

## Defining the Challenge

### Tracking the Most Elusive Factor

Of the three key factors that drive stock prices, the most elusive is investor confidence. Investors often use such terms as *psychology, sentiment,* or *fear and greed* to articulate their views concerning investor confidence. They recognize its powerful influence on stock prices but do not agree on how to measure it. Consequently, they not only face the challenge of appraising the future course of investor confidence, but they begin their effort with no reliable method of quantifying even the current level.

The concept of a risk premium provides a theoretical framework for quantification of investor confidence. As indicated in Chap. 5, complete certainty concerning the future dividend-growth rate and the long-term risk-free rate would determine stock prices. The present value of the stock market, under these hypothetical circumstances, would equal the sum of the future dividends discounted by the risk-free rate. In the absence of risk, the risk premium would be zero. Since no one can project either the dividend stream or the long-term risk-free rate with a high degree of assurance, stock prices must allow for risk. In actual practice, investors price stocks to provide for a discount rate considerably higher than the risk-free rate. The difference between the risk-free rate and the total return expected for equities defines the risk premium.

## Drawing Inferences from the Historical Record

Estimates of the risk premium depend on inferences from the historical record. Chapter 5 explains the approach used to develop an estimate of the *average level* of the risk premium over an extended period of years. Such estimates, based on the excess return generated by stocks over a long period, are useful, as described in Chap. 3, in developing the long-term policy plan. They contribute little insight, however, concerning the *change* in the risk premium over the time horizon relevant to active asset allocation. While policy may focus on the next 10 years—or longer—active asset allocation ordinarily looks to the coming 6 to 18 months.

## Clues Which Bear on Change in the Risk Premium

To accommodate the requirements of active asset allocation, we aim to identify clues which bear on the likelihood of change in the risk premium over the year ahead. In a highly efficient market, most of the information that appears intuitively helpful turns out to be useless, since investors collectively, acting in their own self-interest, so quickly discount it. We therefore look for clues which qualify as slow information. The significance of slow information depends on relationships that are not so immediately obvious. Widespread indifference to the information—or general skepticism concerning its value—provides opportunity to make use of it. The goal, through continuing analysis, is to sort out the significance of slow information before it is fully discounted by market prices.

To gauge investor confidence, we study the most basic measure of market price—how price relates to earnings. For this purpose, we review data for the S&P 500, which accounts for about 70 percent of the market value of publicly traded stocks. Figure 9-1, covering the first quarter of 1955 through the first

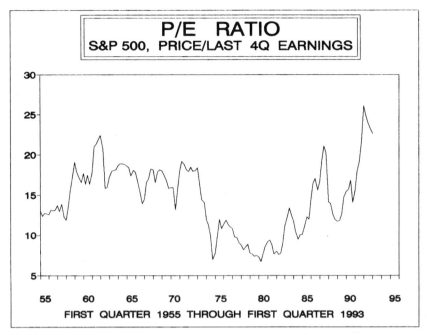

**Figure 9-1.** Tracing the price-earnings ratio based on four-quarter trailing earnings from the first quarter of 1955 through the first quarter of 1993.

quarter of 1993, traces the price-earnings ratio (P/E) based on four-quarter trailing earnings. Our focus on trailing earnings (in contrast to forecasts of future results) separates our measure of investor confidence from estimates of future earnings. We recognize that a very favorable (or extremely unfavorable) outlook for earnings in the year ahead may warrant a very high (or very low) P/E based on trailing earnings. To assess investor confidence, however, we view P/E independently of the estimated earnings outlook. The ratio of price to trailing earnings, particularly as it moves toward historical extremes, provides insight into the state of investor optimism or pessimism. We rely on other measures of the business outlook and interest rates, as presented in Chaps. 7 and 8, to assess the likelihood that the investor confidence represented by the P/E (trailing earnings) is warranted.

# Interpreting the
# Price-Earnings Ratio

## Confronting Two
## Conflicting Views

To explain how we see the relationship between P/E and risk, we first look at the two conflicting views discussed below.* They reflect the very different concepts, as described in Chaps. 1 and 2, concerning how the stock market works. Our conclusion, based on the understanding that the stock market is highly efficient but not completely efficient, differs from both of these extremes.

The *efficient market hypothesis* represents the view at one end of the spectrum. It holds that the P/E for the publicly traded stock market, as a basic measure that is easily understood and widely followed, is high or low for good reason. Since investors compete intensely to take advantage of *perceived* excesses, their collective actions maintain market prices at rational levels in terms of the available information. Although one investor may profit from a current transaction, the advantage next time is likely to go to another investor. *On average,* no investor can expect to gain, since the market P/E, in the framework of the efficient market hypothesis, can provide no useful information. Figure 9-2 supports this point of view. It compares the market P/E from the first quarter of 1955 through the first quarter of 1992 with subsequent market-price change. The P/E, based on trailing four-quarter earnings, is computed at the beginning of each quarter, while percent change in market price is measured over the next four quarters. As displayed in Fig. 9-2, the correlation between P/E and subsequent market-price change appears far too weak to be meaningful.

*Contrarian logic* provides a view in sharp contrast to that which flows from the efficient market hypothesis. It rejects the rationality attributed to the investor consensus by the efficient

---

*This discussion draws on a previously published article: Walter R. Good, "When Are Price/Earnings Ratios Too High—or Too Low?" *Financial Analysts Journal,* July–August 1991, pp. 9–12, 25.

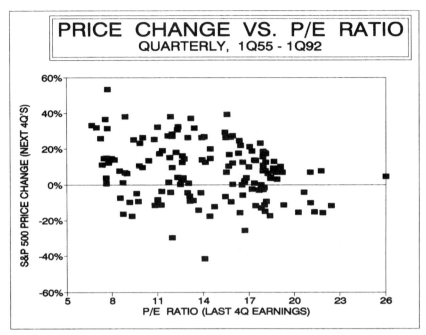

**Figure 9-2.** Comparing the beginning price-earnings ratio from the first quarter of 1955 through the first quarter of 1992 with market-price change over the subsequent four quarters. (*Source:* The Analysts Handbook *issued by Standard & Poor's Corporation.*)

market hypothesis. Rather, it views investors as subject to periodic swings in mass psychology which push stock prices to unwarranted levels. Contrarians, as a general principle, expect to gain advantage by buying when P/Es are low and selling when they are high. Figure 9-3 organizes the data shown in Fig. 9-2 to highlight evidence consistent with contrarian logic. Panel A includes the 127 of the 148 quarterly data points over the first quarter of 1955 through the first quarter of 1992 when the P/E ranged between 8 and 20. The resulting scatter diagram, in accord with the efficient-market position, shows little evidence that buying low or selling high—at least in terms of four-quarter trailing earnings—has been advantageous. Panel B, which displays the 21 quarterly data points not shown in Panel A, presents a very different pattern, clearly consistent with contrarian logic. Very low P/Es (under 8) are without exception associated with market-price gains over the subsequent year. Very high P/Es (over 20) show the opposite result for six of the nine data points. For the three exceptions, the subsequent four-quarter gain averaged less than 8 percent.*

## Alternative 1: Dismiss the Data

One explanation of the disparity between the two panels of Fig. 9-3 stresses shortcomings in the underlying data. We first consider this point of view before addressing, in the next section, an alternative explanation which we consider more persuasive. We recognize that the data is less than perfect, and, for this reason, direct attention to the three limitations listed below. Allowance for these limitations, nevertheless, does not materially change the broad historical pattern. The data still support the contrarian principle as it applies to the extreme P/Es shown in Panel B.

**Hindsight Bias.**   We review the historical relationship between market price and trailing earnings, as shown in Figs. 9-2 and 9-3, in the light of possible hindsight bias. On the first day of the quarter, only earnings for the first three of the trailing four quarters have been reported. The consensus view of the P/E reflects an estimate of four-quarter trailing earnings rather than the final figure still to be reported. The consensus estimate is likely to differ at least slightly from reported earnings when they become available. Consequently, the borderline P/Es (close to either 20 or 8) may not always be appropriately classified by investors until the last-quarter earnings of the four-quarter trailing earnings are actually reported.

   To identify the potential for hindsight bias, we direct attention to two alternative methods of estimating the last-quarter earnings of the four-quarter trailing earnings. One method makes use of consensus estimates. This approach takes into account the continuing flow of information already available and likely to influence earnings for quarters not yet reported. Most institu-

---

*Appendix 9-1 lists the data plotted in Panels A and B of Fig. 9-3.

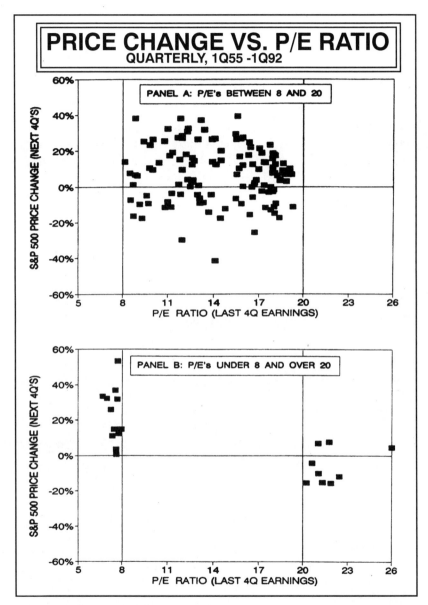

**Figure 9-3.**   Organizing the data in Fig. 9-2 to show separately (*a*)
P/Es between 8 and 20 and (*b*) P/Es under 8 and over 20.

tional fund managers, by relying on the institutional brokers and portfolio managers who serve them, have ready access to necessary estimates on a regular basis. In the absence of help from such outside sources, a completely objective alternative is readily available. It avoids the need for a consensus estimate, since it makes use of the earnings for the last four quarters as already reported. At the beginning of each calendar quarter, these earnings cover the period which lags one quarter behind the four quarters just ended (last quarter earnings not yet reported). *Barron's* provides the required information on a weekly basis, as shown in Fig. 9-4. Although this method ignores information relating to the quarter last ended but not yet reported, the disadvantage, as we shall demonstrate, is marginal.

Our analysis indicates that hindsight bias, although a legitimate concern, does not account for the pattern of data points shown by Panel B. The earnings estimate at the end of a quarter, although more than a month in advance of reported earnings, benefits from the flow of relevant information that has become

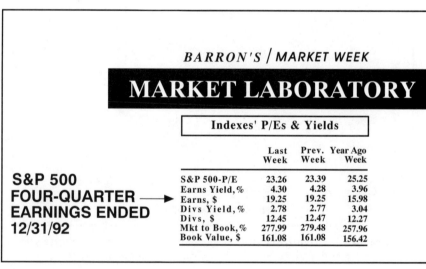

**BARRON'S / MARKET WEEK**

## MARKET LABORATORY

Indexes' P/Es & Yields

**S&P 500**
**FOUR-QUARTER** →
**EARNINGS ENDED**
**12/31/92**

|  | Last Week | Prev. Week | Year Ago Week |
|---|---|---|---|
| S&P 500-P/E | 23.26 | 23.39 | 25.25 |
| Earns Yield, % | 4.30 | 4.28 | 3.96 |
| Earns, $ | 19.25 | 19.25 | 15.98 |
| Divs Yield, % | 2.78 | 2.77 | 3.04 |
| Divs, $ | 12.45 | 12.47 | 12.27 |
| Mkt to Book, % | 277.99 | 279.48 | 257.96 |
| Book Value, $ | 161.08 | 161.08 | 156.42 |

**Figure 9-4.** An example from *Barron's* showing the last reported four-quarter earnings for the S&P 500. (*Source:* Barron's *National Financial and Business Weekly, March 29, 1993.*)

available during the quarter. Such information covers a wide range of items required by business forecasters, including revisions in estimates of overall business activity, sales data for major industries, and comments by company managements concerning profit prospects. At the same time, combining the fourth-quarter estimate with reported results for the three previous quarters sharply diminishes the relative error. In our experience, about two-thirds of the errors in the final-quarter estimate are 12 percent or less, which translates into an error of 3 percent or less for the full year. Figure 9-5 adjusts the scatter diagram in Panel B of Fig. 9-3 to reflect arbitrary reduction by 3 percent of each P/E over 20 and arbitrary increase by 3 percent of each P/E under 8. The scatter diagram also includes any borderline P/E, previously in the middle category, which increases to more than 20 or reduces to less than 8 as a result of a 3 percent adjust-

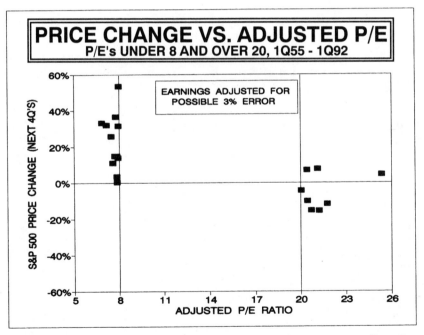

**Figure 9-5.** Adjusting the data in Panel B of Fig. 9-3 to allow for possible error of 3 percent in estimated four-quarter trailing earnings.

ment in the appropriate direction. These adjustments identify erroneous P/E estimates that might have misled investors before fourth-quarter earnings were actually reported. For P/Es over 20, revisions result in the loss of one data point and no additions. For P/Es under 8, there is also one reduction and no additions. The pattern of P/E and subsequent market-price change remains essentially the same.

Note that the adjustments incorporated in Fig. 9-5 are designed to overstate the probable effect of hindsight bias. In every case, Fig. 9-5 assumes that the error is in the direction which would change the classification of the P/E. About 50 percent of the errors might be expected in the opposite direction, reinforcing the initial classification. For the remaining 50 percent, the assumption of a 3 percent error in the four-quarter total overstates the error most of the time. About 34 percent of the total represent errors between 0 and 3 percent (rather than 3 percent), while only about 16 percent are likely to exceed 3 percent.

The alternative method of calculating P/E, based on completely objective information, provides further reason to reject hindsight bias as the explanation for the historical data. Figure 9-6 duplicates Fig. 9-3 except for the identification of four-quarter trailing earnings. The calculation of P/E for Fig. 9-6 reflects *reported* four-quarter trailing earnings.* These earnings lag by one quarter the earnings for the four quarters just ended (last quarter not yet reported) as shown in Fig. 9-3. The respective patterns of the scatter diagrams shown in Panels A and B of Fig. 9-6, nevertheless, are virtually unchanged from those shown for the two panels of Fig. 9-3. The number of quarters with P/Es in excess of 20 is eight instead of nine, reflecting two deletions and one addition. Market price declined over the subsequent four quarters in seven of the eight instances. At the other extreme, data points with P/Es under 8 show a net reduction of three, as a result of three subtractions but no additions. For each of the 10 remaining P/Es under 8, the market price rose over the four quarters ahead.

*Appendix 9-2 lists the data plotted in Fig. 9-6.

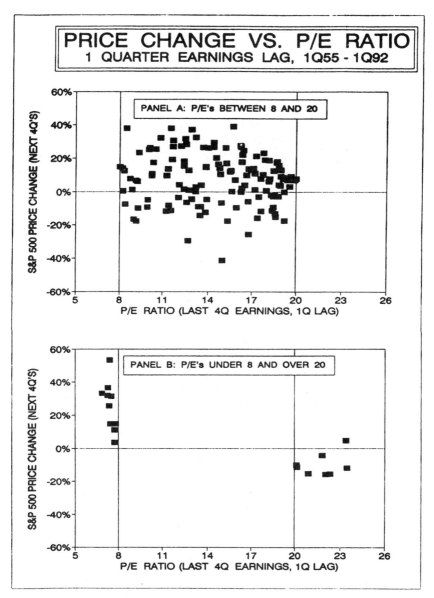

**Figure 9-6.** Adjusting P/Es shown in Fig. 9-3 by substituting last four-quarters *reported* earnings for last four-quarters *trailing* earnings.

**Overlapping Measurement Periods.**  For both very high and very low P/Es, earnings of several of the four-quarter periods overlap, limiting the independence of the data points. For example, the P/E exceeded 20 at the beginning of both the third and fourth quarters of 1987. In each case, stock prices declined sharply over the subsequent four quarters as a result of the same event—the October 1987 stock market crash.

To address the question of overlap, we have also reviewed P/Es at the beginning of each calendar year. Our analysis extends as far back as data are available (starting with a base year for earnings of 1926). From 1927 to 1992, P/Es were under 8 at the beginning of 8 years, all of which experienced a rise in market price over the subsequent year. When P/Es exceeded 20, 3 of the 4 years registered a subsequent decline in market price. For the 1 year when the market price rose, the gain was 4 percent. The annual data, although including only 12 extreme data points, show the same broad pattern as the 22 extreme data points generated by the quarterly data. To check for the effects of hindsight bias, we applied the same adjustments to the annual data as shown in Fig. 9-5 for the quarterly data. The only change is the reduction of the P/Es in the under-8 category from eight to seven. For the completely objective approach (which makes use of four-quarter *reported* earnings) the results are also much the same. The four data points with P/Es in excess of 20 were reduced to three but only because data for quarterly S&P 500 earnings are unavailable prior to 1936. For the eight P/Es under 8, two eliminations brought the total to six. The relationship between P/E and subsequent market-price change, nevertheless, remains approximately the same as before. For P/Es over 20, the subsequent four-quarter market-price change was negative in 2 of the 3 years. For P/Es under 8, market-price change over the comparable four-quarter interval was positive in each instance.

**Changing Earnings Quality.**  The earnings figures, as reported, do not mean precisely the same from one reporting period to the next. Earnings calculations depend on changing accounting rules and reflect management judgments concerning write-offs and loss reserves. They may be distorted significantly by changing levels of inflation. Uncertainty concerning true earnings translates directly into uncertainty concerning the true P/E.

Despite these limitations, the burden of proof rests with the assumption that the P/E based on reported earnings will mean something very different in the future than in the past. For the S&P 500, differences in the quality of aggregate earnings from year to year are much less significant than the much wider variations for individual issues. There is no broad agreement, meanwhile, concerning a better way to calculate earnings. Since many adjustments unrelated to current operations routinely affect reported earnings each year, concern centers on the limited number of blockbuster write-offs which may occur from time to time. They may be sufficiently large to burden overall S&P 500 earnings in a significant way in a particular year. By way of example, in the third quarter of 1991, AT&T and Westinghouse experienced write-offs that together reduced S&P 500 earnings by about $0.60 to $3.74. Solely as a result of these write-offs, the P/E at year end (based on last four-quarter reported earnings) increased from 22.6 to 23.4. Note that this specific adjustment does not change the classification of the P/E, which remains in the very high category (over 20). While such adjustments may prove misleading on occasion, reported earnings remain a widely accepted benchmark. In the light of the historical record, decision makers can hardly ignore extreme P/Es based on trailing earnings as actually reported. The challenge is how to interpret such information for the purpose of valuing the stock market.

## Alternative 2: Reconciling the Disparity

The very different explanation which we favor reconciles the contrasting scatter diagrams presented by Panels A and B of Fig. 9-3. The central issue is the relationship, *on average*, between investor confidence and the P/E. Although other factors also relate to investor confidence, the P/E provides a particularly visible measure. In general, the investor consensus is optimistic (highly confident) when the P/E is high and pessimistic (lacking in confidence) when the P/E is low.

Our position takes issue with the assumption of a straight-line relationship between investor confidence and market P/E, as illustrated by Panel A of Fig. 9-7. The horizontal scale, ranging from 6 to 22, covers most of the P/Es recorded for the S&P 500 since 1926. The vertical scale, representing investor confidence, is qualitative. It ranges from very low to very high, since we recognize that there is no precise quantitative measure of investor confidence. The graph associates the midpoint of investor confidence with the long-term average P/E of about 14. Given the relationship plotted in Panel A of Fig. 9-7, investor confidence would increase just as much when the P/E rises from 14 to 18 as when the P/E increases from 18 to 22. This straight-line relationship provides no help in explaining the disparity between Panels A and B of Fig. 9-3.

Panel B of Fig. 9-7, in sharp contrast to Panel A, illustrates the relationship between investor confidence and P/E as we envision it. Both the vertical and horizontal scales are identical to those shown in Fig. 9-7, Panel A, but the curve tracing the average relationship between the two variables is very different. Investor confidence demonstrates an accelerating rate of change as P/E moves in either direction from the midpoint of 14. It rises very little as the P/E increases from 14 to 18 but much more rapidly over the interval 18 to 22. The implication is that investor confidence need be only moderately above average to support a P/E of 18. A P/E of 22, in contrast, requires extraordinary investor confidence. The process operates in reverse as P/Es move to the lower extremes.

This explanation identifies a fundamental reason for the differing patterns shown in the two panels of Fig. 9-3. It is consistent with the operation of the contrarian principle in one panel (extreme P/Es) but not in the other (P/Es between 20 and 8). Two factors, working together, determine the shape of the curve. When the P/E is above average, investor confidence must increase sufficiently to offset two negative considerations. One negative consideration focuses on how much might be lost if the P/E, currently high, returns to a more normal level. The other

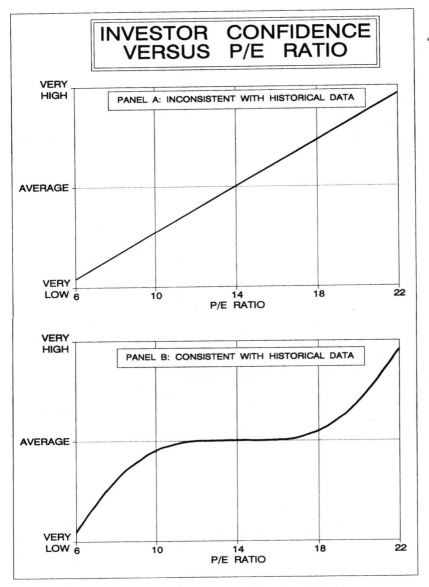

**Figure 9-7.** Two ways of viewing the relationship between investor confidence and P/E: (*a*) inconsistent with historical data and (*b*) consistent with historical data.

negative consideration concerns the risk that a near-term correction in the P/E will actually take place. Both considerations, on average, become more worrisome as the P/E rises toward the upper end of the range. We do not pretend to know the exact shape of either curve. Because of compounding, however, the two factors together produce a curve which rises at a rapidly accelerating rate. Consequently, change in the P/E, as it moves near the upper extremes, is accompanied by a rapidly accelerating rise in investor confidence. As the P/E moves toward the lower extremes, investor confidence demonstrates a reverse pattern. Under these circumstances, the reduction of investor confidence is sufficient to offset two positives, the reverse of the two factors described above. As the P/E declines toward the lower end of the historical range, prospects for gain associated with recovery to a more normal P/E accelerate. Other things equal, the probability that such a rebound will take place also increases sharply.

Our explanation applies the contrarian principle within the framework of a highly efficient market. The investor-confidence curve plotted in Panel B of Fig. 9-7 serves to explain the changing market response to surprises as market P/Es move toward the extremes. Within the broad intermediate range, the level of the P/E in itself provides little help in determining the probable course of stock prices. Under these circumstances—prevailing about 85 percent of the time—changes in key factors other than investor confidence are more likely to explain market-price change. Extreme P/Es, in contrast, provide a useful perspective for assessing the probability of changing investor confidence. The extraordinary optimism implied by very high P/Es leaves limited room for further improvement in confidence. At the same time, such optimism provides a great deal of room for confidence to return to a more normal level. Similarly, extremes in pessimism, reflected in very low P/Es, favor the probability of a positive market-price response. The historical record suggests that, under such circumstances, even a highly rational investor consensus may become increasingly vulnerable to sudden reversal as unexpected new information materializes.

## P/E in Future Operations

Despite the generally consistent historical relationships between extreme market P/Es and subsequent market-price change, we stress the inappropriateness of viewing the P/E in isolation. One reason is the possibility that accounting for earnings will become at some point in the future a much bigger issue than it has been during our back-test period. Under such circumstances, the dividend yield provides a useful "second opinion." Even more important, the historical patterns relating P/E and subsequent market-price change reflect partial correlations between extreme P/Es and other influences that have been related to subsequent market-price change. Active management of asset allocation therefore pays attention not only to the P/E but also to the relationship of the P/E to other prime variables.

## Dividend Yield as a Second Opinion

Dividend yield for the S&P 500 and the corresponding market P/E are closely related. Both measures depend on the same market price. Dividends do not move in lock step with earnings but, for a broad market average, they almost always reflect significant changes in earnings. Figure 9-8, displaying data since 1955, underscores the historical relationship between extreme P/Es and dividend yield. Over these years, the dividend yield has registered less than 3.25 percent each time the P/E exceeded 20. Similarly, the dividend yield has exceeded 5.25 percent in every instance when the P/E declined to less than 8. This pattern has held for more than 4 decades whether the P/E relates the S&P 500 to the last four quarters of reported earnings, as shown in Fig. 9-8, or, alternatively, the P/E is based on four-quarter trailing earnings (last quarter subsequently reported). For the years since 1967, the IDR (see Chap. 7) serves as the numerator in the dividend yield calculation. For the years prior to 1967, when the IDR was not yet available, the yield calculation reflects dividend payments for the four quarters ended 6 months ahead.

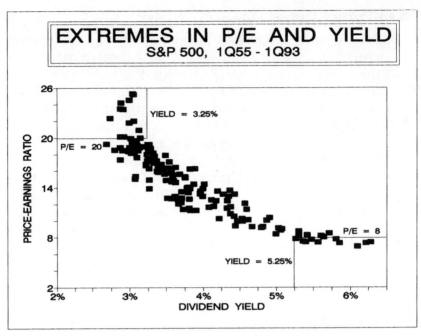

**Figure 9-8.** Comparing extremes in S&P 500 price-earnings ratio and dividend yield from the first quarter of 1955 to the first quarter of 1993. (*Source:* The Analysts Handbook *issued by Standard & Poor's Corporation.*)

The second opinion concerning an extreme P/E, as provided by dividend yield, could be helpful at a point in the future when the significance of reported earnings becomes an important issue. Suppose, for example, massive write-offs (or other common factor) temporarily distort earnings of a large number of companies included in the S&P 500. Since write-offs occur every year, a certain level of charges for this reason are normally recurring. Our concern centers on an exceptional convergence of write-offs. One possibility is a change in accounting rules which results in widespread charges for expenses incurred but not recognized in previous years. Suppose, under such circumstances, the market P/E based on reported earnings exceeds 20 by a considerable margin but the decision maker does not have the necessary information to determine how much of the P/E reflects write-offs. As a routine check on the P/E, a dividend yield of less than 3.25 percent provides reason to confirm the P/E classification as "very high." A yield higher than 3.25 percent, in contrast, means that the "very high" P/E classification is suspect. The decision maker therefore has reason to reject it. In a similar way, the decision maker is able to make use of the dividend yield to confirm or reject a P/E that would otherwise qualify as "very low."

### Relating P/E to the Other Prime Variables

Very high and very low market P/Es, even in the absence of special concern for earnings quality, require continuing analysis in relation to the other two prime variables. Table 9-1 summarizes the historical relationships between the P/E based on four-quarter trailing earnings and subsequent market-price change, as discussed earlier in the chapter.* The annual data compare the P/E at the beginning of each calendar year for the period

**Table 9-1.** P/E versus Four-Quarter Market-Price Change

| | Four-quarter change, S&P 500 | | | |
|---|---|---|---|---|
| P/E | Annually (1927–1992) | | Quarterly (1955–1992) | |
| (trailing earnings) | Up | Down | Up | Down |
| Over 20 | 1 | 3 | 3 | 6 |
| 8–20 | 34 | 20 | 87 | 40 |
| Under 8 | 8 | 0 | 13 | 0 |
| Total | 43 | 23 | 103 | 46 |

*Appendix 9-3 lists the annual data included in Table 9-1. Appendix 9-1, as identified previously, provides the supporting quarterly data.

1927 to 1992 with the subsequent four-quarter market-price change. The quarterly data compare the P/E at the beginning of each quarter for the period 1955 to 1992 with the subsequent four-quarter market-price change. The pattern of the comparisons is much the same in each case. For either series, the broad middle range of P/Es provides little useful information concerning subsequent market-price action. For P/Es over 20 or under 8, in contrast, the pattern of subsequent market-price change in each case is consistent with the contrarian principle in operation. These patterns, nevertheless, reflect a considerable correlation between market P/Es and the other prime variables. Very high P/Es (over 20) have usually accompanied what we identify as neutral-to-unfavorable measures of the business outlook and interest rates. Similarly, very low P/Es (under 8) have accompanied, with few exceptions, measures of business activity and interest rates conducive to a neutral-to-favorable outlook for stock prices. Stock market valuation therefore accords weight to the market P/E but only in the context of the other two prime variables. Chapter 10 presents the details.

## Appendix 9-1
## Measuring Current P/E
## Based on Four-Quarter
## Trailing Earnings
## (First Quarter 1955 to
## First Quarter 1992)

Table 9-2 lists the data plotted in Figs. 9-2 and 9-3. It compares the market P/E at the beginning of each calendar quarter from the first quarter of 1955 through the first quarter of 1992 with the market-price change in the subsequent four quarters. Since the calculation of P/E reflects earnings for the four quarters just ended, in real-time operations earnings for only the first three of the trailing four quarters would have been reported on the date indicated. The data shown here therefore assume that the last-quarter earnings not yet reported will be accurately estimated.

**Table 9-2.** P/E versus Price Change (Next Four Quarters), Quarterly, 1Q55 to 1Q92
Four-Quarter Trailing Earnings

| \|\| P/E < 8 | | | \|\| 8 < P/E < 20 | | | | | | \|\| P/E > 20 | | |
|---|---|---|---|---|---|---|---|---|---|---|---|
| Quarter | P/E | Price change, % | Quarter | P/E | Price change, % | Quarter | P/E | Price change, % | Quarter | P/E | Price change, % |
| 80.2 | 6.68 | 33.2 | 78.2 | 8.17 | 13.9 | 57.4 | 12.22 | 18.0 | 87.4 | 20.29 | −15.5 |
| 74.4 | 6.97 | 32.0 | 78.3 | 8.51 | 7.7 | 85.3 | 12.29 | 30.7 | 62.2 | 20.64 | −4.3 |
| 80.1 | 7.26 | 25.8 | 80.4 | 8.57 | −7.4 | 83.2 | 12.32 | 4.1 | 61.2 | 21.06 | 6.9 |
| 79.3 | 7.36 | 11.0 | 78.1 | 8.73 | 1.1 | 55.2 | 12.36 | 32.5 | 87.3 | 21.08 | −10.0 |
| 79.4 | 7.47 | 14.8 | 81.3 | 8.74 | −16.5 | 83.4 | 12.49 | 0.0 | 61.3 | 21.33 | −15.3 |
| 82.2 | 7.56 | 36.6 | 78.4 | 8.86 | 6.6 | 56.1 | 12.56 | 2.6 | 91.4 | 21.77 | 7.7 |
| 81.4 | 7.61 | 3.6 | 82.4 | 8.88 | 37.9 | 89.3 | 12.61 | 12.6 | 61.4 | 21.88 | −15.7 |
| 79.2 | 7.64 | 0.5 | 77.4 | 9.01 | 6.2 | 88.3 | 12.62 | 16.3 | 62.1 | 22.43 | −11.8 |
| 80.3 | 7.65 | 14.9 | 81.1 | 9.16 | −9.7 | 55.4 | 12.69 | 3.8 | 92.1 | 26.12 | 4.5 |
| 75.1 | 7.71 | 31.5 | 81.2 | 9.33 | −17.7 | 55.3 | 12.74 | 14.5 | | | |
| 82.3 | 7.74 | 53.4 | 84.3 | 9.46 | 25.2 | 57.2 | 12.97 | −4.6 | | | |
| 79.1 | 7.79 | 12.3 | 77.3 | 9.64 | −4.9 | 55.1 | 12.99 | 26.4 | | | |
| 82.1 | 7.98 | 14.8 | 77.2 | 9.76 | −9.4 | 56.3 | 13.05 | 0.9 | | | |
| | | | 74.3 | 9.84 | 10.7 | 56.4 | 13.11 | −6.5 | | | |
| | | | 75.2 | 9.87 | 23.3 | 56.2 | 13.14 | −9.0 | | | |
| | | | 84.4 | 10.03 | 9.6 | 70.3 | 13.17 | 37.1 | | | |
| | | | 85.1 | 10.05 | 26.3 | 83.3 | 13.35 | −8.9 | | | |
| | | | 84.2 | 10.43 | 13.5 | 58.2 | 13.41 | 31.7 | | | |
| | | | 75.4 | 10.81 | 25.5 | 57.1 | 13.69 | −14.3 | | | |
| | | | 77.1 | 10.84 | −11.5 | 57.3 | 13.85 | −4.5 | | | |
| | | | 76.4 | 11.02 | −8.3 | 66.4 | 13.89 | 26.3 | | | |
| | | | 85.2 | 11.02 | 32.2 | 88.2 | 13.93 | 13.9 | | | |
| | | | 83.1 | 11.13 | 17.3 | 90.4 | 14.08 | 26.7 | | | |
| | | | 74.2 | 11.24 | −11.3 | 73.4 | 14.10 | −41.4 | | | |
| | | | 76.3 | 11.27 | −3.6 | 88.1 | 14.12 | 12.4 | | | |
| | | | 76.1 | 11.33 | 19.1 | 73.3 | 14.42 | −17.5 | | | |
| | | | 89.1 | 11.69 | 27.3 | 86.1 | 14.46 | 14.6 | | | |
| | | | 84.1 | 11.76 | 1.4 | 67.1 | 14.47 | 20.1 | | | |
| | | | 89.2 | 11.81 | 15.3 | 89.4 | 14.74 | −12.3 | | | |
| | | | 58.1 | 11.87 | 38.1 | 58.3 | 15.44 | 29.2 | | | |
| | | | 76.2 | 11.87 | −4.2 | 90.1 | 15.45 | −6.6 | | | |
| | | | 74.1 | 11.95 | −29.7 | 91.1 | 15.47 | 26.3 | | | |
| | | | 85.4 | 11.96 | 27.0 | 66.3 | 15.52 | 7.0 | | | |
| | | | 75.3 | 11.96 | 9.5 | 86.4 | 15.58 | 39.1 | | | |
| | | | 88.4 | 11.96 | 28.4 | 90.2 | 15.69 | 10.4 | | | |

(*Continued*)

**Table 9-2.** P/E versus Price Change (Next Four Quarters),
Quarterly, 1Q55 to 1Q92 (*Continued*)

Four-Quarter Trailing Earnings

| P/E < 8 | | | 8 < P/E < 20 | | | | | | P/E > 20 | | |
|---|---|---|---|---|---|---|---|---|---|---|---|
| Quarter | P/E | Price change, % | Quarter | P/E | Price change, % | Quarter | P/E | Price change, % | Quarter | P/E | Price change, % |
| | | | 70.4 | 15.71 | 16.8 | 68.3 | 17.88 | -1.9 | | | |
| | | | 62.3 | 15.78 | 26.7 | 72.1 | 17.91 | 15.6 | | | |
| | | | 69.4 | 15.81 | -9.6 | 91.2 | 17.92 | 7.6 | | | |
| | | | 70.2 | 15.92 | 11.9 | 63.2 | 17.94 | 18.6 | | | |
| | | | 70.1 | 15.93 | 0.1 | 72.3 | 17.95 | -2.7 | | | |
| | | | 62.4 | 15.94 | 27.4 | 71.1 | 17.96 | 10.8 | | | |
| | | | 60.2 | 16.32 | 17.6 | 72.4 | 18.00 | -1.9 | | | |
| | | | 60.4 | 16.37 | 24.7 | 69.1 | 18.03 | -11.4 | | | |
| | | | 73.2 | 16.40 | -15.7 | 65.4 | 18.06 | -14.9 | | | |
| | | | 86.2 | 16.45 | 22.1 | 63.3 | 18.07 | 17.8 | | | |
| | | | 67.2 | 16.55 | 0.0 | 68.1 | 18.10 | 7.7 | | | |
| | | | 68.2 | 16.58 | 12.5 | 63.4 | 18.11 | 17.4 | | | |
| | | | 59.4 | 16.58 | -5.9 | 71.4 | 18.11 | 12.4 | | | |
| | | | 66.2 | 16.71 | 1.1 | 68.4 | 18.14 | -9.3 | | | |
| | | | 87.1 | 16.72 | 2.0 | 67.4 | 18.25 | 6.2 | | | |
| | | | 69.3 | 16.73 | -25.6 | 73.1 | 18.39 | -17.4 | | | |
| | | | 90.3 | 16.84 | 3.7 | 65.2 | 18.41 | 3.6 | | | |
| | | | 67.3 | 17.01 | 9.9 | 72.2 | 18.45 | 4.0 | | | |
| | | | 86.3 | 17.05 | 21.2 | 65.1 | 18.63 | 9.1 | | | |
| | | | 63.1 | 17.19 | 18.9 | 64.1 | 18.66 | 13.0 | | | |
| | | | 59.3 | 17.20 | -2.7 | 71.3 | 18.74 | 7.5 | | | |
| | | | 65.3 | 17.38 | 0.7 | 64.4 | 18.83 | 6.9 | | | |
| | | | 58.4 | 17.38 | 13.6 | 64.3 | 18.87 | 3.0 | | | |
| | | | 69.2 | 17.44 | -11.7 | 64.2 | 18.89 | 9.1 | | | |
| | | | 60.3 | 17.46 | 13.6 | 59.1 | 19.10 | 8.5 | | | |
| | | | 60.1 | 17.67 | -3.0 | 91.3 | 19.12 | 10.0 | | | |
| | | | 61.1 | 17.77 | 23.1 | 71.2 | 19.22 | 6.9 | | | |
| | | | 66.1 | 17.81 | -13.1 | 87.2 | 19.32 | -11.2 | | | |
| | | | 59.2 | 17.83 | -0.2 | | | | | | |

As discussed in Chap. 9, errors in the consensus estimate for a
quarter already completed are unlikely to change the identification of extreme P/Es in a major way. For comparisons which
rely entirely on earnings data already reported, see App. 9-2.

## Appendix 9-2
## Measuring Current P/E
## Based on Earnings
## Already Reported (First
## Quarter 1955 to First
## Quarter 1992)

Table 9-3 lists data plotted in Fig. 9-6. It compares P/E at the
beginning of each calendar quarter from the first quarter of 1955
through the first quarter of 1992 with the market-price change in
the subsequent four quarters. In order to confine the P/E calculation to information already reported, it reflects earnings for
the four quarters ended 3 months earlier. (Earnings for the quarter just ended will not be reported for at least several weeks.)
These reported earnings do not take into account information
concerning earnings for last quarter that may already be available even though the final earnings report is not. As a practical
matter, the average error for the reported earnings (discussed in
Chap. 9) has been only marginally greater than we have experienced from the use of consensus estimates.

## Appendix 9-3
## Measuring Current P/E
## Based on Four-Quarter
## Trailing Earnings (Annual
## Data, 1927 to 1992)

Table 9-4 lists the the annual data summarized in Table 9-1. It
compares P/E at the beginning of each year from 1927 to 1992
with the subsequent market-price change for the year. Since the
calculation of P/E reflects earnings for the four quarters just
ended, earnings for only the first three of the trailing four quar-

**Table 9-3.** P/E versus Price Change (Next Four Quarters), Quarterly, 1Q55 to 1Q92

*Reported* Four-Quarter Trailing Earnings (One Quarter Lag)

| P/E < 8 | | | 8 < P/E < 20 | | | | | | P/E > 20 | | |
|---|---|---|---|---|---|---|---|---|---|---|---|
| Quarter | P/E | Price change, % | Quarter | P/E | Price change, % | Quarter | P/E | Price change, % | Quarter | P/E | Price change, % |
| 80.2 | 6.87 | 33.2 | 82.1 | 8.03 | 14.8 | 83.2 | 12.10 | 4.1 | 87.3 | 20.13 | −10.0 |
| 74.4 | 7.27 | 32.0 | 78.2 | 8.19 | 13.9 | 89.1 | 12.22 | 27.3 | 87.2 | 20.15 | −11.2 |
| 82.2 | 7.29 | 36.6 | 79.2 | 8.24 | 0.5 | 84.1 | 12.40 | 1.4 | 61.3 | 20.92 | −15.3 |
| 80.1 | 7.38 | 25.8 | 79.1 | 8.31 | 12.3 | 57.4 | 12.40 | 18.0 | 62.2 | 21.80 | −4.3 |
| 82.3 | 7.40 | 53.4 | 80.4 | 8.40 | −7.4 | 89.2 | 12.42 | 15.3 | 61.4 | 22.02 | −15.7 |
| 80.3 | 7.47 | 14.9 | 82.4 | 8.50 | 37.9 | 58.2 | 12.49 | 31.7 | 87.4 | 22.32 | −15.5 |
| 75.1 | 7.53 | 31.5 | 78.3 | 8.75 | 7.7 | 88.4 | 12.55 | 28.4 | 92.1 | 23.41 | 4.5 |
| 79.3 | 7.74 | 11.0 | 78.1 | 8.88 | 1.1 | 56.4 | 12.60 | −6.5 | 62.1 | 23.46 | −11.8 |
| 81.4 | 7.74 | 3.6 | 81.3 | 9.00 | −16.5 | 74.1 | 12.69 | −29.7 | | | |
| 79.4 | 7.82 | 14.8 | 78.4 | 9.13 | 6.6 | 56.3 | 12.73 | 0.9 | | | |
| | | | 81.2 | 9.18 | −17.7 | 89.3 | 12.74 | 12.6 | | | |
| | | | 77.4 | 9.26 | 6.2 | 76.2 | 12.91 | −4.2 | | | |
| | | | 81.1 | 9.27 | −9.7 | 70.3 | 12.92 | 37.1 | | | |
| | | | 75.2 | 9.38 | 23.3 | 57.2 | 12.94 | −4.6 | | | |
| | | | 77.2 | 9.93 | −9.4 | 83.4 | 13.19 | 0.0 | | | |
| | | | 77.3 | 9.97 | −4.9 | 55.2 | 13.21 | 32.5 | | | |
| | | | 84.3 | 10.04 | 25.2 | 56.1 | 13.22 | 2.6 | | | |
| | | | 85.1 | 10.10 | 26.3 | 56.2 | 13.39 | −9.0 | | | |
| | | | 84.4 | 10.25 | 9.6 | 57.1 | 13.49 | −14.3 | | | |
| | | | 74.3 | 10.29 | 10.7 | 83.3 | 13.54 | −8.9 | | | |
| | | | 83.1 | 10.37 | 17.3 | 55.4 | 13.56 | 3.8 | | | |
| | | | 75.4 | 10.54 | 25.5 | 55.1 | 13.68 | 26.4 | | | |
| | | | 85.2 | 10.86 | 32.2 | 89.4 | 13.84 | −12.3 | | | |
| | | | 77.1 | 11.25 | −11.5 | 55.3 | 13.86 | 14.5 | | | |
| | | | 75.3 | 11.27 | 9.5 | 86.1 | 13.87 | 14.6 | | | |
| | | | 84.2 | 11.35 | 13.5 | 57.3 | 13.93 | −4.5 | | | |
| | | | 76.4 | 11.38 | −8.3 | 66.4 | 14.02 | 26.3 | | | |
| | | | 74.2 | 11.52 | −11.3 | 90.4 | 14.40 | 26.7 | | | |
| | | | 58.1 | 11.52 | 38.1 | 58.3 | 14.41 | 29.2 | | | |
| | | | 76.1 | 11.62 | 19.1 | 67.1 | 14.58 | 20.1 | | | |
| | | | 85.4 | 11.66 | 27.0 | 88.3 | 14.71 | 16.3 | | | |
| | | | 85.3 | 11.71 | 30.7 | 88.2 | 14.79 | 13.9 | | | |
| | | | 76.3 | 12.04 | −3.6 | 90.2 | 14.86 | 10.4 | | | |

**Table 9-3.** P/E versus Price Change (Next Four Quarters),
Quarterly, 1Q55 to 1Q92 (*Continued*)
*Reported* Four-Quarter Trailing Earnings (One Quarter Lag)

| P/E < 8 | | | 8 < P/E < 20 | | | | | | P/E > 20 | | |
|---|---|---|---|---|---|---|---|---|---|---|---|
| Quar-ter | P/E | Price change, % | Quar-ter | P/E | Price change, % | Quar-ter | P/E | Price change, % | Quar-ter | P/E | Price change, % |
| | | | 90.1 | 14.92 | –6.6 | 61.1 | 17.77 | 23.1 | | | |
| | | | 73.4 | 15.00 | –41.4 | 63.1 | 17.88 | 18.9 | | | |
| | | | 91.1 | 15.19 | 26.3 | 65.3 | 17.97 | 0.7 | | | |
| | | | 70.4 | 15.26 | 16.8 | 63.2 | 18.14 | 18.6 | | | |
| | | | 73.3 | 15.33 | –17.5 | 67.4 | 18.14 | 6.2 | | | |
| | | | 70.2 | 15.51 | 11.9 | 68.1 | 18.20 | 7.7 | | | |
| | | | 88.1 | 15.58 | 12.4 | 68.3 | 18.31 | –1.9 | | | |
| | | | 70.1 | 15.63 | 0.1 | 69.1 | 18.35 | –11.4 | | | |
| | | | 86.4 | 15.73 | 39.1 | 68.4 | 18.43 | –9.3 | | | |
| | | | 66.3 | 15.87 | 7.0 | 72.3 | 18.44 | –2.7 | | | |
| | | | 69.4 | 15.95 | –9.6 | 71.4 | 18.48 | 12.4 | | | |
| | | | 62.4 | 16.22 | 27.4 | 72.4 | 18.52 | –1.9 | | | |
| | | | 62.3 | 16.25 | 26.7 | 66.1 | 18.56 | –13.1 | | | |
| | | | 67.2 | 16.25 | 0.0 | 65.4 | 18.59 | –14.9 | | | |
| | | | 87.1 | 16.31 | 2.0 | 63.4 | 18.67 | 17.4 | | | |
| | | | 60.2 | 16.32 | 17.6 | 63.3 | 18.70 | 17.8 | | | |
| | | | 86.2 | 16.35 | 22.1 | 59.3 | 18.80 | –2.7 | | | |
| | | | 60.4 | 16.42 | 24.7 | 72.1 | 18.80 | 15.6 | | | |
| | | | 90.3 | 16.52 | 3.7 | 72.2 | 18.81 | 4.0 | | | |
| | | | 67.3 | 16.63 | 9.9 | 65.2 | 18.94 | 3.6 | | | |
| | | | 59.4 | 16.73 | –5.9 | 64.1 | 18.94 | 13.0 | | | |
| | | | 69.3 | 16.79 | –25.6 | 65.1 | 18.96 | 9.1 | | | |
| | | | 60.3 | 16.79 | 13.6 | 71.3 | 19.10 | 7.5 | | | |
| | | | 68.2 | 16.92 | 12.5 | 59.1 | 19.17 | 8.5 | | | |
| | | | 58.4 | 17.09 | 13.6 | 59.2 | 19.18 | –0.2 | | | |
| | | | 71.1 | 17.19 | 10.8 | 73.1 | 19.23 | –17.4 | | | |
| | | | 66.2 | 17.19 | 1.1 | 64.4 | 19.44 | 6.9 | | | |
| | | | 86.3 | 17.28 | 21.2 | 64.3 | 19.54 | 3.0 | | | |
| | | | 73.2 | 17.37 | –15.7 | 71.2 | 19.55 | 6.9 | | | |
| | | | 60.1 | 17.46 | –3.0 | 64.2 | 19.65 | 9.1 | | | |
| | | | 91.2 | 17.58 | 7.6 | 61.2 | 19.90 | 6.9 | | | |
| | | | 69.2 | 17.62 | –11.7 | 91.4 | 19.98 | 7.7 | | | |
| | | | 91.3 | 17.72 | 10.0 | | | | | | |

---

**Table 9-4.** P/E versus Price Change, Annually, 1927 to 1992

| P/E < 8 | | | 8 < P/E < 20 | | | | | | P/E > 20 | | |
|---|---|---|---|---|---|---|---|---|---|---|---|
| Year | P/E | Price change, % | Year | P/E | Price change, % | Year | P/E | Price change, % | Year | P/E | Price change, % |
| 1949 | 6.64 | 10.3 | 1978 | 8.73 | 1.1 | 1947 | 14.43 | 0.0 | 1939 | 20.64 | −5.5 |
| 1951 | 7.19 | 16.5 | 1981 | 9.16 | −9.7 | 1986 | 14.46 | 14.6 | 1962 | 22.43 | −11.8 |
| 1950 | 7.22 | 21.8 | 1938 | 9.34 | 25.2 | 1967 | 14.47 | 20.1 | 1934 | 22.95 | −5.9 |
| 1980 | 7.26 | 25.8 | 1943 | 9.49 | 19.4 | 1990 | 15.45 | −6.6 | 1992 | 26.12 | 4.5 |
| 1942 | 7.49 | 12.4 | 1948 | 9.50 | −0.7 | 1991 | 15.47 | 26.3 | | | |
| 1975 | 7.71 | 31.5 | 1952 | 9.74 | 11.8 | 1931 | 15.81 | −47.1 | | | |
| 1979 | 7.79 | 12.3 | 1954 | 9.88 | 45.0 | 1928 | 15.91 | 37.9 | | | |
| 1982 | 7.98 | 14.8 | 1985 | 10.05 | 26.3 | 1970 | 15.93 | 0.2 | | | |
| | | | 1941 | 10.08 | −17.9 | 1987 | 16.72 | 2.0 | | | |
| | | | 1977 | 10.84 | −11.5 | 1933 | 16.80 | 46.6 | | | |
| | | | 1927 | 10.88 | 30.9 | 1937 | 16.84 | −38.6 | | | |
| | | | 1953 | 11.07 | −6.6 | 1963 | 17.19 | 18.9 | | | |
| | | | 1983 | 11.13 | 17.3 | 1929 | 17.64 | −11.9 | | | |
| | | | 1976 | 11.33 | 19.1 | 1960 | 17.67 | −3.0 | | | |
| | | | 1989 | 11.69 | 27.3 | 1936 | 17.67 | 27.9 | | | |
| | | | 1984 | 11.76 | 1.4 | 1961 | 17.77 | 23.1 | | | |
| | | | 1958 | 11.87 | 38.1 | 1966 | 17.81 | −13.1 | | | |
| | | | 1974 | 11.95 | −29.7 | 1972 | 17.91 | 15.6 | | | |
| | | | 1944 | 12.41 | 13.8 | 1971 | 17.96 | 10.8 | | | |
| | | | 1956 | 12.56 | 2.6 | 1969 | 18.03 | −11.4 | | | |
| | | | 1955 | 12.99 | 26.4 | 1946 | 18.08 | −11.9 | | | |
| | | | 1932 | 13.31 | −15.1 | 1968 | 18.10 | 7.7 | | | |
| | | | 1930 | 13.32 | −28.5 | 1973 | 18.39 | −17.4 | | | |
| | | | 1957 | 13.69 | −14.3 | 1965 | 18.63 | 9.1 | | | |
| | | | 1940 | 13.88 | −15.3 | 1964 | 18.66 | 13.0 | | | |
| | | | 1988 | 14.12 | 12.4 | 1959 | 19.10 | 8.5 | | | |
| | | | 1945 | 14.28 | 30.7 | 1935 | 19.39 | 41.4 | | | |

ters would have been reported on the date indicated. The data shown here, as in App. 9-1, assume that the last-quarter earnings not yet reported will be accurately estimated. While assumption of complete accuracy is unrealistic, Chap. 9 explains why errors in consensus estimates for the quarter already completed are unlikely to change the identification of extreme P/Es in a significant way.

# 10
# Putting It
# All Together

## Learning from History

### Demonstrating the Underlying Logic

Three prime variables, when reviewed in relation to each other, provide a framework for valuing the stock market. Chapters 7 to 9 review each of these variables individually. This chapter addresses their interaction—in real-time operations as well as in extensive back-testing. We have operated a stock market model in real time since 1982, and our back-tests have covered an accumulation of stock market and economic data since 1926. We direct special attention to our back-test covering 1970 to date, since it is for these years that the necessary array of contemporary data is available.

We explain the valuation rules, as outlined in Table 10-1, in the sections relating to undervaluation, overvaluation, and neutral valuation. The valuation date for the 1970 to 1992 back-test is routinely the first day of each calendar quarter. Table 10-2, summarizing the more detailed information provided in Chaps. 7 to 9, lists the sources currently used to update each prime variable. For the 1970 to 1992 back-test, as explained in Chap. 8, consensus estimates for Treasury bill rates for the four quarters ahead reflect data collected contemporaneously by the *Washington Bond & Money Market Report*.

Consensus estimates based on Treasury bill futures, which

**Table 10-1.** Valuation Rules—Three Prime Variables

| | Dividend growth* | Treasury bill yield change† | P/E‡ |
|---|---|---|---|
| Undervaluation | Weak | Decline 25 BP or more | Under 20 |
| | Neutral/strong | No requirement | Under 8 |
| Overvaluation | Weak | Rise 50 BP or more | Over 8 |
| | Neutral/strong | No requirement | Over 20 |
| Neutral valuation | All combinations not included above | | |

*Dividend growth is weak when the annual rate of change derived from the indicated dividend rate (IDR) is at least 200 basis points less than the current yield on the long Treasury bond.

†Basis points (BP) change refers to the yield on short Treasury bills for the next four quarters less the yield for the last four quarters.

‡P/E is the current market price for the S&P 500 divided by four-quarter trailing earnings.

**Table 10-2.** Sources for Estimates of Prime Variables

| Estimate | Source |
|---|---|
| Dividend % change (Chap. 7) | |
| Second 4 quarters ahead | Benchmark provided by long Treasury bond yield less 1 percent |
| Next 4 quarters | Indicated dividend rate versus last reported 4 quarters, annualized |
| Treasury bill yield (Chap. 8) | |
| Next 4 quarters | Treasury bill futures |
| Last 4 quarters | As reported |
| P/E (Chap. 9) | |
| Current market price | S&P 500 |
| 4-quarter trailing earnings | First 3 reported, last estimated |
| | *or* |
| | Last 4 quarters reported |

have served this purpose in recent years, were not available over most of this period. Note also that our back-test makes use of the alternative method of calculating P/Es, as listed in Table 10-2 and described in Chap. 9. The alternative method leaves no room for ambiguity, since it avoids the need to track consensus estimates to determine the four-quarter earnings just ended (last quarter not yet reported). Rather, it focuses on four-quarter earnings *already reported*, which lag the four-quarter earnings *just ended* by one quarter. The one-quarter lag in earnings may represent a marginal disadvantage, depending on the accuracy imputed to consensus estimates for the quarter just ended. Over the period for which we have data, nevertheless, our studies indicate that both approaches achieve almost the same results.

**How to Identify
Undervaluation**

It is not hard to imagine, in terms of the three measures considered here, the ideal conditions to favor a rise in market price over the subsequent four quarters. First, *business is depressed,* allowing considerable room for recovery. To provide a measure of current business, we assess the potential for dividend growth from the year immediately ahead to the following year (see Chap. 7). The rate of dividend growth in real terms is weak when it drops more than two percentage points below the current yield on long Treasury bonds. The bond yield provides a practical basis of comparison because it adjusts for the same inflationary expectations that enter into appraisal of the rate of nominal dividend growth. Second, *financial conditions favor a business recovery,* implying significant quickening in dividend growth over the second year ahead. At least since World War II, a decline in the four-quarter average of Treasury bill yields by at least 25 basis points (Chap. 8) has signaled business recovery within the framework of a year. Third, *pricing of the stock market* indicates a large potential for improvement in investor confidence. The record suggests that a P/E ratio under 8 implies highly favorable odds (for reasons explained in Chap. 9).

As spelled out in Chap. 7, measures of overvaluation as well as undervaluation include a weak rate of dividend growth. The critical issue is whether the weak rate of dividend growth will soon be followed by a significant upturn (bullish for stock prices) or whether it will persist (bearish for stock prices). In combination with declining interest rates, weak dividend growth implies undervaluation, since dividend growth is likely soon to improve. In combination with rising interest rates, weak dividend growth indicates the opposite conclusion. With the business outlook already poor, rising interest rates—at best—defer prospects for improvement.

## Positive Patterns Signal Average Gain of 20 Percent

Of the 89 quarterly valuation dates since 1970, 36 show positive combinations as described below. In each case, calculation of the prime variables reflects the then-available information (rather than data still to be reported). The stock market rose over 35 of the subsequent 1-year periods and recorded a moderate decline in one. The net market-price gain, on average, was 20 percent.

**Three Favorable Conditions.** Our back-test shows that all three favorable conditions have been met very rarely—at the beginning of only four quarters. Specific valuation dates were the first day of the month for January 1975, October 1981, and April and July 1982. One year later, the stock market was higher in each case, with an average market-price gain of 31 percent.

**Favorable Combination.** For 26 additional valuation dates, the benchmarks were almost as favorable. Again, the rate of dividend growth was depressed, and the consensus looked for a significant decline in interest rates. Although the P/E was above 8, it remained below the 20 level that has proved so vulnerable over the years. The stock market rose in 25 of the 26 one-year periods. The single decline was moderate (–7 percent), and the net gain for the 26 years averaged 18 percent.

**Severely Depressed P/E.** An extremely depressed P/E, accompanied by neutral-to-strong dividend growth, has also provided evidence of undervaluation. On six additional valuation dates, the P/E registered below 8, and the combination of dividend growth and interest rates, viewed independently of the P/E, indicated the neutral category. The stock market rose in each year subsequent to the valuation date, and the gain for the six measurement periods averaged 22 percent.

## Recognizing Overvaluation

In a similar way, the three prime variables outline conditions associated with overvaluation. In total, the three prime variables indicated negative valuation on 22 valuation dates. The stock market subsequently rose in 9 years and declined in 13. The net average *decline* exceeded 3 percent.

**Uniformly Negative Pattern.** At the extreme, a negative reading includes a combination of weak dividend growth and the outlook for rising interest rates. In addition, the P/E is very high—at least 20. In short, (1) the business outlook is worrisome, (2) rising interest rates both hamper business recovery and add to the discount rate applied to investment income, and (3) extreme investor optimism greatly increases the risk of a sudden reversal of expectations. Although highly unlikely, the three prime variables presented a uniformly negative pattern at the beginning of both the third and fourth quarters of 1987. For the two subsequent four-quarter periods, both of which included the October 19 market crash, the market-price *decline* averaged 13 percent.

**Rising Interest Rates Plus Weak Dividend Growth.** Negative valuations were indicated on 20 additional valuation dates. In each case, rising interest rates accompanied weak dividend growth. The P/E remained in the intermediate zone, between 20 and 8. Over the subsequent year, the market price rose 9 times and declined 11 times. The average *decline* was 2 percent.

## Responding to Mixed Signals

For the remaining 31 quarters, the three prime variables provided evidence of neither overvaluation nor undervaluation. As shown below, the neutral category includes all the readings that do not meet the standards established for undervaluation or overvaluation. In the year subsequent to these valuation dates, market price rose 21 times and declined 10 times, with the average gain amounting to 4 percent.

**Price-Earnings Ratio.** The P/E, in all but two instances, was between 20 and 8. The P/E exceeded 20 in one quarter when declining interest rates and weak dividend growth would have otherwise implied a favorable market outlook. On the other occasion, neutral interest rates accompanied weak dividend growth. This combination, although lacking the favorable implications of clearly declining interest rates, still implies significant potential for business recovery. The coincidence of offsetting measures, in each case, explains the neutral valuation. Similarly, a neutral valuation would apply to a P/E under 8 if either rising or neutral interest rates accompanied weak dividend growth. There were no examples during our back-test period.

**Dividend Growth and Interest Rates.** When the P/E is between 20 and 8, market valuation depends on dividend growth and interest rates. For 22 valuation dates, the prospective rate of dividend growth over the four quarters ahead is classified as either neutral or strong. Under these circumstances, the three prime variables attach no significance to short interest rates. Market price, supported by neutral-to-strong dividend growth, often rises in the face of increasing short rates. Even under these conditions, however, rising interest rates continue to bear on stock market valuation. Classification of dividend growth as neutral-to-strong depends on comparison with the *level* of long bond yields. If long bond yields rise sufficiently, reclassification of dividend growth as weak would mean that stock market valuation depends on the consensus estimate for short rates. The neutral valuation also applies when the dividend is weak but expected interest rates are in the neutral range. This combination determined a neutral valuation on seven valuation dates.

## Gaining Advantage with
## Shorter Decision Frequency

Since the three prime variables involve 1-year estimates subject to revision before the year ends, a shorter decision frequency is likely to be advantageous. Our historical simulation, as reported thus far, has been based on annual decision frequency. Although we have provided quarterly valuations, the results cited in our discussion allow a full year for subsequent market-price change. Portfolio implementation consistent with our data would require division of the portfolio into four equal parts. An asset allocation decision for one-fourth of the portfolio would be made each quarter so that each individual decision would remain in force for a year. Our data show that quarterly decision frequency not only avoids partitioning of the portfolio but also may contribute positively to performance. Over 1970 to 1992, quarterly decisions, reflecting diminished influence on valuation of estimate error, added value at a moderately better rate than annual decisions.

Table 10-3 compares the results for quarterly decision frequency with annual decision frequency. The data for annual decision frequency, as described in the previous section, reflect the relevant market change over a 1-year time horizon. For quarterly decision frequency, in contrast, the relevant market change takes place over the next 3 months. The quarterly market-price change is annualized (item 4 of the table), so that it compares directly with the data for four-quarter periods (item 2). Over the back-test period, quarterly decision frequency produced an annualized rate of price change that moderately surpasses the rate indicated for annual decision frequency. These examples omit allowance for transaction costs, which would be too small to alter significantly the comparisons.*

---

*Appendix 10-1 provides in greater detail the 1970 to 1992 data summarized in Table 10-3.

**Table 10-3.** Contemporary Estimates, 1970 to 1992

|  | Stock market valuation | | | |
| --- | --- | --- | --- | --- |
|  | Under | Neutral | Over | Total |
| Annual decision frequency: | | | | |
| 1. S&P 500 (change, next 4Q*) | | | | |
| Number up | 35 | 21 | 9 | 65 |
| Number down | 1 | 10 | 13 | 24 |
| Total 4Q periods | 36 | 31 | 22 | 89 |
| 2. Price change, 4Q average | 20% | 4% | –3% | 9% |
| Quarterly decision frequency: | | | | |
| 3. S&P 500 (change, next Q) | | | | |
| Number up | 26 | 17 | 11 | 54 |
| Number down | 10 | 14 | 11 | 35 |
| Total 1Q periods | 36 | 31 | 22 | 89 |
| 4. Price change | | | | |
| 1Q average | 6% | 0% | –1% | 2% |
| Annualized rate | 25% | 0% | –4% | 9% |

*4Q = four quarters

# How Can These Simple Measures Compete?

### David and Goliath

How can an approach as simple as the three prime variables provide useful information? Dedicated students of the stock market with impressive credentials in economics or investment management generate comprehensive studies of the outlook for stock prices. Isn't it simplistic to expect three simple measures, readily available to everyone, to compete with the thorough efforts of such experts?

Our response takes issue with the premise of the question. The three prime variables never assume a point of view that differs from the collective views of the experts concerning economic prospects. Rather than compete with the experts, the three prime variables rely on the information that they generate. The three prime variables provide a way of organizing and interpreting such information. The current market price is the starting point. Because the stock market is highly efficient, the collective wisdom of the experts—represented by the investor consensus—is rapidly discounted by market prices. Their wisdom also produces the consensus estimates that are embedded in the financial markets. All investment decision makers, irrespective of their investment skill or other resources, have equal access to the consensus information which serves as inputs to the three prime variables.

Note that our position closely, but not completely, parallels the arguments made by the hard-line supporters of the efficient market hypothesis. They argue that the stock market is so efficient that no one should expect to gain advantage. We reply that the stock market is highly efficient but not completely efficient. Within this framework, market prices, on average, have already discounted most of the information relating to the market outlook. The stock market itself, as a storehouse of information, provides the starting point for our analysis. Only a thin margin of slow information is likely to offer opportunity to gain advantage. The challenge in a highly efficient market is to monitor the limited number of clues which help to identify such information. Individually, each clue will likely mean little, but the goal is to identify a combination of clues that, analyzed in relation to each other, provide useful insights.

## What About Other Variables?

Aren't there many other items of information which, if added to the analysis, would improve the valuation? In reply, we stress the trade-off between complexity of implementation and potential for improvement in valuation. Three prime variables cannot incorporate all potentially useful information bearing on the valuation of the stock market. They fill a special role, nevertheless, because they address the three key factors that drive stock prices (business outlook, interest rates, and investor confidence). The investment decision maker would like to assess directly the changes in prospect for each of these three key factors, but they are hidden from view. In their stead, the three prime variables provide visible measures that relate to these three key factors. Other variables may add useful information but at a cost. The search for additional information quickly encounters diminishing returns while rendering the decision process exponentially more complex.

Consider, by way of illustration, a significant change in the foreign-exchange market—specifically, a sharp decline in the foreign-exchange value of the dollar. Following the logic presented in earlier chapters, the importance of this development for stock market valuation will depend on its impact on the business outlook, interest rates, and investor confidence. Clearly, no decision maker can know in advance the full implications, but the three prime variables provide a framework for analysis. The market for Treasury bill futures gauges the likely response of short interest rates, as viewed by the investor consensus, in comparison with interest rates already discounted by market prices. As a practical matter, Treasury bill futures may well begin to anticipate events in foreign-exchange markets before they fully come into view. The long bond yield, incorporated in the analysis of dividend growth, takes into account the influence of foreign-exchange developments on inflation expectations as measured by long rates. The accompanying impact on investor confidence relates in part to the degree of optimism or pessimism already reflected in the relation of market price to earnings and dividends. A change in investor confidence is likely to be especially dangerous when investor optimism is extraordinarily high, as measured by a high P/E (and low dividend yield). The probabilities shift in the other direction when the P/E and dividend yield already give evidence of deep pessimism.

Inflation provides another example of an economic measure which is largely, but not completely, reflected in the three prime variables. At least in recent years, changing levels of inflation have rather quickly translated into changing levels of interest rates. The three prime variables accord considerable weight to both short rates (incorporated in the interest-rate prime variable) and long bond yields (a significant measure included in the dividend-growth prime variable). As indicated in Chap. 6, the two supplemental variables incorporated in our computerized version of the dynamic model include a continuing comparison of inflation with short interest rates. Our work recognizes a contribution from this variable, most likely when the rate of inflation (or deflation) diverges sharply from the level of short interest rates. Such divergences were particularly pronounced in the early 1930s and again shortly after World War II. In view of the sensitivity of interest rates to inflation as demonstrated over the past quarter century, such extreme divergences seem unlikely to be soon repeated.

## This Time Is Different

Will the future repeat the past? Why should the relationships between the three prime variables and the stock market valuation, as documented in the past, apply to a future that will likely differ in many respects?

Our answer restates the question in terms of probability. In financial affairs, surprises will occur at times and past performance cannot guarantee future results. The practical question addresses the probability that relationships observed in the past will continue into the future. Our response accords precedence to the underlying logic. We argue that the logic addresses fundamental relationships which are basic to the valuation of a highly efficient stock market. The breadth of the statistical data, meanwhile, supports the logic. Extended simulation over the 15 years 1955 to 1969 provides essentially the same results as the 23-year (1970 to 1992) back-test that we discussed earlier in this chapter. For real-time operations, moreover, we offer the record of our computerized model over the 11 years from 1982 to 1992. Since the three prime variables are the core of the computerized model, its record, as we shall show, closely parallels the valuations generated by the three prime variables.

Table 10-4, which follows the same format as the 1970 to 1992 back-test shown in Table 10-3, summarizes comparable data over the years 1955 to 1969. In this earlier period, we substituted for the two inputs which did not become available until the later period. In the absence of consensus estimates for Treasury bill yields, we assumed that the estimate for the four quarters ahead

**Table 10-4.** Supplementary Back-Test, 1955 to 1969

|  | Stock market valuation | | | |
|---|---|---|---|---|
|  | Under | Neutral | Over | Total |
| Annual decision frequency: | | | | |
| 1. S&P 500 (change, next 4Q*) | | | | |
| Number up | 6 | 29 | 3 | 38 |
| Number down | 1 | 12 | 9 | 22 |
| Total 4Q periods | 7 | 41 | 12 | 60 |
| 2. Price change, 4Q average | 19% | 8% | –7% | 6% |
| Quarterly decision frequency: | | | | |
| 3. S&P 500 (change, next Q) | | | | |
| Number up | 6 | 29 | 4 | 39 |
| Number down | 1 | 12 | 8 | 21 |
| Total 1Q periods | 7 | 41 | 12 | 60 |
| 4. Price change | | | | |
| 1Q average | 6% | 2% | –2% | 2% |
| Annualized rate | 25% | 9% | –8% | 7% |

*4Q = four quarters

would be the same as the current spot rate. The interest-rate prime variable, therefore, compares the current spot rate with the average yield for the previous four quarters. We also approximated the IDR. We assumed that, if it had been available in these earlier years, it would have anticipated the actual payments over the four quarters to end 6 months ahead (see Chap. 7). The dividend-growth prime variable annualizes the difference between the IDR and four-quarter dividend payments ended 3 months earlier. Following this pattern, the 1955 to 1969 simulation annualizes the difference between dividend payments for the period ended 6 months ahead and the four-quarter dividend payments ended 3 months earlier.*

For a real-time record of the three prime variables in operation,

*Appendix 10-2, following the same format as App. 10-1, provides the detailed data supporting the 1955 to 1969 data summarized in Table 10-4.

we turn to the results of our computerized valuation model. Development of the model takes into account the dynamics of the stock market over the 55 years from 1927 to 1981. We have operated the model in real time since 1982, making use of daily inputs (including supplemental consensus estimates identified in Chap. 6). The model delivers daily assessment of stock market valuation and routinely estimates the degree of overvaluation or undervaluation. Yet, no matter the extent of the refinements, the three prime variables are central to the decision process. The underlying logic concerning their interaction remains essentially the same, whether inputs are processed daily in a computer model or are tracked quarterly with the aid of a pencil and a sheet of paper.

As shown in Fig. 10-1, stock market valuations based on the three prime variables trace over the back-test period the same

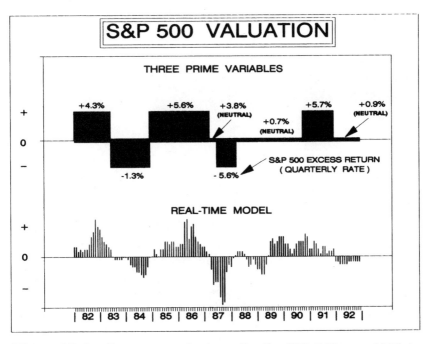

**Figure 10-1.** Comparing valuations for the S&P 500 over 1982 to 1992 as generated by the three prime variables and by the computerized real-time model.

broad pattern as do valuations provided by the real-time model. The two series plotted in Fig. 10-1 indicate valuations (vertical scale) from the beginning of 1982 through 1992 (horizontal scale). The solid black rectangles in the upper segment of the graph represent the valuations (undervalued, overvalued, or neutral) generated by the three prime variables, as determined on the first day of the calendar quarter. In the lower part of the graph, the narrow bars extending in either direction from the baseline display the valuation estimates provided on the first day of each month by the real-time model. For both series, neutral valuation coincides with the baseline. The graph indicates the performance of the stock market for each level of valuation included in the upper series. Over each valuation period, the associated percentage represents the compound *quarterly* rate of excess return for the S&P 500 (total investment return in excess of that for short Treasury bills).*

# Appendix 10-1
# Valuation Data,
# 1970 to 1992

Tables 10-5 and 10-6 list valuation data covering the years 1970 to 1992, as summarized in Table 10-3. Table 10-5 orders the data by valuation, while Table 10-6 lists the same data chronologically. For each table, "1Q70–4Q92" indicates "the first quarter of 1970 to the fourth quarter of 1992." The notation in the first column identifies the year and quarter (i.e., "70.1" signifies "1970, first quarter"). The three prime variables are derived as specified in Table 10-2 with one modification. Next four-quarter Treasury bill yields are derived from consensus surveys compiled by the *Washington Bond & Money Market Report*, as detailed in Table 8-6, rather than Treasury bill futures. $\Delta D_2 - \Delta D_1$ repre-

---

*Appendix 10-3, following the format of Apps. 10-1 and 10-2, lists the 1982 to 1992 quarterly valuations for the three prime variables as plotted in Fig. 10-1.

**Table 10-5.** Stock Market Valuation: Historical Simulation, Contemporary Consensus Estimates for 1Q70–4Q92, Ordered by Valuation

| | Prime variables | | | | | | | Price change | |
| | $\Delta D_2-$ | | | | | | | | |
| Qtr. | $\Delta D_1$ (BP) | $T_1-T_0$ (BP) | $P/E_0$ (-1Q) | Business outlook | Interest rates | Investor confidence | Valuation | Next 4Q % | Next Q % |
|---|---|---|---|---|---|---|---|---|---|
| 75.1 | 326 | –161 | 7.53 | Weak | Declining | Very low | Undervalued | 31.5 | 21.6 |
| 81.4 | 631 | –61 | 7.74 | Weak | Declining | Very low | Undervalued | 3.6 | 5.5 |
| 82.2 | 623 | –102 | 7.29 | Weak | Declining | Very low | Undervalued | 36.6 | –2.1 |
| 82.3 | 975 | –65 | 7.40 | Weak | Declining | Very low | Undervalued | 53.4 | 9.9 |
| 70.2 | 350 | –94 | 15.51 | Weak | Declining | Midrange | Undervalued | 11.9 | –18.9 |
| 70.3 | 651 | –81 | 12.92 | Weak | Declining | Midrange | Undervalued | 37.1 | 15.8 |
| 70.4 | 664 | –111 | 15.26 | Weak | Declining | Midrange | Undervalued | 16.8 | 9.4 |
| 71.1 | 924 | –163 | 17.19 | Weak | Declining | Midrange | Undervalued | 10.8 | 8.9 |
| 71.2 | 748 | –178 | 19.55 | Weak | Declining | Midrange | Undervalued | 6.9 | –0.6 |
| 75.2 | 354 | –223 | 9.38 | Weak | Declining | Midrange | Undervalued | 23.3 | 14.2 |
| 75.3 | 531 | –48 | 11.27 | Weak | Declining | Midrange | Undervalued | 9.5 | –11.9 |
| 80.4 | 344 | –35 | 8.40 | Weak | Declining | Midrange | Undervalued | –7.4 | 8.2 |
| 82.1 | 436 | –352 | 8.03 | Weak | Declining | Midrange | Undervalued | 14.8 | –8.6 |
| 82.4 | 946 | –352 | 8.50 | Weak | Declining | Midrange | Undervalued | 37.9 | 16.8 |
| 83.1 | 878 | –263 | 10.37 | Weak | Declining | Midrange | Undervalued | 17.3 | 8.8 |
| 83.2 | 750 | –98 | 12.10 | Weak | Declining | Midrange | Undervalued | 4.1 | 9.9 |
| 85.1 | 456 | –129 | 10.10 | Weak | Declining | Midrange | Undervalued | 26.3 | 8.0 |
| 85.2 | 426 | –38 | 10.86 | Weak | Declining | Midrange | Undervalued | 32.2 | 6.2 |
| 85.3 | 450 | –139 | 11.71 | Weak | Declining | Midrange | Undervalued | 30.7 | –5.1 |
| 85.4 | 586 | –43 | 11.66 | Weak | Declining | Midrange | Undervalued | 27.0 | 16.0 |
| 86.1 | 465 | –33 | 13.87 | Weak | Declining | Midrange | Undervalued | 14.6 | 13.1 |
| 86.2 | 227 | –88 | 16.35 | Weak | Declining | Midrange | Undervalued | 22.1 | 5.0 |
| 86.3 | 258 | –55 | 17.28 | Weak | Declining | Midrange | Undervalued | 21.2 | –7.8 |
| 86.4 | 480 | –131 | 15.73 | Weak | Declining | Midrange | Undervalued | 39.1 | 4.7 |
| 87.1 | 414 | –77 | 16.31 | Weak | Declining | Midrange | Undervalued | 2.0 | 20.5 |
| 90.4 | 117 | –76 | 14.40 | Weak | Declining | Midrange | Undervalued | 26.7 | 7.9 |
| 91.1 | 113 | –134 | 15.19 | Weak | Declining | Midrange | Undervalued | 26.3 | 13.6 |
| 91.2 | 634 | –154 | 17.58 | Weak | Declining | Midrange | Undervalued | 7.6 | –1.1 |
| 91.3 | 714 | –90 | 17.72 | Weak | Declining | Midrange | Undervalued | 10.0 | 4.5 |
| 91.4 | 657 | –100 | 19.98 | Weak | Declining | Midrange | Undervalued | 7.7 | 7.5 |
| 74.4 | –101 | –72 | 7.27 | Neutral/ strong | Declining | Very low | Undervalued | 32.0 | 7.9 |
| 80.3 | 55 | –423 | 7.47 | Neutral/ strong | Declining | Very low | Undervalued | 14.9 | 9.8 |

Qtr. = Quarter (beginning)
BP = Basis points

*(Continued)*

**Table 10-5.** Stock Market Valuation: Historical Simulation, Contemporary Consensus Estimates for 1Q70–4Q92, Ordered by Valuation (*Continued*)

| | Prime variables | | | | | | | Price change | |
|---|---|---|---|---|---|---|---|---|---|
| Qtr. | $\Delta D_2-$ $\Delta D_1$ (BP) | $T_1-T_0$ (BP) | $P/E_0$ (–1Q) | Business outlook | Interest rates | Investor confidence | Valuation | Next 4Q % | Next Q % |
| 79.3 | –351 | 3 | 7.74 | Neutral/ strong | Neutral | Very low | Undervalued | 11.0 | 6.2 |
| 79.4 | –222 | 33 | 7.82 | Neutral/ strong | Neutral | Very low | Undervalued | 14.8 | –1.3 |
| 80.1 | –298 | 91 | 7.38 | Neutral/ strong | Rising | Very low | Undervalued | 25.8 | –5.4 |
| 80.2 | –230 | 299 | 6.87 | Neutral/ strong | Rising | Very low | Undervalued | 33.2 | 11.9 |
| 92.1 | 793 | –156 | 23.41 | Weak | Declining | Very high | Neutral | 4.5 | –3.2 |
| 92.2 | 611 | –33 | 25.28 | Weak | Declining | Very high | Neutral | | 1.1 |
| 92.3 | 537 | –56 | 25.21 | Weak | Declining | Very high | Neutral | | 2.4 |
| 92.4 | 442 | –101 | 24.50 | Weak | Declining | Very high | Neutral | | 4.3 |
| 70.1 | 375 | 39 | 15.63 | Weak | Neutral | Midrange | Neutral | 0.1 | –2.6 |
| 71.3 | 627 | 47 | 19.10 | Weak | Neutral | Midrange | Neutral | 7.5 | –1.4 |
| 71.4 | 670 | 42 | 18.48 | Weak | Neutral | Midrange | Neutral | 12.4 | 3.8 |
| 72.1 | 626 | –7 | 18.80 | Weak | Neutral | Midrange | Neutral | 15.6 | 5.0 |
| 76.1 | 813 | 25 | 11.62 | Weak | Neutral | Midrange | Neutral | 19.1 | 13.9 |
| 76.2 | 583 | 13 | 12.91 | Weak | Neutral | Midrange | Neutral | –4.2 | 1.5 |
| 76.4 | 114 | 40 | 11.38 | Weak | Neutral | Midrange | Neutral | –8.3 | 2.1 |
| 87.2 | 309 | 3 | 20.15 | Weak | Neutral | Very high | Neutral | –11.2 | 4.2 |
| 74.3 | –24 | –49 | 10.29 | Neutral/ strong | Declining | Midrange | Neutral | 10.7 | –26.1 |
| 89.4 | –690 | –26 | 13.84 | Neutral/ strong | Declining | Midrange | Neutral | –12.3 | 1.2 |
| 90.1 | –384 | –83 | 14.92 | Neutral/ strong | Declining | Midrange | Neutral | –6.6 | –3.8 |
| 90.2 | –213 | –27 | 14.86 | Neutral/ strong | Declining | Midrange | Neutral | 10.4 | 5.3 |
| 90.3 | –190 | –39 | 16.52 | Neutral/ strong | Declining | Midrange | Neutral | 3.7 | –14.5 |
| 74.1 | –230 | –4 | 12.69 | Neutral/ strong | Neutral | Midrange | Neutral | –29.7 | –3.7 |
| 74.2 | –106 | 7 | 11.52 | Neutral/ strong | Neutral | Midrange | Neutral | –11.3 | –8.5 |

Qtr. = Quarter (beginning)
BP = Basis points

**Table 10-5.** Stock Market Valuation: Historical Simulation, Contemporary Consensus Estimates for 1Q70–4Q92, Ordered by Valuation (*Continued*)

| | Prime variables | | | | | | | Price change | |
|---|---|---|---|---|---|---|---|---|---|
| | $\Delta D_2-$ | | | | | | | Next | Next |
| Qtr. | $\Delta D_1$ (BP) | $T_1-T_0$ (BP) | $P/E_0$ (–1Q) | Business outlook | Interest rates | Investor confidence | Valuation | 4Q % | Q % |
| 77.1 | –279 | –16 | 11.25 | Neutral/ strong | Neutral | Midrange | Neutral | –11.5 | –8.4 |
| 77.2 | –480 | 40 | 9.93 | Neutral/ strong | Neutral | Midrange | Neutral | –9.4 | 2.1 |
| 89.3 | –868 | 40 | 12.74 | Neutral/ strong | Neutral | Midrange | Neutral | 12.6 | 9.8 |
| 77.3 | –523 | 78 | 9.97 | Neutral/ strong | Rising | Midrange | Neutral | –4.9 | –3.9 |
| 77.4 | –223 | 161 | 9.26 | Neutral/ strong | Rising | Midrange | Neutral | 6.2 | –1.5 |
| 78.1 | –216 | 154 | 8.88 | Neutral/ strong | Rising | Midrange | Neutral | 1.1 | –6.2 |
| 78.2 | –211 | 133 | 8.19 | Neutral/ strong | Rising | Midrange | Neutral | 13.9 | 7.1 |
| 78.3 | 15 | 163 | 8.75 | Neutral/ strong | Rising | Midrange | Neutral | 7.7 | 7.3 |
| 78.4 | 81 | 224 | 9.13 | Neutral/ strong | Rising | Midrange | Neutral | 6.6 | –6.3 |
| 79.2 | –40 | 178 | 8.24 | Neutral/ strong | Rising | Midrange | Neutral | 0.5 | 1.3 |
| 88.2 | 59 | 85 | 14.79 | Neutral/ strong | Rising | Midrange | Neutral | 13.9 | 5.6 |
| 88.3 | –405 | 162 | 14.71 | Neutral/ strong | Rising | Midrange | Neutral | 16.3 | –0.6 |
| 88.4 | –209 | 195 | 12.55 | Neutral/ strong | Rising | Midrange | Neutral | 28.4 | 2.1 |
| 89.1 | –323 | 237 | 12.22 | Neutral/ strong | Rising | Midrange | Neutral | 27.3 | 6.2 |
| 89.2 | –651 | 222 | 12.42 | Neutral/ strong | Rising | Midrange | Neutral | 15.3 | 7.8 |
| 72.2 | 470 | 50 | 18.81 | Weak | Rising | Midrange | Overvalued | 4.0 | –0.1 |
| 72.3 | 333 | 91 | 18.44 | Weak | Rising | Midrange | Overvalued | –2.7 | 3.2 |
| 72.4 | 419 | 164 | 18.52 | Weak | Rising | Midrange | Overvalued | –1.9 | 6.8 |
| 73.1 | 109 | 186 | 19.23 | Weak | Rising | Midrange | Overvalued | –17.4 | –5.5 |
| 73.2 | 374 | 243 | 17.37 | Weak | Rising | Midrange | Overvalued | –15.7 | –6.5 |

Qtr. = Quarter (beginning)                                              (*Continued*)
BP = Basis points

**Table 10-5.** Stock Market Valuation: Historical Simulation, Contemporary Consensus Estimates for 1Q70–4Q92, Ordered by Valuation (*Continued*)

| | Prime variables | | | | | | | Price change | |
|---|---|---|---|---|---|---|---|---|---|
| Qtr. | $\Delta D_2-$ $\Delta D_1$ (BP) | $T_1-T_0$ (BP) | $P/E_0$ $(-1Q)$ | Business outlook | Interest rates | Investor confidence | Valuation | Next 4Q % | Next Q % |
| 73.3 | 442 | 262 | 15.33 | Weak | Rising | Midrange | Overvalued | −17.5 | 4.0 |
| 73.4 | 148 | 93 | 15.00 | Weak | Rising | Midrange | Overvalued | −41.4 | −10.0 |
| 75.4 | 762 | 96 | 10.54 | Weak | Rising | Midrange | Overvalued | 25.5 | 7.5 |
| 76.3 | 237 | 55 | 12.04 | Weak | Rising | Midrange | Overvalued | −3.6 | 0.9 |
| 79.1 | 293 | 260 | 8.31 | Weak | Rising | Midrange | Overvalued | 12.3 | 5.7 |
| 81.1 | 506 | 194 | 9.27 | Weak | Rising | Midrange | Overvalued | −9.7 | 0.2 |
| 81.2 | 369 | 74 | 9.18 | Weak | Rising | Midrange | Overvalued | −17.7 | −3.5 |
| 81.3 | 397 | 127 | 9.00 | Weak | Rising | Midrange | Overvalued | −16.5 | −11.5 |
| 83.3 | 730 | 59 | 13.54 | Weak | Rising | Midrange | Overvalued | −8.9 | −1.2 |
| 83.4 | 750 | 70 | 13.19 | Weak | Rising | Midrange | Overvalued | 0.0 | −0.7 |
| 84.1 | 830 | 81 | 12.40 | Weak | Rising | Midrange | Overvalued | 1.4 | −3.5 |
| 84.2 | 739 | 124 | 11.35 | Weak | Rising | Midrange | Overvalued | 13.5 | −3.8 |
| 84.3 | 754 | 156 | 10.04 | Weak | Rising | Midrange | Overvalued | 25.2 | 8.4 |
| 84.4 | 734 | 156 | 10.25 | Weak | Rising | Midrange | Overvalued | 9.6 | 0.7 |
| 88.1 | 158 | 69 | 15.58 | Weak | Rising | Midrange | Overvalued | 12.4 | 4.8 |
| 87.3 | 138 | 52 | 20.13 | Weak | Rising | Very high | Overvalued | −10.0 | 5.9 |
| 87.4 | 423 | 175 | 22.32 | Weak | Rising | Very high | Overvalued | −15.5 | −23.2 |

Qtr. = Quarter (beginning)
BP = Basis points

sents dividend change second four quarters ahead less dividend change over the next four quarters. $T_1-T_0$ identifies average Treasury bill yield next four quarters less average over last four quarters. "$P/E_0(-1Q)$" measures the price-earnings ratio based on current price and last-reported four-quarter earnings. "$(-1Q)$" indicates that last-reported four-quarter earnings are lagged by one quarter. The last two columns detail the S&P 500 price change for the next four quarters and the next quarter, respectively.

**Table 10-6.** Stock Market Valuation: Historical Simulation,
Contemporary Consensus Estimates, 1Q70–4Q92, Chronological

| Qtr. | $\Delta D_1$ (BP) | $\Delta D_2-$ $T_1-T_0$ (BP) | Prime variables P/E$_0$ (–1Q) | Business outlook | Interest rates | Investor confidence | Valuation | Price change Next 4Q % | Next Q % |
|------|------|------|------|------|------|------|------|------|------|
| 70.1 | 375 | 39 | 15.63 | Weak | Neutral | Midrange | Neutral | 0.1 | –2.6 |
| 70.2 | 350 | –94 | 15.51 | Weak | Declining | Midrange | Undervalued | 11.9 | –18.9 |
| 70.3 | 651 | –81 | 12.92 | Weak | Declining | Midrange | Undervalued | 37.1 | 15.8 |
| 70.4 | 664 | –111 | 15.26 | Weak | Declining | Midrange | Undervalued | 16.8 | 9.4 |
| 71.1 | 924 | –163 | 17.19 | Weak | Declining | Midrange | Undervalued | 10.8 | 8.9 |
| 71.2 | 748 | –178 | 19.55 | Weak | Declining | Midrange | Undervalued | 6.9 | –0.6 |
| 71.3 | 627 | 47 | 19.10 | Weak | Neutral | Midrange | Neutral | 7.5 | –1.4 |
| 71.4 | 670 | 42 | 18.48 | Weak | Neutral | Midrange | Neutral | 12.4 | 3.8 |
| 72.1 | 626 | –7 | 18.80 | Weak | Neutral | Midrange | Neutral | 15.6 | 5.0 |
| 72.2 | 470 | 50 | 18.81 | Weak | Rising | Midrange | Overvalued | 4.0 | –0.1 |
| 72.3 | 333 | 91 | 18.44 | Weak | Rising | Midrange | Overvalued | –2.7 | 3.2 |
| 72.4 | 419 | 164 | 18.52 | Weak | Rising | Midrange | Overvalued | –1.9 | 6.8 |
| 73.1 | 109 | 186 | 19.23 | Weak | Rising | Midrange | Overvalued | –17.4 | –5.5 |
| 73.2 | 374 | 243 | 17.37 | Weak | Rising | Midrange | Overvalued | –15.7 | –6.5 |
| 73.3 | 442 | 262 | 15.33 | Weak | Rising | Midrange | Overvalued | –17.5 | 4.0 |
| 73.4 | 148 | 93 | 15.00 | Weak | Rising | Midrange | Overvalued | –41.4 | –10.0 |
| 74.1 | –230 | –4 | 12.69 | Neutral/ strong | Neutral | Midrange | Neutral | –29.7 | –3.7 |
| 74.2 | –106 | 7 | 11.52 | Neutral/ strong | Neutral | Midrange | Neutral | –11.3 | –8.5 |
| 74.3 | –24 | –49 | 10.29 | Neutral/ strong | Declining | Midrange | Neutral | 10.7 | –26.1 |
| 74.4 | –101 | –72 | 7.27 | Neutral/ strong | Declining | Very low | Undervalued | 32.0 | 7.9 |
| 75.1 | 326 | –161 | 7.53 | Weak | Declining | Very low | Undervalued | 31.5 | 21.6 |
| 75.2 | 354 | –223 | 9.38 | Weak | Declining | Midrange | Undervalued | 23.3 | 14.2 |
| 75.3 | 531 | –48 | 11.27 | Weak | Declining | Midrange | Undervalued | 9.5 | –11.9 |
| 75.4 | 762 | 96 | 10.54 | Weak | Rising | Midrange | Overvalued | 25.5 | 7.5 |
| 76.1 | 813 | 25 | 11.62 | Weak | Neutral | Midrange | Neutral | 19.1 | 13.9 |
| 76.2 | 583 | 13 | 12.91 | Weak | Neutral | Midrange | Neutral | –4.2 | 1.5 |
| 76.3 | 237 | 55 | 12.04 | Weak | Rising | Midrange | Overvalued | –3.6 | 0.9 |
| 76.4 | 114 | 40 | 11.38 | Weak | Neutral | Midrange | Neutral | –8.3 | 2.1 |

Qtr. = Quarter (beginning)    (*Continued*)
BP = Basis points

**Table 10-6.** Stock Market Valuation: Historical Simulation, Contemporary Consensus Estimates, 1Q70–4Q92, Chronological (*Continued*)

| Qtr. | $\Delta D_2-$ $\Delta D_1$ (BP) | $T_1-T_0$ (BP) | $P/E_0$ (–1Q) | Business outlook | Interest rates | Investor confidence | Valuation | Next 4Q % | Next Q % |
|------|------|------|------|------|------|------|------|------|------|
| 77.1 | –279 | –16 | 11.25 | Neutral/ strong | Neutral | Midrange | Neutral | –11.5 | –8.4 |
| 77.2 | –480 | 40 | 9.93 | Neutral/ strong | Neutral | Midrange | Neutral | –9.4 | 2.1 |
| 77.3 | –523 | 78 | 9.97 | Neutral/ strong | Rising | Midrange | Neutral | –4.9 | –3.9 |
| 77.4 | –223 | 161 | 9.26 | Neutral/ strong | Rising | Midrange | Neutral | 6.2 | –1.5 |
| 78.1 | –216 | 154 | 8.88 | Neutral/ strong | Rising | Midrange | Neutral | 1.1 | –6.2 |
| 78.2 | –211 | 133 | 8.19 | Neutral/ strong | Rising | Midrange | Neutral | 13.9 | 7.1 |
| 78.3 | 15 | 163 | 8.75 | Neutral/ strong | Rising | Midrange | Neutral | 7.7 | 7.3 |
| 78.4 | 81 | 224 | 9.13 | Neutral/ strong | Rising | Midrange | Neutral | 6.6 | –6.3 |
| 79.1 | 293 | 260 | 8.31 | Weak | Rising | Midrange | Overvalued | 12.3 | 5.7 |
| 79.2 | –40 | 178 | 8.24 | Neutral/ strong | Rising | Midrange | Neutral | 0.5 | 1.3 |
| 79.3 | –351 | 3 | 7.74 | Neutral/ strong | Neutral | Very low | Undervalued | 11.0 | 6.2 |
| 79.4 | –222 | 33 | 7.82 | Neutral/ strong | Neutral | Very low | Undervalued | 14.8 | –1.3 |
| 80.1 | –298 | 91 | 7.38 | Neutral/ strong | Rising | Very low | Undervalued | 25.8 | –5.4 |
| 80.2 | –230 | 299 | 6.87 | Neutral/ strong | Rising | Very low | Undervalued | 33.2 | 11.9 |
| 80.3 | 55 | –423 | 7.47 | Neutral/ strong | Declining | Very low | Undervalued | 14.9 | 9.8 |
| 80.4 | 344 | –35 | 8.40 | Weak | Declining | Midrange | Undervalued | –7.4 | 8.2 |
| 81.1 | 506 | 194 | 9.27 | Weak | Rising | Midrange | Overvalued | –9.7 | 0.2 |
| 81.2 | 369 | 74 | 9.18 | Weak | Rising | Midrange | Overvalued | –17.7 | –3.5 |

Qtr. = Quarter (beginning)
BP = Basis points

**Table 10-6.** Stock Market Valuation: Historical Simulation, Contemporary Consensus Estimates, 1Q70–4Q92, Chronological (*Continued*)

| Qtr. | $\Delta D_1$ (BP) | $T_1 - T_0$ (BP) | $P/E_0$ (-1Q) | Business outlook | Interest rates | Investor confidence | Valuation | Next 4Q % | Next Q % |
|------|------|------|------|------|------|------|------|------|------|
| | | | | | | | | Price change | |
| | $\Delta D_2-$ $\Delta D_1$ | | | | | | | | |
| 81.3 | 397 | 127 | 9.00 | Weak | Rising | Midrange | Overvalued | –16.5 | –11.5 |
| 81.4 | 631 | –61 | 7.74 | Weak | Declining | Very low | Undervalued | 3.6 | 5.5 |
| 82.1 | 436 | –352 | 8.03 | Weak | Declining | Midrange | Undervalued | 14.8 | –8.6 |
| 82.2 | 623 | –102 | 7.29 | Weak | Declining | Very low | Undervalued | 36.6 | –2.1 |
| 82.3 | 975 | –65 | 7.40 | Weak | Declining | Very low | Undervalued | 53.4 | 9.9 |
| 82.4 | 946 | –352 | 8.50 | Weak | Declining | Midrange | Undervalued | 37.9 | 16.8 |
| 83.1 | 878 | –263 | 10.37 | Weak | Declining | Midrange | Undervalued | 17.3 | 8.8 |
| 83.2 | 750 | –98 | 12.10 | Weak | Declining | Midrange | Undervalued | 4.1 | 9.9 |
| 83.3 | 730 | 59 | 13.54 | Weak | Rising | Midrange | Overvalued | –8.9 | –1.2 |
| 83.4 | 750 | 70 | 13.19 | Weak | Rising | Midrange | Overvalued | 0.0 | –0.7 |
| 84.1 | 830 | 81 | 12.40 | Weak | Rising | Midrange | Overvalued | 1.4 | –3.5 |
| 84.2 | 739 | 124 | 11.35 | Weak | Rising | Midrange | Overvalued | 13.5 | –3.8 |
| 84.3 | 754 | 156 | 10.04 | Weak | Rising | Midrange | Overvalued | 25.2 | 8.4 |
| 84.4 | 734 | 156 | 10.25 | Weak | Rising | Midrange | Overvalued | 9.6 | 0.7 |
| 85.1 | 456 | –129 | 10.10 | Weak | Declining | Midrange | Undervalued | 26.3 | 8.0 |
| 85.2 | 426 | –38 | 10.86 | Weak | Declining | Midrange | Undervalued | 32.2 | 6.2 |
| 85.3 | 450 | –139 | 11.71 | Weak | Declining | Midrange | Undervalued | 30.7 | –5.1 |
| 85.4 | 586 | –43 | 11.66 | Weak | Declining | Midrange | Undervalued | 27.0 | 16.0 |
| 86.1 | 465 | –33 | 13.87 | Weak | Declining | Midrange | Undervalued | 14.6 | 13.1 |
| 86.2 | 227 | –88 | 16.35 | Weak | Declining | Midrange | Undervalued | 22.1 | 5.0 |
| 86.3 | 258 | –55 | 17.28 | Weak | Declining | Midrange | Undervalued | 21.2 | –7.8 |
| 86.4 | 480 | –131 | 15.73 | Weak | Declining | Midrange | Undervalued | 39.1 | 4.7 |
| 87.1 | 414 | –77 | 16.31 | Weak | Declining | Midrange | Undervalued | 2.0 | 20.5 |
| 87.2 | 309 | 3 | 20.15 | Weak | Neutral | Very high | Neutral | –11.2 | 4.2 |
| 87.3 | 138 | 52 | 20.13 | Weak | Rising | Very high | Overvalued | –10.0 | 5.9 |
| 87.4 | 423 | 175 | 22.32 | Weak | Rising | Very high | Overvalued | –15.5 | –23.2 |
| 88.1 | 158 | 69 | 15.58 | Weak | Rising | Midrange | Overvalued | 12.4 | 4.8 |
| 88.2 | 59 | 85 | 14.79 | Neutral/ strong | Rising | Midrange | Neutral | 13.9 | 5.6 |
| 88.3 | –405 | 162 | 14.71 | Neutral/ strong | Rising | Midrange | Neutral | 16.3 | –0.6 |

Qtr. = Quarter (beginning)                                           (*Continued*)
BP = Basis points

Understanding the Pitfalls and Opportunities

**Table 10-6.** Stock Market Valuation: Historical Simulation, Contemporary Consensus Estimates, 1Q70–4Q92, Chronological (*Continued*)

| | Prime variables | | | | | | | Price change | |
|---|---|---|---|---|---|---|---|---|---|
| | $\Delta D_2-$ $\Delta D_1$ | $T_1-T_0$ | $P/E_0$ | Business | Interest | Investor | | Next | Next |
| Qtr. | (BP) | (BP) | (–1Q) | outlook | rates | confidence | Valuation | 4Q % | Q % |
| 88.4 | –209 | 195 | 12.55 | Neutral/ strong | Rising | Midrange | Neutral | 28.4 | 2.1 |
| 89.1 | –323 | 237 | 12.22 | Neutral/ strong | Rising | Midrange | Neutral | 27.3 | 6.2 |
| 89.2 | –651 | 222 | 12.42 | Neutral/ strong | Rising | Midrange | Neutral | 15.3 | 7.8 |
| 89.3 | –868 | 40 | 12.74 | Neutral/ strong | Neutral | Midrange | Neutral | 12.6 | 9.8 |
| 89.4 | –690 | –26 | 13.84 | Neutral/ strong | Declining | Midrange | Neutral | –12.3 | 1.2 |
| 90.1 | –384 | –83 | 14.92 | Neutral/ strong | Declining | Midrange | Neutral | –6.6 | –3.8 |
| 90.2 | –213 | –27 | 14.86 | Neutral/ strong | Declining | Midrange | Neutral | 10.4 | 5.3 |
| 90.3 | –190 | –39 | 16.52 | Neutral/ strong | Declining | Midrange | Neutral | 3.7 | –14.5 |
| 90.4 | 117 | –76 | 14.40 | Weak | Declining | Midrange | Undervalued | 26.7 | 7.9 |
| 91.1 | 113 | –134 | 15.19 | Weak | Declining | Midrange | Undervalued | 26.3 | 13.6 |
| 91.2 | 634 | –154 | 17.58 | Weak | Declining | Midrange | Undervalued | 7.6 | –1.1 |
| 91.3 | 714 | –90 | 17.72 | Weak | Declining | Midrange | Undervalued | 10.0 | 4.5 |
| 91.4 | 657 | –100 | 19.98 | Weak | Declining | Midrange | Undervalued | 7.7 | 7.5 |
| 92.1 | 793 | –156 | 23.41 | Weak | Declining | Very high | Neutral | 4.5 | –3.2 |
| 92.2 | 611 | –33 | 25.28 | Weak | Declining | Very high | Neutral | | 1.1 |
| 92.3 | 537 | –56 | 25.21 | Weak | Declining | Very high | Neutral | | 2.4 |
| 92.4 | 442 | –101 | 24.50 | Weak | Declining | Very high | Neutral | | 4.3 |

Qtr. = Quarter (beginning)

BP = Basis points

# Appendix 10-2
# Valuation Data,
# 1955 to 1969

Tables 10-7 and 10-8 list valuation data covering the years 1955 to 1969, as summarized in Table 10-4. Table 10-7 orders the data

**Table 10-7.** Stock Market Valuation: Historical Simulation, 1Q55–4Q69, Ordered by Valuation

| | Prime variables | | | | | | | Price change | |
| | $\Delta D_2-$ | | | | | | | | |
| Qtr. | $\Delta D_1$ (BP) | $T_1-T_0$ (BP) | $P/E_0$ (−1Q) | Business outlook | Interest rates | Investor confidence | Valuation | Next 4Q % | Next Q % |
|---|---|---|---|---|---|---|---|---|---|
| 58.2 | 668 | −197 | 12.49 | Weak | Declining | Midrange | Undervalued | 31.7 | 7.5 |
| 58.3 | 375 | −156 | 14.41 | Weak | Declining | Midrange | Undervalued | 29.2 | 10.7 |
| 60.3 | 238 | −172 | 16.79 | Weak | Declining | Midrange | Undervalued | 13.6 | −6.0 |
| 60.4 | 355 | −42 | 16.42 | Weak | Declining | Midrange | Undervalued | 24.7 | 8.6 |
| 61.1 | 348 | −35 | 17.77 | Weak | Declining | Midrange | Undervalued | 23.1 | 12.0 |
| 67.2 | 123 | −86 | 16.25 | Weak | Declining | Midrange | Undervalued | 0.0 | 0.5 |
| 67.3 | 315 | −77 | 16.63 | Weak | Declining | Midrange | Undervalued | 9.9 | 6.7 |
| 58.1 | 450 | 26 | 11.52 | Weak | Neutral | Midrange | Neutral | 38.1 | 5.3 |
| 61.2 | 229 | −16 | 19.90 | Weak | Neutral | Midrange | Neutral | 6.9 | −0.6 |
| 67.4 | 187 | 43 | 18.14 | Weak | Neutral | Midrange | Neutral | 6.2 | −0.2 |
| 60.2 | −563 | −93 | 16.32 | Neutral/ strong | Declining | Midrange | Neutral | 17.6 | 2.9 |
| 55.1 | −735 | 11 | 13.68 | Neutral/ strong | Neutral | Midrange | Neutral | 26.4 | 1.7 |
| 55.2 | −505 | 45 | 13.21 | Neutral/ strong | Neutral | Midrange | Neutral | 32.5 | 12.2 |
| 55.3 | −491 | 18 | 13.86 | Neutral/ strong | Neutral | Midrange | Neutral | 14.5 | 6.4 |
| 56.2 | −1423 | 34 | 13.39 | Neutral/ strong | Neutral | Midrange | Neutral | −9.0 | −3.1 |
| 57.2 | 78 | 47 | 12.94 | Neutral/ strong | Neutral | Midrange | Neutral | −4.6 | 7.4 |
| 57.4 | −44 | 47 | 12.40 | Neutral/ strong | Neutral | Midrange | Neutral | 18.0 | −5.7 |
| 58.4 | −28 | 43 | 17.09 | Neutral/ strong | Neutral | Midrange | Neutral | 13.6 | 10.3 |
| 63.1 | −474 | 36 | 17.88 | Neutral/ strong | Neutral | Midrange | Neutral | 18.9 | 5.5 |
| 63.2 | −200 | 29 | 18.14 | Neutral/ strong | Neutral | Midrange | Neutral | 18.6 | 4.2 |
| 63.3 | −499 | 43 | 18.70 | Neutral/ strong | Neutral | Midrange | Neutral | 17.8 | 3.4 |

Qtr. = Quarter (beginning)                                                    (*Continued*)
BP = Basis points

**Table 10-7.** Stock Market Valuation: Historical Simulation, 1Q55–4Q69, Ordered by Valuation (*Continued*)

| | Prime variables | | | | | | | Price change | |
| | $\Delta D_2$– | | | | | | | | |
| Qtr. | $\Delta D_1$ (BP) | $T_1$–$T_0$ (BP) | $P/E_0$ (–1Q) | Business outlook | Interest rates | Investor confidence | Valuation | Next 4Q % | Next Q % |
|---|---|---|---|---|---|---|---|---|---|
| 64.1 | –709 | 44 | 18.94 | Neutral/ strong | Neutral | Midrange | Neutral | 13.0 | 5.3 |
| 64.2 | –612 | 31 | 19.65 | Neutral/ strong | Neutral | Midrange | Neutral | 9.1 | 3.4 |
| 64.3 | –654 | 20 | 19.54 | Neutral/ strong | Neutral | Midrange | Neutral | 3.0 | 3.0 |
| 64.4 | –631 | 6 | 19.44 | Neutral/ strong | Neutral | Midrange | Neutral | 6.9 | 0.7 |
| 65.1 | –606 | –3 | 18.96 | Neutral/ strong | Neutral | Midrange | Neutral | 9.1 | 1.7 |
| 65.2 | –531 | 10 | 18.94 | Neutral/ strong | Neutral | Midrange | Neutral | 3.6 | –2.4 |
| 65.3 | –566 | 7 | 17.97 | Neutral/ strong | Neutral | Midrange | Neutral | 0.7 | 6.9 |
| 65.4 | –535 | 5 | 18.59 | Neutral/ strong | Neutral | Midrange | Neutral | –14.9 | 2.7 |
| 66.2 | –473 | 6 | 17.19 | Neutral/ strong | Neutral | Midrange | Neutral | 1.1 | –5.0 |
| 66.3 | –55 | 3 | 15.87 | Neutral/ strong | Neutral | Midrange | Neutral | 7.0 | –9.7 |
| 68.4 | –60 | 39 | 18.43 | Neutral/ strong | Neutral | Midrange | Neutral | –9.3 | 1.2 |
| 55.4 | –1161 | 95 | 13.56 | Neutral/ strong | Rising | Midrange | Neutral | 3.8 | 4.1 |
| 56.1 | –1286 | 114 | 13.22 | Neutral/ strong | Rising | Midrange | Neutral | 2.6 | 6.6 |
| 57.3 | –201 | 81 | 13.93 | Neutral/ strong | Rising | Midrange | Neutral | –4.5 | –10.4 |
| 59.1 | –180 | 91 | 19.17 | Neutral/ strong | Rising | Midrange | Neutral | 8.5 | 0.4 |
| 59.2 | –154 | 78 | 19.18 | Neutral/ strong | Rising | Midrange | Neutral | –0.2 | 5.5 |
| 59.3 | –133 | 96 | 18.80 | Neutral/ strong | Rising | Midrange | Neutral | –2.7 | –2.7 |

Qtr. = Quarter (beginning)
BP = Basis points

**Table 10-7.** Stock Market Valuation: Historical Simulation, 1Q55–4Q69, Ordered by Valuation (*Continued*)

| | Prime variables | | | | | | | Price change | |
| Qtr. | $\Delta D_2-$ $\Delta D_1$ (BP) | $T_1-T_0$ (BP) | $P/E_0$ (-1Q) | Business outlook | Interest rates | Investor confidence | Valuation | Next 4Q % | Next Q % |
|---|---|---|---|---|---|---|---|---|---|
| 59.4 | −788 | 110 | 16.73 | Neutral/ strong | Rising | Midrange | Neutral | −5.9 | 5.3 |
| 60.1 | −684 | 109 | 17.46 | Neutral/ strong | Rising | Midrange | Neutral | −3.0 | −7.6 |
| 62.3 | −287 | 84 | 16.25 | Neutral/ strong | Rising | Midrange | Neutral | 26.7 | 2.8 |
| 62.4 | −285 | 53 | 16.22 | Neutral/ strong | Rising | Midrange | Neutral | 27.4 | 12.1 |
| 63.4 | −478 | 62 | 18.67 | Neutral/ strong | Rising | Midrange | Neutral | 17.4 | 4.6 |
| 66.1 | −502 | 71 | 18.56 | Neutral/ strong | Rising | Midrange | Neutral | −13.1 | −3.5 |
| 66.4 | 50 | 109 | 14.02 | Neutral/ strong | Rising | Midrange | Neutral | 26.3 | 4.9 |
| 68.2 | −42 | 108 | 16.92 | Neutral/ strong | Rising | Midrange | Neutral | 12.5 | 10.4 |
| 68.3 | −108 | 132 | 18.31 | Neutral/ strong | Rising | Midrange | Neutral | −1.9 | 3.1 |
| 69.1 | 58 | 133 | 18.35 | Neutral/ strong | Rising | Midrange | Neutral | −11.4 | −2.3 |
| 56.3 | 122 | 50 | 12.73 | Weak | Rising | Midrange | Overvalued | 0.9 | −3.4 |
| 56.4 | 743 | 76 | 12.60 | Weak | Rising | Midrange | Overvalued | −6.5 | 2.9 |
| 57.1 | 1042 | 78 | 13.49 | Weak | Rising | Midrange | Overvalued | −14.3 | −5.5 |
| 67.1 | 309 | 53 | 14.58 | Weak | Rising | Midrange | Overvalued | 20.1 | 12.3 |
| 68.1 | 136 | 72 | 18.20 | Weak | Rising | Midrange | Overvalued | 7.7 | −6.5 |
| 69.2 | 173 | 108 | 17.62 | Weak | Rising | Midrange | Overvalued | −11.7 | −3.7 |
| 69.3 | 265 | 83 | 16.79 | Weak | Rising | Midrange | Overvalued | −25.6 | −4.7 |
| 69.4 | 407 | 130 | 15.95 | Weak | Rising | Midrange | Overvalued | −9.6 | −1.1 |
| 61.3 | −246 | 15 | 20.92 | Neutral/ strong | Neutral | Very high | Overvalued | −15.3 | 3.2 |
| 61.4 | −384 | 13 | 22.02 | Neutral/ strong | Neutral | Very high | Overvalued | −15.7 | 7.2 |
| 62.1 | −365 | 76 | 23.46 | Neutral/ strong | Rising | Very high | Overvalued | −11.8 | −2.8 |
| 62.2 | −98 | 51 | 21.80 | Neutral/ strong | Rising | Very high | Overvalued | −4.3 | −21.3 |

Qtr. = Quarter (beginning)
BP = Basis points

**Table 10-8.** Stock Market Valuation: Historical Simulation, 1Q55–4Q69, Chronological

| Qtr. | Prime variables | | | Business outlook | Interest rates | Investor confidence | Valuation | Price change | |
|---|---|---|---|---|---|---|---|---|---|
| | $\Delta D_2 - \Delta D_1$ (BP) | $T_1 - T_0$ (BP) | $P/E_0$ (−1Q) | | | | | Next 4Q % | Next Q % |
| 55.1 | −735 | 11 | 13.68 | Neutral/strong | Neutral | Midrange | Neutral | 26.4 | 1.7 |
| 55.2 | −505 | 45 | 13.21 | Neutral/strong | Neutral | Midrange | Neutral | 32.5 | 12.2 |
| 55.3 | −491 | 18 | 13.86 | Neutral/strong | Neutral | Midrange | Neutral | 14.5 | 6.4 |
| 55.4 | −1161 | 95 | 13.56 | Neutral/strong | Rising | Midrange | Neutral | 3.8 | 4.1 |
| 56.1 | −1286 | 114 | 13.22 | Neutral/strong | Rising | Midrange | Neutral | 2.6 | 6.6 |
| 56.2 | −1423 | 34 | 13.39 | Neutral/strong | Neutral | Midrange | Neutral | −9.0 | −3.1 |
| 56.3 | 122 | 50 | 12.73 | Weak | Rising | Midrange | Overvalued | 0.9 | −3.4 |
| 56.4 | 743 | 76 | 12.60 | Weak | Rising | Midrange | Overvalued | −6.5 | 2.9 |
| 57.1 | 1042 | 78 | 13.49 | Weak | Rising | Midrange | Overvalued | −14.3 | −5.5 |
| 57.2 | 78 | 47 | 12.94 | Neutral/strong | Neutral | Midrange | Neutral | −4.6 | 7.4 |
| 57.3 | −201 | 81 | 13.93 | Neutral/strong | Rising | Midrange | Neutral | −4.5 | −10.4 |
| 57.4 | −44 | 47 | 12.40 | Neutral/strong | Neutral | Midrange | Neutral | 18.0 | −5.7 |
| 58.1 | 450 | 26 | 11.52 | Weak | Neutral | Midrange | Neutral | 38.1 | 5.3 |
| 58.2 | 668 | −197 | 12.49 | Weak | Declining | Midrange | Undervalued | 31.7 | 7.5 |
| 58.3 | 375 | −156 | 14.41 | Weak | Declining | Midrange | Undervalued | 29.2 | 10.7 |
| 58.4 | −28 | 43 | 17.09 | Neutral/strong | Neutral | Midrange | Neutral | 13.6 | 10.3 |
| 59.1 | −180 | 91 | 19.17 | Neutral/strong | Rising | Midrange | Neutral | 8.5 | 0.4 |
| 59.2 | −154 | 78 | 19.18 | Neutral/strong | Rising | Midrange | Neutral | −0.2 | 5.5 |
| 59.3 | −133 | 96 | 18.80 | Neutral/strong | Rising | Midrange | Neutral | −2.7 | −2.7 |
| 59.4 | −788 | 110 | 16.73 | Neutral/strong | Rising | Midrange | Neutral | −5.9 | 5.3 |

Qtr. = Quarter (beginning)

BP = Basis points

**Table 10-8.** Stock Market Valuation: Historical Simulation, 1Q55–4Q69, Chronological (*Continued*)

| | Prime variables | | | | | | Price change | |
|---|---|---|---|---|---|---|---|---|
| Qtr. | $\Delta D_2-$ $\Delta D_1$ (BP) | $T_1-T_0$ (BP) | $P/E_0$ (–1Q) | Business outlook | Interest rates | Investor confidence | Valuation | Next 4Q % | Next Q % |
| 60.1 | –684 | 109 | 17.46 | Neutral/ strong | Rising | Midrange | Neutral | –3.0 | –7.6 |
| 60.2 | –563 | –93 | 16.32 | Neutral/ strong | Declining | Midrange | Neutral | 17.6 | 2.9 |
| 60.3 | 238 | –172 | 16.79 | Weak | Declining | Midrange | Undervalued | 13.6 | –6.0 |
| 60.4 | 355 | –42 | 16.42 | Weak | Declining | Midrange | Undervalued | 24.7 | 8.6 |
| 61.1 | 348 | –35 | 17.77 | Weak | Declining | Midrange | Undervalued | 23.1 | 12.0 |
| 61.2 | 229 | –16 | 19.90 | Weak | Neutral | Midrange | Neutral | 6.9 | –0.6 |
| 61.3 | –246 | 15 | 20.92 | Neutral/ strong | Neutral | Very high | Overvalued | –15.3 | 3.2 |
| 61.4 | –384 | 13 | 22.02 | Neutral/ strong | Neutral | Very high | Overvalued | –15.7 | 7.2 |
| 62.1 | –365 | 76 | 23.46 | Neutral/ strong | Rising | Very high | Overvalued | –11.8 | –2.8 |
| 62.2 | –98 | 51 | 21.80 | Neutral/ strong | Rising | Very high | Overvalued | –4.3 | –21.3 |
| 62.3 | –287 | 84 | 16.25 | Neutral/ strong | Rising | Midrange | Neutral | 26.7 | 2.8 |
| 62.4 | –285 | 53 | 16.22 | Neutral/ strong | Rising | Midrange | Neutral | 27.4 | 12.1 |
| 63.1 | –474 | 36 | 17.88 | Neutral/ strong | Neutral | Midrange | Neutral | 18.9 | 5.5 |
| 63.2 | –200 | 29 | 18.14 | Neutral/ strong | Neutral | Midrange | Neutral | 18.6 | 4.2 |
| 63.3 | –499 | 43 | 18.70 | Neutral/ strong | Neutral | Midrange | Neutral | 17.8 | 3.4 |
| 63.4 | –478 | 62 | 18.67 | Neutral/ strong | Rising | Midrange | Neutral | 17.4 | 4.6 |
| 64.1 | –709 | 44 | 18.94 | Neutral/ strong | Neutral | Midrange | Neutral | 13.0 | 5.3 |
| 64.2 | –612 | 31 | 19.65 | Neutral/ strong | Neutral | Midrange | Neutral | 9.1 | 3.4 |
| 64.3 | –654 | 20 | 19.54 | Neutral/ strong | Neutral | Midrange | Neutral | 3.0 | 3.0 |
| 64.4 | –631 | 6 | 19.44 | Neutral/ strong | Neutral | Midrange | Neutral | 6.9 | 0.7 |

Qtr. = Quarter (beginning)
BP = Basis points

(*Continued*)

**Table 10-8.** Stock Market Valuation: Historical Simulation, 1Q55–4Q69, Chronological (*Continued*)

| | Prime variables | | | | | | | Price change | |
|---|---|---|---|---|---|---|---|---|---|
| Qtr. | $\Delta D_2-$ $\Delta D_1$ (BP) | $T_1-T_0$ (BP) | $P/E_0$ (–1Q) | Business outlook | Interest rates | Investor confidence | Valuation | Next 4Q % | Next Q % |
| 65.1 | –606 | –3 | 18.96 | Neutral/ strong | Neutral | Midrange | Neutral | 9.1 | 1.7 |
| 65.2 | –531 | 10 | 18.94 | Neutral/ strong | Neutral | Midrange | Neutral | 3.6 | –2.4 |
| 65.3 | –566 | 7 | 17.97 | Neutral/ strong | Neutral | Midrange | Neutral | 0.7 | 6.9 |
| 65.4 | –535 | 5 | 18.59 | Neutral/ strong | Neutral | Midrange | Neutral | –14.9 | 2.7 |
| 66.1 | –502 | 71 | 18.56 | Neutral/ strong | Rising | Midrange | Neutral | –13.1 | –3.5 |
| 66.2 | –473 | 6 | 17.19 | Neutral/ strong | Neutral | Midrange | Neutral | 1.1 | –5.0 |
| 66.3 | –55 | 3 | 15.87 | Neutral/ strong | Neutral | Midrange | Neutral | 7.0 | –9.7 |
| 66.4 | 50 | 109 | 14.02 | Neutral/ strong | Rising | Midrange | Neutral | 26.3 | 4.9 |
| 67.1 | 309 | 53 | 14.58 | Weak | Rising | Midrange | Overvalued | 20.1 | 12.3 |
| 67.2 | 123 | –86 | 16.25 | Weak | Declining | Midrange | Undervalued | 0.0 | 0.5 |
| 67.3 | 315 | –77 | 16.63 | Weak | Declining | Midrange | Undervalued | 9.9 | 6.7 |
| 67.4 | 187 | 43 | 18.14 | Weak | Neutral | Midrange | Neutral | 6.2 | –0.2 |
| 68.1 | 136 | 72 | 18.20 | Weak | Rising | Midrange | Overvalued | 7.7 | –6.5 |
| 68.2 | –42 | 108 | 16.92 | Neutral/ strong | Rising | Midrange | Neutral | 12.5 | 10.4 |
| 68.3 | –108 | 132 | 18.31 | Neutral/ strong | Rising | Midrange | Neutral | –1.9 | 3.1 |
| 68.4 | –60 | 39 | 18.43 | Neutral/ strong | Neutral | Midrange | Neutral | –9.3 | 1.2 |
| 69.1 | 58 | 133 | 18.35 | Neutral/ strong | Rising | Midrange | Neutral | –11.4 | –2.3 |
| 69.2 | 173 | 108 | 17.62 | Weak | Rising | Midrange | Overvalued | –11.7 | –3.7 |
| 69.3 | 265 | 83 | 16.79 | Weak | Rising | Midrange | Overvalued | –25.6 | –4.7 |
| 69.4 | 407 | 130 | 15.95 | Weak | Rising | Midrange | Overvalued | –9.6 | –1.1 |

Qtr. = Quarter (beginning)
BP = Basis points

by valuation, while Table 10-8 lists the same data chronologically. For each table, "1Q55–4Q69" indicates "the first quarter of
1955 to the fourth quarter of 1969." The notation in the first column identifies the year and quarter (i.e., "55.1" signifies "1955,
first quarter"). The three prime variables, designated as
"$\Delta D_2 - \Delta D_1$," "$T_1 - T_0$," and "$P/E_0(-1Q)$" are derived as specified
in Table 10-2 with two modifications. Over the period 1955 to
1969 the indicated dividend rate and consensus expectations of
Treasury bill yields were not available. In their absence, we substitute for the IDR actual dividend payments for the period
ended 6 months ahead and, for Treasury bill futures, the current
spot Treasury bill rate. "$P/E_0(-1Q)$" measures the price-earnings
ratio based on current price and last-reported four-quarter earnings. "$(-1Q)$" indicates that last-reported four-quarter earnings
are lagged by one quarter. The last two columns detail the S&P
500 price change for the next four quarters and the next quarter,
respectively.

## Appendix 10-3
## Valuation Data,
## 1982 to 1992

Table 10-9 chronologically lists the valuation data for the three
prime variables over the years 1982 to 1992, as plotted in Fig.
10-1. Following the format of App. 10-1, "1Q82–4Q92" indicates
"the first quarter of 1982 to the fourth quarter of 1992." The notation in the first column identifies the year and quarter (i.e., "82.1"
signifies "1982, first quarter"). The three prime variables, desig-
nated as "$\Delta D_2 - \Delta D_1$," "$T_1 - T_0$," and $P/E_0(-1Q)$ are derived as specified in Table 10-2 with one modification. Next four-quarter
Treasury bill yields are derived from consensus surveys of the
*Washington Bond & Money Market Report,* as detailed in Table 8-6,
rather than from Treasury bill futures. "$P/E_0(-1Q)$" measures the
price-earnings ratio based on current price and last-reported four-
quarter earnings. "$(-1Q)$" indicates that last-reported four-quarter
earnings are lagged by one quarter. The last column lists the
quarterly excess return for the S&P 500 (total investment return in
excess of that for short Treasury bills).

**Table 10-9.** Stock Market Valuation: Historical Simulation, Contemporary Consensus Estimates, 1Q82–4Q92, Chronological

| Qtr. | $\Delta D_2-$ $\Delta D_1$ (BP) | $T_1-T_0$ (BP) | $P/E_0$ (–1Q) | Business outlook | Interest rates | Investor confidence | Valuation | S&P 500 % excess return* |
|---|---|---|---|---|---|---|---|---|
| 82.1 | 436 | –352 | 8.03 | Weak | Declining | Midrange | Undervalued | –9.7 |
| 82.2 | 623 | –102 | 7.29 | Weak | Declining | Very low | Undervalued | –3.7 |
| 82.3 | 975 | –65 | 7.40 | Weak | Declining | Very low | Undervalued | 8.9 |
| 82.4 | 946 | –352 | 8.50 | Weak | Declining | Midrange | Undervalued | 15.9 |
| 83.1 | 878 | –263 | 10.37 | Weak | Declining | Midrange | Undervalued | 7.9 |
| 83.2 | 750 | –98 | 12.10 | Weak | Declining | Midrange | Undervalued | 8.8 |
| 83.3 | 730 | 59 | 13.54 | Weak | Rising | Midrange | Overvalued | –2.4 |
| 83.4 | 750 | 70 | 13.19 | Weak | Rising | Midrange | Overvalued | –1.8 |
| 84.1 | 830 | 81 | 12.40 | Weak | Rising | Midrange | Overvalued | –4.4 |
| 84.2 | 739 | 124 | 11.35 | Weak | Rising | Midrange | Overvalued | –4.8 |
| 84.3 | 754 | 156 | 10.04 | Weak | Rising | Midrange | Overvalued | 7.0 |
| 84.4 | 734 | 156 | 10.25 | Weak | Rising | Midrange | Overvalued | –0.6 |
| 85.1 | 456 | –129 | 10.10 | Weak | Declining | Midrange | Undervalued | 7.4 |
| 85.2 | 426 | –38 | 10.86 | Weak | Declining | Midrange | Undervalued | 5.4 |
| 85.3 | 450 | –139 | 11.71 | Weak | Declining | Midrange | Undervalued | –5.7 |
| 85.4 | 586 | –43 | 11.66 | Weak | Declining | Midrange | Undervalued | 15.0 |
| 86.1 | 465 | –33 | 13.87 | Weak | Declining | Midrange | Undervalued | 12.2 |
| 86.2 | 227 | –88 | 16.35 | Weak | Declining | Midrange | Undervalued | 4.3 |
| 86.3 | 258 | –55 | 17.28 | Weak | Declining | Midrange | Undervalued | –8.3 |
| 86.4 | 480 | –131 | 15.73 | Weak | Declining | Midrange | Undervalued | 4.0 |
| 87.1 | 414 | –77 | 16.31 | Weak | Declining | Midrange | Undervalued | 19.7 |
| 87.2 | 309 | 3 | 20.15 | Weak | Neutral | Very high | Neutral | 3.8 |
| 87.3 | 138 | 52 | 20.13 | Weak | Rising | Very high | Overvalued | 5.2 |
| 87.4 | 423 | 175 | 22.32 | Weak | Rising | Very high | Overvalued | –23.7 |
| 88.1 | 158 | 69 | 15.58 | Weak | Rising | Midrange | Overvalued | 4.6 |
| 88.2 | 59 | 85 | 14.79 | Neutral/ strong | Rising | Midrange | Neutral | 5.1 |
| 88.3 | –405 | 162 | 14.71 | Neutral/ strong | Rising | Midrange | Neutral | –1.3 |
| 88.4 | –209 | 195 | 12.55 | Neutral/ strong | Rising | Midrange | Neutral | 1.3 |
| 89.1 | –323 | 237 | 12.22 | Neutral/ strong | Rising | Midrange | Neutral | 5.1 |

Qtr. = Quarter (beginning)
BP = Basis points
*Total S&P 500 return less Treasury bill return, over the indicated quarter.

**Table 10-9.** Stock Market Valuation: Historical Simulation, Contemporary Consensus Estimates, 1Q82–4Q92, Chronological (*Continued*)

| Qtr. | Prime variables $\Delta D_1$ (BP) | $\Delta D_2-$ $T_1-T_0$ (BP) | $P/E_0$ (−1Q) | Business outlook | Interest rates | Investor confidence | Valuation | S&P 500 % excess return* |
|---|---|---|---|---|---|---|---|---|
| 89.2 | −651 | 222 | 12.42 | Neutral/ strong | Rising | Midrange | Neutral | 6.5 |
| 89.3 | −868 | 40 | 12.74 | Neutral/ strong | Neutral | Midrange | Neutral | 8.4 |
| 89.4 | −690 | −26 | 13.84 | Neutral/ strong | Declining | Midrange | Neutral | 0.1 |
| 90.1 | −384 | −83 | 14.92 | Neutral/ strong | Declining | Midrange | Neutral | −4.7 |
| 90.2 | −213 | −27 | 14.86 | Neutral/ strong | Declining | Midrange | Neutral | 4.2 |
| 90.3 | −190 | −39 | 16.52 | Neutral/ strong | Declining | Midrange | Neutral | −15.4 |
| 90.4 | 117 | −76 | 14.40 | Weak | Declining | Midrange | Undervalued | 7.0 |
| 91.1 | 113 | −134 | 15.19 | Weak | Declining | Midrange | Undervalued | 12.9 |
| 91.2 | 634 | −154 | 17.58 | Weak | Declining | Midrange | Undervalued | −1.6 |
| 91.3 | 714 | −90 | 17.72 | Weak | Declining | Midrange | Undervalued | 3.9 |
| 91.4 | 657 | −100 | 19.98 | Weak | Declining | Midrange | Undervalued | 7.1 |
| 92.1 | 793 | −156 | 23.41 | Weak | Declining | Very high | Neutral | −3.5 |
| 92.2 | 611 | −33 | 25.28 | Weak | Declining | Very high | Neutral | 0.9 |
| 92.3 | 537 | −56 | 25.21 | Weak | Declining | Very high | Neutral | 2.3 |
| 92.4 | 442 | −101 | 24.50 | Weak | Declining | Very high | Neutral | 4.3 |

Qtr. = Quarter (beginning)
BP = Basis points
*Total S&P 500 return less Treasury bill return, over the indicated quarter.

# PART 4
## Confronting the Future

# 11

# The Three
# Prime Variables
# in Operation

## Managing Exposure to
## the Stock Market

### Identifying the Practical
### Applications

This chapter addresses the practical application of the three prime variables to day-to-day active management of asset allocation. Previous chapters explain how the three prime variables serve to value the stock market. A measure of market valuation, however, does not automatically translate into an investment decision. The initial section of this chapter describes the operation of a decision process based on the three prime variables. The necessary inputs routinely appear in the financial press. The second section addresses the decision maker who weighs a range of competing forecasts in order to reach his or her own judgment. In this application, the three prime variables serve as a screen to aid in controlling bias. They identify forecasts that fail adequately to address all three key factors that drive stock prices.

## Making Sure the Framework Is in Place

The decision process for managing exposure to the stock market requires a clearly defined framework. Market valuation aims to assess the likelihood of a particular market-price outcome. Translation into a specific asset allocation decision, as discussed in Chap. 3, depends on the policy framework in which the fund operates. We summarize below the three essential components.

**Policy Plan.** The starting point is an unambiguously defined long-term policy plan. As described in Chap. 3, the objectives of the fund, not the current assessment of the financial markets, determine policy. Active asset allocation, since it is a departure from policy, requires a definition of policy. The policy plan specifies the normal position for each asset group.

**Active Ranges.** The second step determines the ranges around the policy norm in which active asset allocation may operate. Although skillful active asset allocation expects to add value over a series of decisions, any one decision may turn out wrong. To control risk in a highly efficient market, decision makers therefore operate within moderate ranges. By way of illustration, suppose the policy norm for common stocks is 50 percent. Ranges for active asset allocation might be set at 40 to 60 percent, or perhaps 35 to 65 percent. The precise extent of the range depends on the fund's tolerance for risk related to active asset allocation. (Establishment of a swing portfolio, as described in Chap. 3, provides an alternative way of controlling deviations from policy.)

**Decision Frequency.** Our studies of the decision process based on the three prime variables, as indicated by data presented in Chap. 10, favor quarterly decision frequency. The first day of each calendar quarter is convenient because it coincides with the beginning of the standard quarterly period for performance measurement. Apart from this consideration, consistent observance of any other date would serve about as well. A 3-month interval between decisions, meanwhile, avoids the possibility of day-to-day reversals in weightings as the valuation measure fluctuates around a trigger point. At the same time, a 3-month decision frequency is positioned to catch major moves, since valuations look 6 to 12 months ahead.

## Translating Valuation into Portfolio Weightings

Active management of the allocation of fund assets to the stock market depends on the interaction *between* the weighting decision *and* the policy designed to meet particular fund objectives. We outline the process in the three steps summarized below.

**Worksheet.** Figure 11-1 presents a worksheet that brings together on one page the data defining the three prime variables. Titles on the worksheet briefly identify the information required to fill in each blank. The arrangement of the information facilitates the simple arithmetic needed for its processing. For purpose of illustration, we have filled in the blanks with data available on October 1, 1987, and, on this basis, have checked the status concerning each prime variable.

**Decision Matrix.** Figure 11-2 serves as a decision matrix. The interest-rate prime variable determines which of the three panels applies to the other two prime variables. The worksheet example shows rising interest rates, directing attention to Panel B. The weak dividend growth indicated for the business outlook means that the appropriate decision will be found in the upper row of the matrix in Panel B. Since the worksheet shows very high investor confidence (P/E greater than 20), the right-hand box included in this upper row specifically locates the applicable decision on the worksheet date. For this example, the analysis of market valuation based on the three prime variables results in a decision to underweight common stocks.

**Interaction with Policy.** Fund policy determines the specific implementation of the weighting decision. Suppose that the policy norm for common stocks is 60 percent, the midpoint of a 50 to 70 percent range. Underweighting therefore translates into a com-

DATE: $\boxed{10/1/87}$

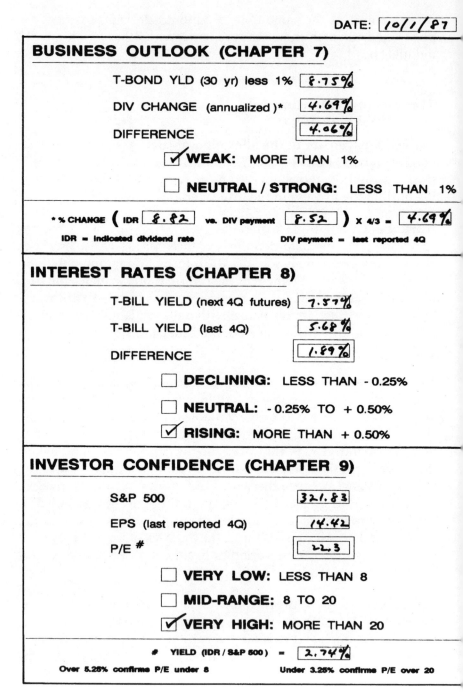

## BUSINESS OUTLOOK (CHAPTER 7)

T-BOND YLD (30 yr) less 1% $\boxed{8.75\%}$

DIV CHANGE (annualized)* $\boxed{4.69\%}$

DIFFERENCE $\boxed{4.06\%}$

☑ **WEAK:** MORE THAN 1%

☐ **NEUTRAL / STRONG:** LESS THAN 1%

* % CHANGE $\left( \text{IDR} \boxed{8.82} \text{ vs. DIV payment } \boxed{8.52} \right) \times 4/3 = \boxed{4.69\%}$

IDR = indicated dividend rate                    DIV payment = last reported 4Q

## INTEREST RATES (CHAPTER 8)

T-BILL YIELD (next 4Q futures) $\boxed{7.57\%}$

T-BILL YIELD (last 4Q) $\boxed{5.68\%}$

DIFFERENCE $\boxed{1.89\%}$

☐ **DECLINING:** LESS THAN - 0.25%

☐ **NEUTRAL:** - 0.25% TO + 0.50%

☑ **RISING:** MORE THAN + 0.50%

## INVESTOR CONFIDENCE (CHAPTER 9)

S&P 500 $\boxed{321.83}$

EPS (last reported 4Q) $\boxed{14.42}$

P/E # $\boxed{22.3}$

☐ **VERY LOW:** LESS THAN 8

☐ **MID-RANGE:** 8 TO 20

☑ **VERY HIGH:** MORE THAN 20

# YIELD (IDR / S&P 500) = $\boxed{2.74\%}$

Over 5.25% confirms P/E under 8          Under 3.25% confirms P/E over 20

**Figure 11-1.** Worksheet that brings together the data defining the three prime variables.

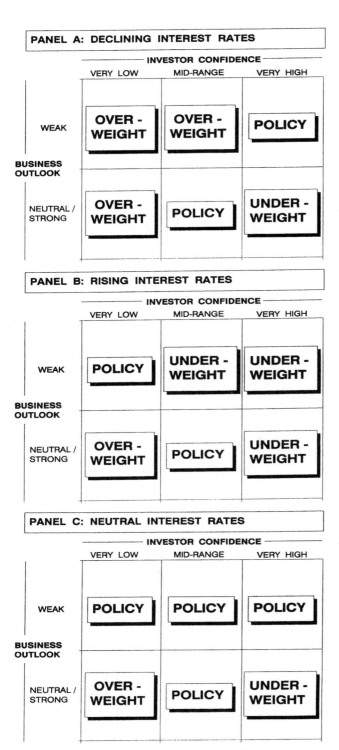

**Figure 11-2.** A decision matrix, specifying when to overweight and when to underweight common stocks.

mon stock percentage of 50 percent. Note, however, that 50 percent might represent the policy norm for a different fund with different objectives. If the policy norm were 40 percent, moreover, 50 percent would represent a 10-percentage-point *overweighting.*

## Limiting Turnover and Transaction Costs

Stock market valuation, although determined on a scheduled date of each quarter, does not result in a weighting change unless it differs from the previous quarter. Over the 1970 to 1992 back-test, for example, valuation changed on 21 of the 89 quarterly valuation dates. At this rate, transaction costs would be incurred, on average, once each year, except for possible interim rebalancing. The purpose of rebalancing is to offset the drift associated with changes in market value due to variations in return for the asset groups that make up the fund. When the stock market environment is particularly volatile, the three prime variables may call for two or three transactions in a single year. At the other extreme, they may provide no reason for a weighting change for a much more extended period, perhaps for as long as several years. In a highly efficient stock market, the burden of proof rests with the argument to depart from the policy weighting.

Recognition that the stock market is highly efficient bears on both the frequency and extent of changes in active asset allocation. Traditional active management, as described in Chap. 1, views the stock market as highly irrational. As a result, active managers are likely to develop strong opinions concerning the difference between market value and market prices. Logically, such strong opinions translate into aggressive overweighting or underweighting. At the other extreme, the hard-liners on the efficient market (Chap. 2) disavow any attempt to disagree with the market prices. They therefore have no reason to adjust asset allocation to perceived changes in the market outlook. Between these two extremes, active asset allocation that operates in a highly efficient stock market occupies an intermediate position. It expects to gain advantage by exploiting a thin margin of slow information. At the same time, it recognizes that market prices already discount most of the readily available information. Historical studies based on the three prime variables are consistent with these conclusions. They suggest that about half the time the three prime variables highlight clues that shift the odds sufficiently in one direction or the other to warrant overweighting or underweighting. On the remainder of the valuation dates, the three prime variables, pointing to the same conclusion as the hard-liners on the efficient market hypothesis, support a neutral weighting.

Costs per transaction depend primarily on the method of implementation. The most economical method is the purchase and sale of futures (Chap. 3). Transactions in index funds are much less expensive than in actively managed portfolios. The least favored alternative is the purchase or sale of actively managed equities, not only because of the transaction costs but also because of the disruption of stock selection strategy. But if a fund manager must implement asset allocation by trading individual stocks, the best way to accomplish a change in the exposure to the stock market will likely involve actions taken for other reasons. For example, delay of reinvestment in the stock market as individual issues are sold because of relative attractiveness effectively reduces overall equity exposure. Increase in equity exposure awaits identification of attractive new alternatives. Meanwhile, cash flows in or out of the fund provide opportunities to change the mix of assets.

## Controlling Risk through Rebalancing

Rebalancing policy adapts to the specific characteristics of the fund. In a large fund using stock market futures, the trigger points for rebalancing may be relatively narrow. Suppose, for example, the stock position rises by more than 0.5 percent over the quarter solely as a result of relative appreciation. In such case, a small adjustment in stock market futures would bring the position back to the target level. For another fund, because of its smaller size and more costly method of implementing transactions, the trigger point for rebalancing may be set at two or three percentage points above the target level. A specifically defined trigger point would be inappropriate for the account which depends on managing cash flow for opportunities to adjust exposure to the stock market. Rebalancing would occur as opportunities develop for other reasons (cash additions or withdrawals or stock selection decisions).

## Controlling Bias

### Approaches That Work
### Part of the Time

The major reason for bias in valuing the stock market is disproportionate emphasis on one or two of the three key factors that drive stock prices. Table 11-1 lists three common approaches along with the key factor that each is likely to emphasize. Each of these approaches is likely to work part of the time. *Economic forecasting* is particularly relevant in periods when the central issue is the course of business activity rather than changing interest rates or extremes of investor optimism or pessimism. A dramatic example is the highly unstable period for the economy in the 1930s. The *dividend discount model*, with its special sensi-

**Table 11-1.** Bias in Active Asset Allocation

|  | Key factors that drive stock prices | | |
|---|---|---|---|
|  | Business outlook (dividend growth) | Interest rates (risk-free rate) | Investor confidence (risk premium) |
| Economic forecasting | X |  |  |
| Dividend-discount model |  | X |  |
| P/E model |  |  | X |

tivity to interest-rate changes, has its best opportunity during periods of extremely volatile interest rates. Note the increasing application of dividend-discount models to active asset allocation as a result of recurring episodes of highly volatile interest rates in the 1970s and early 1980s. Decisions based primarily on the P/E reflect in large measure wide swings in investor confidence. According to this view, an extremely high P/E reflects excessive optimism, while, at the other extreme, the likelihood is that pessimism is overdone. Other approaches with a similar orientation include measures of *price/book* or *price/intrinsic value* (as recommended by Graham and Dodd[1]).

### How a Reliable Approach Suddenly Becomes Irrelevant

Any one of these approaches may suddenly become irrelevant when the primary influence which it addresses is no longer the key factor driving market prices. Market-price action during the 1960s provides a clear example. The three panels of Fig. 11-3 divide the 9 years 1960 to 1968 into three equal periods. Each panel compares the S&P 500 index, plotted quarterly, with a widely followed series that bears on investor assessment of the stock market. Each of these series (P/E, earnings, and interest rates) relates most directly to one of the three key factors that drive stock prices, as identified by the following.

**Investor Confidence, 1960 to 1962.**  Panel A of Fig. 11-3 compares market price with P/E (four-quarter trailing earnings). As suggested by the highlighting, market-price swings in the early 1960s reflected in large part rapid changes in investor confidence. The S&P 500 ran ahead sharply in 1961 (to 22.4 times trailing earnings at year end), broke abruptly in 1962, and then progressively recovered in 1963. There is little evidence, as indicated by comparisons displayed in Panels B and C, that this pattern of market-price change during this period resulted from the changing course of either business activity or interest rates. Rather, the market P/E traces a pattern of extreme investor optimism in 1961, followed by a sharp reaction in 1962, and a gradual rebuilding to a more positive level by 1963.

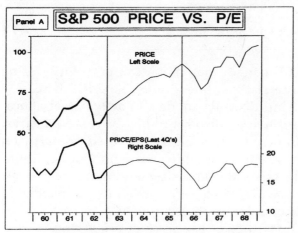

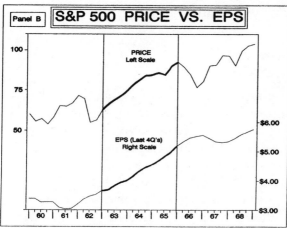

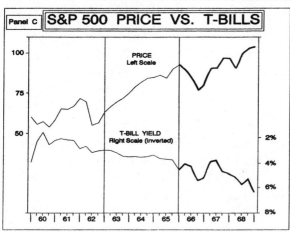

**Figure 11-3.** Examples of changing influences on stock prices: (a) investor confidence, (b) business outlook, and (c) interest rates.

**Business Outlook, 1963 to 1965.** Panel B of Fig. 11-3 compares market price with four-quarter trailing earnings per share. The highlighting during this middle period emphasizes the parallel uptrends for the two series. Note that the market-price trend leads the earnings trend, which extends well into 1966. Changes in P/E and interest rates, meanwhile, remained relatively modest over this period. Taken together, comparisons of data displayed in the three panels of Fig. 11-3 underscore the role of the business outlook in driving stock prices over 1963 to 1965.

**Interest Rates, 1966 to 1968.** Panel C of Fig. 11-3 compares market price with the current yield (inverted) on short Treasury bills. Beginning in 1966, the volatility of interest rates picked up markedly. As emphasized by the highlighting in Panel C, interest rates were a critical factor in explaining the swings in market prices (and, consequently, market P/E) during 1966 and much of 1967. Business activity and earnings subsequently slowed in reaction to financial conditions, but the credit crunch, more than anything, explains the 1966 bear market. In 1967, moreover, declining interest rates supported a vigorous market recovery.

### Checking for Bias

The three prime variables, as an overview of stock market valuation, provide perspective in examining other approaches for bias. By way of example, suppose an economic forecaster is bullish on the stock market because of prospects for rising earnings. Reference to the current state of the three prime variables provides the framework for a checklist as shown below. In a similar way, a conclusion based on a measure of investor confidence or interest rates calls for consideration of the likely role of the other two key factors that drive stock prices.

**Business Outlook.** What is the near-term outlook for dividend growth, as suggested by comparison of the indicated dividend rate with long-term bond yields? Weak dividend growth—in the absence of negatives relating to interest rates and investor confidence—increases the probability of favorable market impact from rising earnings. Strong dividend growth over the coming several quarters, however, is not necessarily negative for the stock market. Under these circumstances, a key issue is likely to be whether the market price is too high or too low (see below, "How Much Optimism?").

**Interest Rates.**   How will interest rates affect the stock market outlook? Rising interest rates are likely to be highly negative if earnings and dividends are already depressed. But rising interest rates are not necessarily bad news if dividend growth is sufficiently strong. The clearly positive combination, as underscored by the record since World War II, is significantly declining interest rates along with depressed business activity.

**How Much Optimism?**   Does the market price already reflect so much investor optimism that stock prices are highly vulnerable to an adverse turn in investor confidence? Are stock prices so low, implying such widespread investor pessimism, that a significant recovery in investor confidence becomes likely in the face of even modest improvement in business activity? Or is the market P/E in the broad middle area, as it has been more than  80 percent of the time? In this middle area, differences in level of P/E are unlikely to shed much light on the current attractiveness of the stock market.

## Who Needs to Guard against Bias?

Who can benefit from keeping in mind the current status of the three prime variables? In our view, everyone who is likely to have a role in determining exposure of fund assets to the risks and returns related to common stocks can benefit. The member of the investment committee, although perhaps not a full-time investment professional, can maintain a broad investment perspective through routine updating of the three prime variables. The fund manager, with access to a full range of guidance concerning stock market valuation, can use the three prime variables as a means of organizing a checklist. The specialist in active asset allocation, reviewing on a daily basis a wide range of prospective influences on stock prices, may look to the three prime variables for continuing perspective. The decision process incorporating the three prime variables can serve, not only as a second opinion, but also as logical framework for analyzing the likelihood that a different point of view will prevail. Even the hard-liners on the efficient market hypothesis may want to monitor the three prime variables, if, as outlined in Chap. 12, they are periodically tempted to engage in back-door market timing.

## Reference

1. Sidney Cottle, Roger F. Murray, and Frank E. Block, *Graham and Dodd's Security Analysis*, McGraw-Hill, New York, 1988.

# 12

# Examining
# the Alternative:
# Back-Door
# Market Timing

## How the "Underground"
## Decision Process
## Takes Over

### Filling the Vacuum

Back-door market timing is "underground" investment management. Investment literature seldom discusses back-door market timing, since, like the underground economy, it hides from official recognition. Yet, its influence is pervasive. It fills the vacuum created when fund management disavows, ignores, or otherwise excludes an explicit role for active asset allocation. Very simply, back-door market timing is active asset allocation disguised as policy asset allocation. It responds to the individual decision maker's view of the outlook for the stock market (active decision) rather than the consensus views already represented by current market prices (as reflected in the passive policy plan). Back-door market timers may go to great lengths to avoid acknowledging the underlying reason for the decision. They frequently explain the cutback (or increase) in stocks on the basis of a change in fund objectives. They may belatedly recognize that the policy had earlier reflected the wrong analysis of the fund's true objectives. Alternatively, they may reconsider the long-term assumptions underlying the policy plan.

## Who Are the Back-Door Market Timers?

A large number of people, each with their own fears and hopes and individual points of view, may contribute—directly or indirectly—to the pressures for back-door market timing. The list includes investment committee members who oversee the operation of the fund, chief executive officers and chief financial officers who have a stake in the outcome of the investment committee decisions, pension officers and other fund managers who recommend changes in asset allocation, outside portfolio managers who influence total fund asset allocation through changes in the composition of the portfolios under their supervision, and consultants who advise on asset allocation. Each of these contributors to the decision process answers in turn to constituents who are far from indifferent concerning the outcome of fund management. The constituent groups range from security analysts, who see pension-fund performance affecting earnings and dividends of the sponsoring corporation, to beneficiaries of endowment funds, who may have to adjust budgets in response to fund investment experience. Participants in retirement plans worry if their retirement income is threatened. For fund managers and portfolio managers, a particularly compelling issue is the relation between investment performance and career advancement—or even job security.

## When 5 Years Are Almost Forever

Back-door market timing feeds on the disparity between the very long time horizons central to policy planning and the much shorter time horizons relevant to decision makers and the constituents that they serve. Our analysis of asset allocation focuses on 5-year periods, aiming to reflect the perspective of the investment decision maker who is held accountable for fund returns. A scholar, assembling data for a doctoral thesis or writing a journal article, may rely on assumptions extending decades into the future. Such assumptions are likely to reflect the historical experience as far back as the inception of the S&P 500 (which, with fewer issues in earlier years, dates back to 1926). The policy plan, since it determines the long-term diversification of the fund, appropriately incorporates such assumptions (or similar assumptions modified for change in such factors as market volatility). For the active decision maker in day-to-day operations, however, a year on the wrong side of the stock market goes very slowly. Under such circumstances, *5 years is the very long term.* Survival of client relationships, perhaps even the decision maker's job, may well depend on fund performance long before the end of 5 years.

## Making It Happen

Although there are no reliable statistics compiled on back-door market timing, it is clearly a powerful influence on overall asset allocation. In every bear market, we see examples as investment committees gather to review fund performance in the light of distressing losses. It suddenly becomes self-evident to one or more participants in the discussion that the long-term policy asset allocation is just plain wrong, whatever the outlook for stock prices. One question, repeated increasingly as the bear market gains momentum, summarizes the challenge: Does the fund, in the light of its true objectives (or "more realistic" policy assumptions), need to hold such a large portion of stocks? We list below various ways in which back-door market timers may respond. While these illustrations of back-door market timing relate to actions taken in bear markets, similar examples characterize bull markets.

**Reduce Policy Allocation to Stocks.** The straightforward alternative is simply to reduce the policy percentage for stocks to bring it in line with a revised definition of the objectives of the fund. Recommendations along these lines often include assurances that the action has nothing to do with prospects for the stock market. The purpose, it now seems, is to correct a past oversight in policy planning.

**Discover Bond Immunization.** Another possibility is to discover the appeal of bond immunization for a portion of liabilities (particularly applicable to the segment of a pension fund representing plan participants who are already retired). The aim is to assemble a fixed-income portfolio which will provide future cash flow sufficient to meet a specified set of future liabilities, as can best be estimated. Implementation requires segregation of part of the fund in an immunized bond portfolio. Although the percentage allocation to stocks in the remainder of the fund may remain the same, the exposure to the stock market of the total fund, including the immunized segment, declines significantly. Table 12-1 provides an illustration. Columns 1 and 2 show a $100 million fund with assets allocated to reflect policy percentages of 60 percent for stocks and 40 percent for bonds. The remaining columns specify the changes in the fund resulting from a shift of $30 million to a bond immunization program. Columns 3 and 4 show the initial policy percentages applied to the $70 million of assets not included in the immunization program. As indicated in columns 5 and 6, the equity percentage for the total fund, including the assets dedicated to bond immunization, drops from 60 to

**Table 12-1.** Market timing Through Bond Immunization

| | Initial fund | | After bond immunization Excluding immunization bonds | | After bond immunization Including immunization bonds | |
|---|---|---|---|---|---|---|
| | Millions | % | Millions | % | Millions | % |
| Stocks | $ 60 | 60% | $42 | 60% | $ 42 | 42% |
| Bonds | 40 | 40 | 28 | 40 | 58 | 58 |
| Total | $100 | 100% | $ 70 | 100% | $100 | 100% |

42 percent, even though there is no change in the stated policy percentage.

**Replacing Portfolio Managers.** A third alternative provides for replacement of one group of aggressive equity managers— those usually fully invested in more volatile issues—with another group which is much more likely to hold defensive issues and cash reserves. In this way, there is no change recorded in the policy commitment to equities even though a significant reduction takes place in the exposure to the stock market. Table 12-2 illustrates how shifting $50 million of portfolio assets from equity manager A to equity manager B reduces exposure to the equity market by $18 million. This calculation highlights significant differences in the normal portfolios of the two managers. Manager A characteristically holds a larger portion of the total assets in equities than does manager B, as indicated by the data displayed in the upper section of the table. Even more important is the beta adjustment included in the lower section of the table. Manager A routinely invests in more aggressive stocks with an average beta of 1.15. Manager B, in contrast, regularly skews stock selection toward conservative income producers, especially telephone

**Table 12-2.** Market timing through Changing Equity Managers

|  | Manager A | | Manager B | | Difference* | |
| --- | --- | --- | --- | --- | --- | --- |
|  | Millions | % | Millions | % | Millions | % |
| Normal portfolio |  |  |  |  |  |  |
| Stocks | $48 | 96% | $44 | 88% | $ −4 | −8% |
| Cash | 2 | 4 | 6 | 12 | 4 | 8 |
| Total | $50 | 100% | $50 | 100% | $ 0 | 0% |
| Beta adjusted |  |  |  |  |  |  |
| Stocks[†] | $55 | 110% | $37 | 74% | $−18 | −36% |
| Cash | −5 | −10 | 13 | 26 | 18 | 36 |
| Total | $50 | 100% | $50 | 100% | $ 0 | 0% |

*Manager B less Manager A
[†]Beta for normal stock segment: manager A = 1.15, manager B = 0.85.

companies and electric utilities. As a result, the average beta for manager B is 0.85. The adjustment for these differing betas, superimposed on the differences in normal cash holdings already identified, explains how the shift in assets from one manager to the other can significantly contribute to back-door market timing. The decision is equivalent to the withdrawal of $18 million from an S&P 500 index fund, with the proceeds invested in cash equivalents.

**Replacing the Fund Manager.** An even more drastic alternative is to replace the manager of the overall fund with someone who is likely to move policy in another direction. The new fund manager, perhaps already selected because of a more cautious approach to investment risk, can hardly overlook the reasons for the predecessor's departure. Policy decisions, as described in Chap. 3, strive to replace subjective judgments concerning the investment outlook with consensus expectations for expected return, variability of returns, and correlation of returns with other asset groups. Under the best of circumstances, however, investment managers cannot achieve the goal of complete objectivity. Passive investing requires certain individual judgments, which, absent necessary discipline, provide significant wiggle room for changing the assumptions underlying policy. History provides guidance in identifying the estimates required for policy planning, but which measure of the past best serves this purpose? William F. Sharpe, in an article published in 1975, makes a judgment concerning the years that would likely best reflect future returns and volatility of the stock market. Note his concluding sentence, which underscores the subjectivity associated with choice of the most appropriate measuring period (our italics):

> Those who feel that recent events portend a future like the early years of The Great Depression are probably excessively pessimistic. On the other hand, the two decades following World War II may have been exceptionally favorable for holders of stocks. To get a balanced view of how a timing strategy might perform in the future, we have chosen the middle road, utilizing the values from the period 1934 to 1972. *Readers who consider this choice unsatisfactory can easily substitute other values in our formulas.*[1]

Figure 12-1 compares stock market returns over three alternative measuring periods. The first bar represents the compound annual rate of excess return for stocks over the 39-year period selected by Sharpe, 1934 to 1972. (Excess return equals total return for stocks less that for short Treasury bills.) The middle bar shows the comparable compound rate of excess return for the full range of available data over 67 years, 1926 to 1992. The third bar reflects a judgment not unlike that made by Sharpe but with an opposite conclusion. It represents results for the entire period 1926 to 1992 except for the 20 years 1940 to 1959. Omission of these middle years recognizes the extremely abnormal conditions associated with World War II and its aftermath.

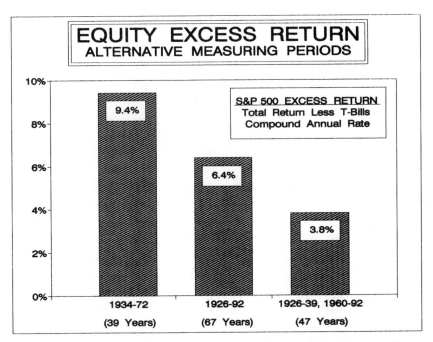

**Figure 12-1.** Compares excess returns for the S&P 500 over three measuring periods: 1934 to 1972; 1926 to 1992; and 1926 to 1992, excluding the period from 1940 to 1959. (*Source:* Stocks, Bonds, Bills, and Inflation 1993 Yearbook, *Ibbotson Associates, Chicago, annually updates the work by Roger G. Ibbotson and Rex A. Sinquefield. Used with permission. All rights reserved.*)

Demand for products of American business surged during the war and subsequently benefited from American political and economic domination in a war-ravaged world. At the same time, the slowness of interest rates to adjust to creeping inflation translated into a huge subsidy for American business and its stockholders.

Differences in stock market returns, other things equal, account for differing allocation of assets to the stock market. The historical returns (compound rate of excess return) vary substantially over the three measuring periods. They range from 9.4 (Sharpe) to 6.4 (entire period) to 3.8 percent (entire period excluding 1940 to 1959). Future expectations based on any one of these periods, each of which has generated a positive compound rate of excess return, support allocation of a portion of the fund to common stocks. The percentage allocation to stocks, nevertheless, depends on assumptions for each asset group concerning expected return, volatility of returns, and correlations of returns with other asset groups. Other things equal, a shift between alternative return estimates for the stock market, as illustrated by Fig. 12-1, opens the door to significant change in policy asset allocation.

While Fig. 12-1 deals specifically with the return for the S&P 500, similar questions apply to the assumptions for each of the asset groups included in the policy plan. For several of these asset groups, moreover, the historical data may pose additional challenging questions. Consider, for example, the expected return for bonds. An extended upward trend in inflationary expectations over most of the postwar period (at least until the early 1980s) has severely limited *average* bond returns. Virtually all policy planners therefore use estimates which attempt to adjust the historical record for this factor. Such adjustments may relate the betas of bond and stock returns, since expected returns in an efficient market are proportional to risk that cannot be diversified away (as measured by beta). Still, there is no way to make such adjustments on a strictly objective basis. For other asset groups, such as real estate, foreign stocks, and venture capital, the historical data are much less adequate than for domestic stocks, bonds, and cash. As a result, policy planners rely heavily on the imposition of constraints, reflecting healthy skepticism concerning the specific estimates. Estimates of correlation based on past experience are particularly tricky, since the future experience may depart drastically from the past record. By way of example, stock and bond returns showed little correlation until the second half of the 1960s, when changing inflationary expectations became a powerful market influence for both asset groups. Although inflation had fluctuated more sharply from year to year in earlier periods, it was not until 1966 that the long-term outlook for inflation, as perceived by the consensus of investors, began to change dramatically. If inflation remains relatively stable at the relatively low levels of recent years, the correlation between stock and bond returns over the years ahead will almost certainly drop well below the average for the past quarter century. While there are many other examples, the conclusion in each case is the same. The new fund manager, by his or her choice of "objective" inputs, enjoys considerable latitude to adjust policy asset allocation.

## Improving the Odds

### Skill Required to Break Even

Back-door market timing, although it may succeed dramatically on occasion, will prove counterproductive most of the time. In a highly efficient stock market, insights superior to those of the investor consensus are not easily achieved. How can back-door market timing, which takes over from time to time without a carefully disciplined decision process, hope to do better than chance? We therefore estimate that the probability of a favorable outcome (before allowance for transaction costs) is the same as for a toss of a coin—50 percent. For fund performance, nevertheless, the negative implications of back-door market timing are far worse than break even. In order to explain why this is so— and what to do about it—we refer to our *barometer of opportunity*.

To construct the barometer of opportunity, we assume that an investment decision maker has one opportunity each quarter to change asset allocation. One option is to commit 100 percent of fund assets to the stock market, as represented by the S&P 500. The alternative is to place 100 percent of fund assets in short Treasury bills. The decision is implemented at the beginning of each calendar quarter based on closing prices for the previous quarter (ending March, June, September, and December). The measure of performance is the *excess return for the fund* (ERF). It represents the difference between the total return of the fund and the return on Treasury bills. When the fund is invested in the stock market, the fund excess return is the same as the *excess return for stocks* (ERS). Investment in Treasury bills, by definition, results in an excess return of zero. The cumulative ERF is therefore the same as the cumulative ERS over periods when the fund is invested in stocks. The equation below states ERF in terms of ERS together with a measure of the skill of the investment decision maker. Cumulative ERS consists of two parts. One part includes the quarters when ERS is positive ($\text{ERS}_p$). The other part includes the quarters when ERS is negative ($\text{ERS}_n$). The measure of skill is the probability (PROB) that the investment decision maker will make the correct decision each quarter.

$$\text{ERF} = \text{PROB} \times (\text{cumulative ERS}_p) + (100\% - \text{PROB}) \times$$
$$(\text{cumulative ERS}_n)$$

For any assumed level of skill, comparison of ERF with the results of a buy-and-hold strategy for stocks provides a measure of the advantage gained by active asset allocation. The buy-and-hold strategy reflects the excess return generated by the S&P 500. Whether the ERF represents a better expected return depends on both the opportunity presented by the ERS in the quarters included in the data set and the level of decision maker skill, as represented by PROB. Given perfect foresight, which means that PROB equals 100 percent, each decision would properly identify the ERS for the coming quarter. As a result, ERF would equal cumulative $\text{ERS}_p$, since the fund would always hold Treasury bills in the quarters designated $\text{ERS}_n$. A PROB of

50 percent, in contrast, represents a complete lack of skill. On average, the fund would hold stocks half the quarters for both cumulative $ERS_p$ and cumulative $ERS_n$. In a similar way, the equation may be used to calculate expected ERF for any assumption relating to the skill of the decision maker, with PROB ranging from 50 (no skill) to 100 percent (perfect skill).

### Addressing the Central Issue

The barometer of opportunity is calibrated to identify the varying levels of skill required of the decision maker in order to break even as the market environment changes. Note that the underlying assumptions do not attempt to take into account the many variations of circumstance which may apply to fund operations. Fund guidelines may permit switching between stocks and fixed-income securities of varying maturities as well as short Treasury bills. They may allow overweighting of stocks when they are undervalued as well as underweighting when they are overvalued. (Overweighting raises the expected return relative to the performance benchmark, but it also introduces incremental risks). Certain back-door market timers may operate with a continuing bullish or bearish bias, and others may characteristically shift from bearish bias in bear markets to bullish bias in bull markets. Since more than one source of back-door market timing may impact the decisions of a given fund, the biases may change as the decision makers change. Other analyses, moreover, may select a shorter or longer time horizon than the 5 years that we consider appropriate for our purposes. Despite such qualifications, the barometer of opportunity addresses the central issue in active asset allocation—the performance implications of shifting assets between the stock market and significantly less risky fixed-income assets. It therefore serves as a broad measure of the decision maker's skill necessary for successful active asset allocation.

Figure 12-2 presents the barometer of opportunity covering the 63 five-year periods beginning with 1926 to 1930. As discussed earlier in this chapter, we focus on a 5-year time horizon

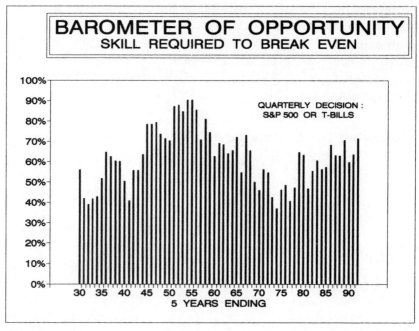

**Figure 12-2.** Barometer of opportunity indicates decision-maker skill required to break even over the 63 five-year periods ending 1930 to 1992.

because of its practical significance to those who share responsibility for fund performance. Each bar represents the 5 years ended with the year marked on the horizontal scale. The vertical scale measures PROB, the probability (in percent) of a correct decision. The height of each bar shows the PROB required for a program of active asset allocation to break even before transaction costs. For an investment fund able to make use of futures contracts, transaction costs would only marginally alter the comparisons shown here. The height of each bar is negatively related to the opportunity to gain performance advantage through active asset allocation. The bars rising to the highest levels represent periods when opportunities are most limited. At the other extreme, the very short bars reflect periods when active asset allocation is likely to look particularly appealing relative to a buy-and-hold strategy for common stocks.

## Gauging the Prospects for
## Back-Door Market Timing

Back-door market timing, despite the complete absence of skill, will likely gain advantage if the stock market environment is sufficiently negative. Figure 12-3 organizes the data previously plotted in Fig. 12-2 to highlight the implications of varying levels of the decision-maker's skill. Panel A establishes the baseline at a skill level of 50 percent. It shows that this level of skill would likely have achieved favorable returns from active asset allocation in only 13 of the 63 five-year periods. During such periods, performance measurement may well identify back-door market timing as astute investment management. The 5 years ended 1974, which included the extreme 1973 to 1974 bear market, provides a particularly dramatic example. Over these 5 years, the S&P 500 registered a compound annual rate of excess return amounting to *negative* 7.8 percent. Note that the bar representing the 5 years ended 1974 indicates only 4 out of 10 correct decisions would have been needed, on average, to break even.

Most of the time, since successful asset allocation will require a level of skill well in excess of 50 percent, the outlook for back-door market timing is dim. Panel B of Fig. 12-3 highlights 5-year periods when the market environment required, on avrege, investment skill of 60 percent to break even. Even though this level of skill is far superior to that provided by tossing a coin, active asset allocation could have expected to achieve success in only 25 of the 63 five-year periods ended between 1930 and 1992. This comparison, taken at face value, underscores the market forces working *against* active asset allocation in general and back-door market timing in particular. Six correct decisions out of 10 would not have been sufficient, on average, to break even for the majority of the 5-year periods included in the historical record. Panel C demonstrates a level of skill (70 percent) which would likely have achieved favorable performance, on balance, in most 5-year periods. Although the World War II period and early postwar years would have been daunting for even this level of skill, the last 33 five-year periods included only three requiring a higher level of skill to expect to break even.

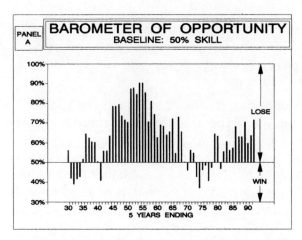

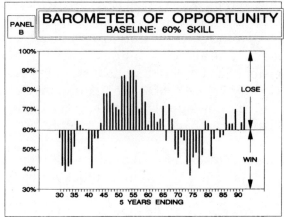

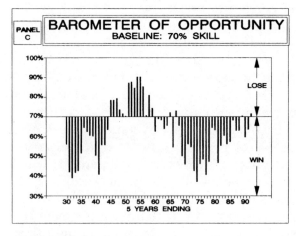

**Figure 12-3.** Highlighting three levels of decision-maker skill: (a) 50 percent, (b) 60 percent, and (c) 70 percent.

## How to Gain Advantage

The barometer of opportunity, in addition to demonstrating the negative implications of back-door market timing, directs attention to the level of skill required to gain advantage. In a highly efficient market, even a highly skilled decision maker will be hard pressed much of the time to demonstrate skill far greater than the PROB of 50 percent which we assign to back-door market timing. Figure 12-4, summarizing 20 quarterly decisions over a 5-year period, provides an example. On the first day of each quarter, the decision maker determines that the stock market is either undervalued or overvalued. The first column classifies each of these 20 decisions according to the probability that it will turn out correctly. The weighted average probability of 60 percent (column A) compares favorably with prospects for back-door market timing. It is still too low, nevertheless, to gain

### DECISION-MAKER SKILL

| 5 Years | | Weight | | |
|---|---|---|---|---|
| # Q's | PROB | A | B | C |
| 2 | 80% | 100% | 100% | 100% |
| 4 | 70% | 100% | 100% | 100% |
| 6 | 60% | 100% | 100% | 0% |
| 8 | 50% | 100% | 0% | 0% |
| 20 | | | | |
| | | | | |
| Weighted Average PROB | | 60% | 67% | 73% |

PROB = probability of correct decision

**Figure 12-4.** Making best use of decision-maker skill: relating weighting of common stocks to probability of correct decision.

advantage over the performance benchmark (buy-and-hold stocks) during more than half the 5-year periods in our historical sample. To make best use of his or her skill, the decision maker exercises restraint, implementing decisions only when the probability of a correct answer is sufficiently high. Column B shows how the average probability of a correct answer rises to 67 percent if the decision maker avoids implementation in eight quarters when the probability of success is low. For column C, the average increases to 73 percent, based on limiting implementation to six quarters with the best prospects of success.

The decision process described in this book aims to benefit from the principle represented by Fig. 12-4. Valuation of the stock market, as determined by the three prime variables, varies widely as the market environment changes. Much of the time, the three prime variables indicate a market valuation which differs only very moderately from the current market price. Decision rules, reflecting the high margin for error under such circumstances, maintain stock market exposure in line with policy. As the discrepancy between indicated market value and current market price widens, so does the probability of a correct decision. Accordingly, decision rules implement overweighting or underweighting to reflect the higher confidence in the correctness of the decision. We aim to increase the average probability of success by limiting implementation, as shown in Fig. 12-4, to the more promising combinations of the three prime variables.

### Strengthening Policy

Our review of back-door market timing underscores the often overlooked connection between active management of asset allocation and the functioning of policy. A highly efficient stock market places policy asset allocation, based on the principles of passive investing, at the center of fund management. Active asset allocation, operating within the limits imposed by policy, aims to add value relative to the policy plan. At the same time, it contributes to the integrity of the policy plan itself by deflecting pressures for back-door market timing. As outlined in Chap. 3, we measure performance of active asset allocation relative to that calculated for the policy plan. We are not, however, able to measure something else that may be as important. We cannot know how much the policy plan benefits, in actual practice, from identification of a specific role for active asset allocation. The advantage for a specific fund depends on both the skill of active management and how much back-door market timing would otherwise be tolerated. Given the widespread influence of back-door market timing, together with its negative implications for fund performance, the potential benefit seems considerable. Fund managers in the 1990s, in our view, will likely pursue one or the other of two alternative approaches to asset allocation. One alternative attempts to rely entirely on a passive policy plan. By excluding a disciplined program of active asset allocation, it virtually assures unplanned episodes of back-door market timing. For the reasons presented in this book, we prefer the alternative. It provides—complementary to the passive policy plan—a carefully developed program of active asset allocation.

# Reference

1. William F. Sharpe, "Likely Gains from Market Timing," *Financial Analysts Journal*, March–April 1975, p. 64.

# About the Authors

WALTER R. GOOD, CFA, is the managing partner of Capital Market Systems. He also serves as associate editor of the *Financial Analysts Journal*. Mr. Good is the coauthor of *Managing Pension Assets*, published in 1990. He has managed institutional investment funds both as plan sponsor and external investment manager, having served as chairman of the pension investment committee for the Continental Group, Inc.; president of Mellon Universe Management Group; and member of the Investment Advisory Panel for the Pension Benefit Guarantee Corporation. He holds undergraduate and MBA degrees from the University of Chicago.

ROY W. HERMANSEN, CFA, is a partner of Capital Market Systems. Previously, he was executive vice president of Mellon Universe Management Group. He holds undergraduate engineering degrees from Lehigh University and an MBA from Columbia University.

JACK R. MEYER is president and CEO of Harvard Management Company, Inc., which manages the University's endowment fund and charitable trusts. He was previously treasurer and chief investment officer of the Rockefeller Foundation. He holds an undergraduate degree from Denison University and an MBA from Harvard Business School.

# Index

*Note:* An *f.* after a page number refers to a figure; a *t.* to a table.